ज्ञान गरिमा के
67 वर्ष

भारतीय ज्ञानपीठ

णाणं
पयासयं
वीर नि.सं. 2470
ई.सन 1944
भारतीय ज्ञानपीठ

The Silent Earth

[Mūkamāṭī]

Epic poem

The Silent Earth

[Mūkamāṭī]

Epic poem

Acharya Vidyasagar

Translated by
Lal Chandra Jain

Bharatiya Jnanpith

Moortidevi Granthamala : English Series No. 22

ISBN 978-81-263-1875-9

THE SILENT EARTH [Mūkamāṭī]
(Epic poem)
by Acharya Vidyasagar

Translated by Lal Chandra Jain

Published by
Bharatiya Jnanpith
18, Institutional Area, Lodi Road
New Delhi-110 003
e-mail : jnanpith@satyam.net.in, sales@jnanpith.net
website : www.jnanpith.net

Printed at : Vikas Computer and Printers, Delhi-110032

First Edition : 2010
Price : Rs. 350, $ 25

The Silent Earth

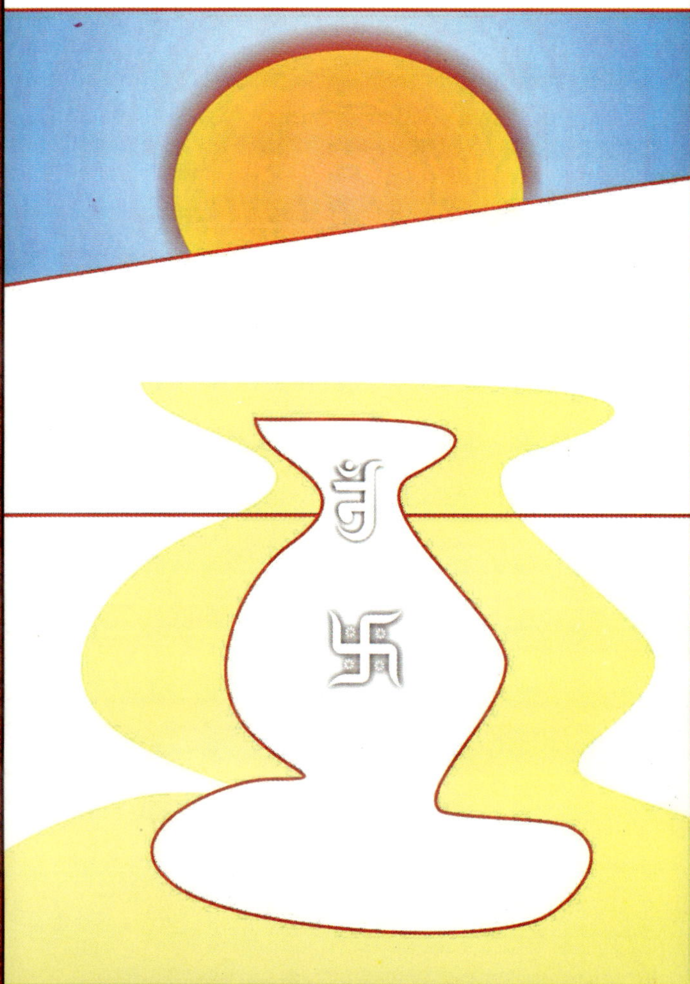

Dedicated most humbly
At the lotus-feet of the great poet-author of
Mūkamāṭī (The Silent Earth)
The spiritual Epic poem
Rev. Acharya Shri Vidyasagar Maharaj

—Lal Chandra Jain

Foreword

'Mūkamāṭī'- The Silent Earth - is a spiritual Epic poem. In the tradition of saintly poetry, it is an incomparable creative work of modern Hindi Literature. Originally born in the non-Hindi speaking Karnataka Province (a Kannada-speaking area), and educated up to High School standard through the medium of Kannada language, Reverend Acharya Shri Vidyasagar Maharaj composed this great Epic poem, which is written in simple charming Hindi, impressive poetic style and easy blank verse. Really, it is an 'Allegory' of the Journey of Emancipation of Soul. Through this literary work, a reader acquires a new insight into 'life' and the 'world', in comprehending its past, present and future; with the help of the discriminating science of the 'real self' along with the 'unreal self' with a new and deeper understanding too of one's 'own true self.'

Though, till now, about three dozens of books, in Hindi, Sanskrit and English, by Rev. Acharya Maharaj have been published; but the Epic poem 'Mūkamāṭī' is the most popular, widely discussed and venerated literary work among all the literary creations produced by him.

Lecturer in Hindi, Sri Lal Chandra Jain, a resident of Lalitpur (U.P.) is a poet of some standing. In the year 1996 an

Āryikā Saṅgha, a holy group of female-ascetics, initiated by Acharya Shri Vidyasagar Maharaj, arrived at Shri Parshva Nath Digamber Jain Temple, Lalitpur. Shri Lal Chandra Jain got a good opportunity for the first hearing of the Epic poem 'Mūkamāṭī', through the religious preceptress Prashāntamatī Mātājī, one of the revered female disciples of Acharya Maharaj.

Thereafter, he put his time and energies into the detailed study of the great Epic poem and, dedicated himself with diligence and devotion to the work of preparing the English Version of the Epic poem. After his efforts for about three years, his labours came to some satisfactory close, and he got the English version computerized in the year 2001.

I myself too had read, and appreciated 'Mūkamāṭī' Epic poem (Hindi edition-1994). I went through his English version; and I found that Shri Lal Chandra Jain had performed the translation-work with due care and understanding. The other good thing is that the translation has been done successfully according to Hindi page-wise.

I do believe that the English translation of the significant 'Eulogium' by the Secretary of Bharatiya Jnanpith, New Delhi, (Late) Shri Lakshmi Chandra Jain, a learned personality, having a deep insight into the Epic poem; and the English version of an essay 'Mānasa Taraṅga' by Rev. Acharya Shri Vidyasagar Maharaj translated under the heading 'The Thought Wave', shall prove to be helpful in the perusal–and comprehension of the 'Book'

Besides it, a Comment Sheet of 155 brief explanatory comments on some special terms and references has also been added at the 'Bookend' according to the progressive serial numbers with their pages, to help the interested readers for an easy understanding of the related points.

In the end, I extend my hearty congratulations to Shri Lal Chandra Jain for his successful attempt in producing the English version of the great Epic poem 'Mūkamāṭī' - 'The Silent Earth'- with the hope that it would be liked by the learned lovers of literature and religiousness.

G.C.Singhai, Lalitpur
Retd. Professor
Govt. Narmada Post-Graduate College
Hoshangabad, M.P.

Acknowledgments

At Siddhodaya Siddha Kshetra, Nemavara, Distt. Devas, M.P., I presented my English version –'The Silent Earth', to the great poet-author of the Epic poem 'Mūkamāṭī', Rev. Acharya Shri Vidyasagar Maharaj, in the annual session of Shri Digamber Jain Mahasamiti, on August 11, 2002.

Thereafter, Rev. Shri Abhayasagar Maharaj, not only favoured me with his kind perusal of the English version 'The Silent Earth', but also blessed me with the due corrections, alterations, valuable suggestions and solid guidance for the betterment of the performance. I very humbly express my heart-felt 'salutation'-'*Namostu*'- to him for it all.

Further, how can I forget the happy remembrance of Shri Sharad Jain (secretary, All India Digamber Jain Tirtha-kshetra Committee) Bhopal, M.P., who recommended the Translation-work (The Silent Earth) for the approval of publication. I hope that he shall keep up his kind favour towards the publication of the Book- The Silent Earth - in future also.

I express my gratitude to the learned Retd. Prof. Gulab Chand Singhai (Head of the Deptt. of Economics, Govt. Narmada Post-Graduate College, Hoshangabad, M.P.), who obliged me by writing the 'Foreword' of 'The Silent Earth'.

I humbly express my hearty gratitude to Sahu Shri

Akhilesh Jain, the managing trustee, Bharatiya Jnanpith, New Delhi, for his acceptance of publishing my translation work 'The Silent Earth'. I am also thankful to Dr. Gulab Chandra Jain, the chief publication officer of Bharatiya Jnanpith, for good production.

I am also thankful to Shri Puspendra Jain Pali, the owner of 'Computer Care, Graphics and Training Centre', Lalitpur, for his good computerization of the work.

In the end, I feel no hesitation in saying that if Rev. Muni Shri Abhayasagar Maharaj, Shri Sharad Jain (Bhopal) and the reputed institution Bharatiya Jnanpith itself had not accorded their help and acceptance to an ordinary man like myself; then, this English version of the spiritual Epic poem 'Mūkamāṭī' won't have become able to see the daylight of publication.

Sincerely Yours
Lal Chandra Jain
(Translator)

Lalitpur (U.P.)
Mahaveer Jayanti
7th of April, 2009

Contents

Foreword VII
Acknowledgments X
By Translator's Pen XV
Eulogium XLIX
Homage to Jñāna-guru LXXIII
The Thought Wave (Mānasa Taraṅga) LXXV

The Silent Earth

1. Canto First -
No Admixture, Gain in Category 01 - 88
2. Canto Second -
The 'Word' is not 'Wisdom' :
The 'Wisdom', not 'Purification' 89 - 187
3. Canto Third -
The Preservation of Virtuousness :
The Purification of Sinfulness 189 - 267
4. Canto Four -
The Fiery Ordeal : The Silvery Ashes 269 - 488

Brief Explanatory Comments 489 - 528

Transliterating Symbols

Vowels

अ	आ	इ	ई	उ	ऊ	ऋ	लृ
a	ā	i	ī	u	ū	ṛ	ḷ

ए	ऐ	ओ	औ	अं	अः
e	ai	o	au	aṁ	aḥ

Constants

क्	ख्	ग्	घ्	ङ्
k	kh	g	gh	ṅ
च्	छ्	ज्	झ्	ञ्
ch	chh	j	jh	ñ
ट्	ठ्	ड्	ढ्	ण्
ṭ	ṭh	ḍ	ḍh	ṇ
त्	थ्	द्	ध्	न्
t	th	d	dh	n
प्	फ्	ब्	भ्	म्
p	ph	b	bh	m

य्	र्	ल्	व्	श्	ष्	स्	ह्
y	r	l	v	ś	ṣ	s	h

क्ष्	त्र्	ज्ञ्
kṣ	tr	jñ

By Translator's Pen

1. The great aim of an Epic–

A famous Acharya of Sanskrit Literature, Shri Mammat, the author of 'Kavyaprakash' has said, "काव्यं यशसे अर्थकृते व्यवहारविदे शिवेतरक्षतये सद्यः परिनिवृत्तये..."–"*Kāvyam yaśase, arthakṛte, vyavahāravide, śivetarakṣataye, sadyaḥ parinivṛttaye...*"This pithy saying carries the sense that poetry is meant to earn fame and money, for the knowledge of personal and social practices, thinking and conduct, and for the removal of all types of evils of personal or social life, to bring in happiness, peace, public welfare and goodness of life, that is the 'Śivatva'. The last objective carries the sense of deliverance of 'Soul' from sins or crimes or worldly bondages, within a due time-span. This aim of literature or poetry, indicates towards a deep inner life-experience, which links poetry with spiritualism; and which acts as a motive-force for our feelings, thoughts and actions to take the journey of life onward upon the path of salvation. Thus, this last point is meant not only to purify, but also to glorify the human consciousness.

From among the above-mentioned five main objectives of poetry, the first two objectives "काव्यं यशसे, अर्थकृते" - that is, 'poetry for fame and money' have been indicated with an ordinary worldly viewpoint. But, the last three aims : "व्यवहारविदे, शिवेतरक्षतये, सद्यः परिनिवृत्तये..." that is, the knowledge of personal and social practices, thinking and conduct, the public welfare, goodness of life and deliverance of 'Soul' from worldly bondages– signify the great aims and objectives of any great literature or poetry. According to my view, the last three sublime aims and objectives carry a deeper insight peculiar to the sacred literature, related to the spiritual excellence of life. With reference to the Epic poem 'Mūkamāṭī' the genuine sense infixed with these last three aims and objectives of great poetry, indicates towards those human values, behaviours and practices, which bring us all upon the path of right faith, right knowledge and right conduct. Ultimately, they help us achieve, along with a better living, the Supreme Goal of life, the 'Śivatva', that is, the Final Liberation.

2. The Spiritual vision, the basic vision of the Spiritual Epic-poem 'Mūkamāṭī'–

From the spiritual point of view, this Creative Work in the form of 'Mūkamāṭī' Epic poem is based upon only one single event, that is, the perfect purification of the 'Soul' hidden within the 'Soil', in which many small stone-pieces or pebbles, flowing into the time-stream have mingled and dissolved. Within the span of this one single event, so many happenings and different dimensions of thought have been brought into its fold. The rough mixture of such a 'Soil', after removing the pebbles by crushing and sifting it, has to be moulded through the 'Artisan–potter' into the fair and bright image of 'Shankar'. Really, the basic purpose of the Saint-poet is the essential insight of 'self-realization', and the expression of the spiritual thoughts and feelings of human consciousness.

Rev. Acharya Shri Vidyasagar Maharaj is fundamentally, a Saint-poet of spiritual life. And, in this life, holy renunciation and penance go to make a great contribution. In the Epic poem

Mūkamāṭī, with reference to the story of the eminent trader devoted to religiousness, the Saint-poet's that very life-view, which is based on 'self-natured spiritualism', finds expression. According to this viewpoint, the importance of the real internal values of life is considered to be far greater than that of the external values of life. The spiritual understanding of the Saint-poet goes on meaningfully indicating towards that very thinking in which the human consciousness should be filled with the sentiments of non-attachment, renunciation and penance. Really, in the Epic poem 'Mūkamāṭī', the process of purification of the impure worldly condition of human consciousness; and, through its perfect accomplishment to establish it ultimately into the, 'Supreme State of Final Emancipation' or 'Salvation' has been exhibited. Not being based upon a mere intellectual hypothesis or a bare consideration of some idealistic principles, all these holy activities have been fixed and valued on the solid ground of a practical thinking and an effective conduct of a known and accepted spiritual-cultural tradition.

Today, there pervades an atmosphere of enmity, aversion and struggle almost everywhere in the world, The Knowledge and Science of modern age, after having dragged upon the track of terrorism, is carrying the whole of the human race towards the dreadful sight of the third world-war. Therefore, we should welcome that resonant voice of 'Mūkamāṭī' which, to make us free from such an atmosphere, makes us keenly eager towards the direction of world-welfare, by awakening the great ideas and ideals within human consciousness through the development of a non-violent mind and a heart filled with human values.

Rev. Acharya Shri Vidyasagar Maharaj is a great spiritual saint and an ascetic in the first instance, and a poetic genius afterwards. Hence, it goes without saying that, in his great 'Creative Work', his clear view is to do social welfare along with the attainment of self-liberation, and to make the extraordinarily good conduct, thoughts and feelings to grow fruitfully within the human consciousness. He wishes to inculcate and develop in our social life such spiritual insight, which may come to the rescue of humanity, caught into the mighty whirlpool of the ocean of worldly existence. By infusing it with 'Right Faith for Right Path' his call of awakening is –

> "The complete uprooting, indeed,
> Of all the shackles
> In the form of the body, the mind and the speech,
> Is *Mokṣa,* that is, the Final Salvation,
> Within the stainless state of this Final Salvation,
> Resides the Eternal Bliss" !

–'Mūkamāṭī', p. - 486

In other words, we can say that, really, under the materialistic and anarchic circumstances of today, in the degenerating conditions of disregard to 'Faith' in the highest values, the great aim of the Saint-poet is to re-establish the entire restless humanity, caught into the terrible trap of vested interests, in a peaceful-progressive and better life-pattern. The higher objective of the Epic-poem is to change the consciousness of extrovert thinking of the human society of today into the 'introvert' form. The Saint-poet wishes to reorganize the heart and mind of generally self-willed and somehow self-conceited man of today in such a manner that, having raised himself from 'selfishness', he could remain steadfast into the highest goodness or the 'Ultimate Reality' and should be able to create new purificatory rites of spiritual life through his clean conscience.

3. An Epic poem, not eventful; but based mainly upon higher thoughts and sentiments–

In the traditional forms of Epics, the poet aims at some historical or mythological events, narrated with an elevated poetic style, and characterization of some heroes and heroines, who are famous for their heroic deeds. But, the Epic poem 'Mūkamāṭī' can not be counted within such traditional poetic performances. In this Epic poem of the Saint-poet, a thin thread of eventful narration runs from the beginning up to the end. The gems and the pearls of great thoughts and sentiments threaded into it go on scattering their matchless lustre at every step. From this point of view, we may consider this Epic poem to be an 'Allegorical narration' in which, 'The Legend of the Soul' has been depicted and analysed in a living, subtle and dynamic manner. While turning round into the labyrinth of the bodily successions of physical world, while seizing and abandoning them, how this individual 'Soul'- enshrined in the body, comes into contact with the music of gods and the light of heavens, after being entangled and disentangled with the hellish darkness of the underworld –all these points are the mainstay of the narrative.

Thenceforth, how its inner journey, having attained the highest splendour of the human consciousness, enthrones itself over the 'Siddha Śilā', [that is, the Eternal Abode]-while enjoying the perfect repose in the state of immortal happiness –all this has been depicted in the rare symbolic utterances. From this point of view, this Spiritual Epic poem is a singular 'Creative Work'. In this Work of poetry the aim of the Saint-poet is not to characterize some special hero, but to depict and prevail upon some particular sentiment, good or evil. The human consciousness is a 'living mass' of fair-passionless and passional feelings, emotions and sentiments. While depicting and evaluating that very 'mass of consciousness'- the Saint-poet has created a particular type of 'Spiritual Romance', by supposing the 'Silent Earth' ('Mūkamāṭī') as the 'heroine' and the 'Artisan potter' as the 'hero' of the Epic poem. Rev. Spiritual Guide or 'Gurudeva' himself may be regarded as the holy 'Artisan potter' and the 'Supreme Personage'–the 'Super Divinity'–is the highly venerable, Shri Arihant Dev–

> "Who live after being liberated from all delusions
> Who are fully free from worldly attachments and
> aversions
> For whom the births and deaths, old age and decay
> Can't touch now,...
> xx xx xx
>
> Those who have neither attachment in belongings
> nor any union of saints
> Those who are alone-only their own True 'selves'
> Whom should they care for ?
> They are always fully beyond all worries,
> Absolved from the *eighteen blemishes....*"

–'Mūkamāṭī', pp. - 326-327

Besides the living beings in the form of 'characters', through the medium of some lifeless 'characters' too–such as golden pitcher, earthen pitcher, utensils, ewers, and the other various objects of worship and adoration–while presenting the heart-touching dialogues– the Saint-poet has also given some interesting analysis and descriptions of the fair or foul qualities of human beings. At such places, the form of the figure of speech–personification', is beautiful. The dialogue of the critic mosquito or the bug with the devotee eminent trader, may be counted within some such dialogues.

4. Inclusion of some important references to modern life–

Though the major part of the Epic poem 'Mūkamāṭī' is relevant from the spiritual point of view; but some particular thought-provoking references related to modern life- patterns enhance the excellence of poetry through their realistic touch. Some special reflections of thought are noteworthy: –

(A) Reference to modern scientific trends–

If modern physical science of today holds the nectar of the development of humanity in one hand, it also holds the deadly poison of the destruction of humanity in the other hand. The Saint-poet says–

> "High above, the force of atom is at work
> Then, hither...downwards
> The power of Manu exists!
> Over and above, the machine is thundering
> Beneath it, the holy incantation is being sung
> The one is a killer
> The other a saviour;
> The one is Science
> Whose subsistence is 'argument',
> The other is Faith
> Which doesn't worry, for a calling !"

–'Mūkamāṭī', p. - 249

The modern physical science somehow rests upon the destructive force of 'Atom', while the 'Faith' has been the saviour force, and shall ever remain so. The root of Science is 'argument,' while the retaining power for Earth and 'Religion' has been the –'Faith' or the true fidelity in the genuine religious beliefs. The passionless supreme 'Soul' of man, in its

'Godliness'-due to it being subtler, than the minutest physical atom of science-has remained supremely powerful, inexhaustive and a perpetual source of auspiciousness for the humanity of the world.

(B) Reference to Literature–

At another place, while indicating towards the true form of literature, the Saint -poet puts his ideas summarily thus–

> "The purport of the benevolent
> Is the profession of literature,
> It really means that
> The true literature is only that
> By studying which
> Happiness should be originated and attained
> Otherwise,
> Like a flower devoid of sweet smell
> It is the deprivation of happiness–
> A cluster of words without sum and substance...!"
>
> –*'Mūkamāṭī', p. - 111*

It means that literature which is good for the public at large, proves its genuineness upon the touch-stone of far-reaching utility for life and general welfare of all the living beings. Through such a beneficial literature, the humanity, while going ahead upon the right track of life may be able to accomplish the individual, as well as, social welfare. The remaining worthless literature is, really, like flowers without fragrance, only a heap of meaningless words.

(C) Terrorism, a formidable curse to world humanity–

Today, the nations equipped with horrible weapons, are engaged in violence and terrorist activities through their hidden armed militants in disguise. The terror of the third World War, which may bring total destruction, is hanging over the head of humanity, like the sword of Damocles. In the Epic poem Mūkamāṭī, there comes a reference about a hard blow by terrorism to a God-believing family The Saint-poet Acharya Vidyasagar Maharaj, says in that very context :

"Till the terrorism is alive,
This Earth
Can't take the breath of peace,
These eyes, now
Can't see the terrorism,
These ears, now
Can't hear the name of terror,
This life too is firmly resolute that
That one–(terror) or this one-(peace) –
Here, the existence of the one shall remain."

–*'Mūkamāṭī', p. - 441*

Violence and Terrorism is the burning problem of the twenty first century. Its right solution can be possible only through the observance of the great principle of 'Non-violence' which is the supreme attribute of the every religion of the world. The terrorist tendencies and the acts of violence shall only add fuel to the fire, Rev, Shri Amrit Chandracharya, giving an excellent definition of 'Non- violence' in his famous holy Book– 'Puruṣārtha-siddhyupāya' says–

"अप्रादुर्भावः खलु रागादीनां भवत्यहिंसेति।
तेषामेवोत्पत्तिः हिंसेति जिनागमस्य संक्षेपः ।। 44 ।।

That is, certainly, the non-origination of passions etc., is non-violence; while, the origination of those very passions etc. is 'violence'. It is the sum and substance of holy Jain Scriptures. How subtle and heart-touching is the above-quoted definition of violence and non-violence, in the materialistic socio-economic contexts of today.

The terrible world-wide 'violence', terrorism and anarchic life-conditions have become rampant, and the tremendously destructive atomic weapons have endangered the future peace and prosperity of all nations. Really, violence and terrorism, at first originate in the human mind. Due to these passional feelings of mental violence and terrorism, our own vital breath of right conduct is primarily hit hard. Then, the tendencies and activities to deliver a fatal blow to others is the aftermath of it. Hence, the 'non-origination' of undue passional feelings of attachment and aversion have rightly been said to be 'non-violence'.

(D) References to some experiences of rare 'Wisdom' and 'Purification'–

In the second canto of the Epic poem Mūkamāṭī the Artisan potter digs out the 'Soil' at the river-bank, far away from his hermitage of his premises. His hoe, all of a sudden fractures the fore-head of a thorn. The feeling of revengefulness arises into its heart. At that very moment, the Artisan potter is filled with a sense of self-aversion. The subtle reaction of such a good sentiment manifests itself in the manner that there arises a sense of pacification of anger, ejection of the sense of retaliation and an uprise of the sense of high wisdom. While discussing such a feeling of good wisdom, the Saint-poet says–

"Without being sprinkled with divine wisdom
These plants of words
Never get flourished,
It's also true that
On the plants of words
Fragrant and pollinated–
The flowers of perfect awakening never smell sweet

xx xx xx

Intellect rears restlessness
Purification bears the fruits of perfect repose,
Not through the flowers, but through the fruits.
Contentment is felt..."

– *Mūkamāṭī, pp. - 106-107*

In the fourth canto of the Epic poem, the detailed depiction of the pious food-taking observance of an ascetic, a vivid description of the joys and sorrows of the bestowers of food-stuffs, the religious preachings by the sages and saints, the immediate indifference of the eminent trader-devotee towards the worldliness etc, have been described minutely. Telling us about the importance of the arrival of the sages and saints, the Saint-poet says –

"It is the very significance of a saint's arrival, indeed,
That the end of the worldliness is visualized,
It matters little if
The one, who makes an approach,
May or may not become at once
A saint, or a person with self-restraint–
There is no rule or regulation whatsoever
But,
He is sure to be a man of self-contentment.
A blessing in the right direction, indeed,
Is a temple in the right condition."

– *Mūkamāṭī, p. - 352*

We find the indications and solutions of so many socio-economic problems of today in the fourth Canto. In a curious reference, we get the understanding of our sense of social responsibility, through the medium of a bug, thus –

> "But it is a pity that
> The greedy and sinful persons
> Turn even the marital hand-taking (ceremony)
> Into the life-taking (formality).
> Generally, the attendants are asked to serve
> In an improper way,
> And
> The disbursement of salaries too, improper indeed.
> –Such persons tell themselves to be
> The progeny of Manu !
> The magnanimous human beings !"

– *Mūkamāṭī, pp.* - *386-387*

The above-quoted extracts have been presented as some of the important extracts from the Epic poem. Really, the whole of the Epic-poem abounds with such numerous heart-touching and religious portions, precepts and maxims.

It is not possible to quote extensively, within an essay of limited space; all the extracts, selected from the Epic poem, widespread into four cantos comprised in about five hundred pages.

5. Excellence in the depictions of the surrounding Nature–

According to ancient definitions, the depiction of natural background and environment has been regarded as necessary in an Epic. Generally, the depiction of natural surroundings has been found in two forms in this Epic poem–

(A) The depiction of Nature for Nature's sake.

(B) To see or establish the reflections of human forms and feelings, thoughts and actions into the objects and atmosphere of natural surroundings or environment.

(A) The depiction of Nature for Nature's sake–

If we scan attentively, the depictions of natural surroundings and atmosphere, the Epic poem –'Mūkamāṭī'– attracts the eye through its various beauty-spots depicted every now and then, Let us see a charming scenic view of Nature on entering a dense forest–

"The various types of fine trees
Kissing the high sky
Are standing with open umbrellas,
The ground is the winner of the weariness
It looks graceful with rich greenery
The shadows have spread a carpet over the ground.
The tiny and huge shrubs and bunches
Laden with flowers, fruits and foliage,
As if scattering smiles
Upon the toiling and wearied way-farers.
Those charming creepers
Embracing the trees from feet to gullet
Seem to be calling and enticing the visitors,
And
Are asking the passers-by, walking constantly,
To take repose for a while."

–'Mūkamāṭī', p. - 423

How fascinating is the pre-quoted, simple and natural mixed–up depiction of Nature !

(B) To see or establish the reflections of human forms and feelings, thoughts and actions into the objects and atmosphere of natural surroundings or

environment–

The auspicious beginning of the Epic poem Mūkamāṭī has been done with the figure of speech 'Personification' of the natural surroundings of the early morning hour. On seeing the shadows of human gestures and emotions reflected into the movements of the 'Nature-dancer', we get an easy remembrance of the beauty of expression of Romantic Trend (Chhāyāvādī kāvya-dhārā) of Hindi poetry–

"The sun is slumbering no more indeed
Yet he is
Still reclining
Into the gentle lap of the mother,
Is changing sides
While drawing the garment over his face.

On the lips of the Eastern horizon
There lurks a light graceful smile
No hem on the head is there
And
Like the scattered scarlet dust
The splendour of the colourful tint
Appears agreeable, dear brother...!

The water-lily as if sinking
Behind the veil of shyness
Wishes to evade
The finger-touch of the Sun;
She tries to give a covering of the petals
To her pollen–
To her emotional countenance !"

Mūkamāṭī', pp. 01-02

The splendour of the young rising Sun, the Eastern horizon

with colourful tint of the 'scattered scarlet dust', and the picturesque depiction of the bashfully shrinking water-lily like a lovely shy lady at the early morning hour-all is so charming !

In the swelling and scattering of the dark and white cloudiness, the Saint-poet discerns reflected the 'six coloured emotions,'–(Ṣaṭ Leśyāyen) and their gestures and moods. In discovering and depicting their-images and identities also in their various forms and appearances, while comparing them with different ladies, the human activities have been held 'primary' and the natural surroundings of comparison as 'secondary'. Here, the spiritual thinking of the Saint-poet becomes resonant through the touch with natural surroundings. The Saint-poet reads sermons into the environmental phenomena. Such emotional depictions of the feelings are found at so many spots in the Epic poem Mūkamāṭī'. But the subtle thought–seeking investigating insight and the spiritual thinking of the Saint-poet explores and expresses an element of innate pious thought or sentiment behind the multiple objects of the visible 'Nature' almost everywhere.

6. The Super-natural element in the Epic poem–

In the fourth canto, the Golden pitcher feels uneasy because of the Earthen Pitcher being held in high esteem. The Golden pitcher, on being prompted by the feeling of jealousy, invites a gang of terrorists. That gang creates havoc into the peaceful family-life of the devout eminent trader. The devout trader has to pass through so many extra-ordinary calamities. But, he succeeds in protecting his family-members with the wonderful help of the co-operative forces of his natural surroundings and the creatures other than human beings-such as, a group of elephants and serpents, In the case of the boat sinking into the fast current of the river, the whole of the family is also saved. Ultimately, a change of heart takes place among the terrorists. This entire incidence is in itself an awe-inspiring and amazing scenic view, which is no less than a miracle. But, from the view of the dignity of the firm religious Faith and genuine devotion, the narrative of the event under reference is true. The devotees with hearty dedication and unflinching Faith in God have often been blessed with protective fearlessness. It is an example of that very superhuman miracle, which manifests itself in the form of 'Divine Compassion'.

7.The accomplishment of asceticism (*Śramaṇa Sādhanā*), manners and morals of a votary house-holder (*Bhakta Śrāvaka*) –

In the fourth canto, the attainment of an ascetic (*Śramaṇa Yogī*) and his holy routine has been described in its details. This canto seems a charming confluence of new ideas, curiosities and the thought-situations of this world; as well as the next world too. In this canto, even the lifeless objects-[the helping objects for worship]-too are seen to be seeking indulgence in the living dialogues, and throwing light upon the minute good or bad folds of the human heart and mind. At proper spots of the Epic poem, the appearance of dramatic sensibility imparts liveliness to brief and substantial conversations. A 'Bug' says to the devout eminent-trader–

"Don't try to confer dry temptations,
A self-dependent life should be lived up,
Offer away the watery libations
To the skill of cunningness !
Pay, homage
To humility which is the mother of eminence !
The sky should be contained
Within the largeness of decorum
And–
The life should become an example of liberality !

Without any pretext–
The troubles of the others should be removed !"

— *Mūkamāṭī', pp. 387-388*

The votary house-holders (*Bhakta Śrāvaka*) have been depicted making preparations for the dietal invitation (*Pratigrahaṇ*) of the ascetics-the great saints (*Munirājs*). The votary house-holders show their readiness for getting the holy routine of the ascetics performed. They form a square designed 'space' with coloured meal at their own doorways. Then, they stand in rows, with coconuts and various other fruits in their hands or in platters etc. Thus, they try to receive the venerable saints, arriving from a distance, through their humble calls with holy utterances. Along with it, this canto includes the description and analysis of the worthy or unworthy holy personages (*Supātra/Kupātra)*. It also presents the minute and lively analysis of- the feelings and sentiments of the 'bestowers of food' (*Āhāradātās*). References have also been made to the holy calls and the prescribed pious utterances at the time of the dietal invitation of the ascetics. Thus the whole of the process of sacred alms-giving (*Āhāradāna)* has been described in a lively way.

The votary house-holders and the alms-givers (*Āhāradātās*) while eulogizing the venerable saints, sing thus–

"Protect us, your holy feet are
The ship which floats as well as rescues.
O compassionate sage of sages !
Carry us to the shores of the ocean of existence !"

— *Mūkamāṭī', p. 325*

While describing the holy bestowal of food-stuffs to the reverend ascetics in due manner and with proper arrangements, the Saint-poet has also referred to a philosophic investigation of the 'pain of hunger; and the different obstacles (*Antarāya)* in the process of sacred alms-giving (*Āhāradāna).* These obstacles should not be allowed to vitiate the happy occasion. To have a look at the pious routine of holy food-taking by the venerable saints, the groups of votary house-holders in the neighbourhood gather around in large numbers. In the end, the venerable ascetic, after preaching them with a brief sermon, departs for his stay at some hermitage (or some solitary abode).– The head of the votary house-holder's family too, with the wooden water-jar in hand, follows him like a shadow. The holy ascetic's sermonizing at that moment is remarkable. He utters thus –

> "From outside
> Whatever is being seen
> That...I...am...not...indeed
> And all that
> Doesn't really belong to me.
> These eyes
> Can't see me
> The power to see
> Is there within me;
> I was...am...and shall be
> The maker of that power,
> The seer of all
> I was...am...and shall be.
> From outside
> Whatever is being seen
> That...I...am...not...indeed !"

–Mūkamāṭī', p. 345

Thus, in this fourth canto, the attainment of asceticism and the attributes of saintliness have been presented with subtle and splendid analysis. While going through this canto from beginning to end, the reader feels highly delighted.

Some poetic lines spring up into my feelings and thoughts.

Those lines are as follows –

Through the words of the Holy Saint
Mūkamāṭī speaks in such a way-
That by the vital message thus delivered
Has uprooted the order of senselessness !

On the peak of renunciation and penance
As if appears there a new dawn,
The body seems to be an abode of clay-
Which is a night-resort for the eternal Soul !

The venerable Saint-poet thus exhorts-
This clay be turned into a holy pitcher, yes,
Wherein be filled the waters of Knowledge True,
And let it be dedicated at the Feet of God !

—Lines from the Translator's own Hindi Poem

8. The artistic aspects of the poetic form in the Epic poem Mūkamāṭī –

(A) Language and versification –

The established basic theme of the Spiritual Epic poem Mūkamāṭī and the viewpoint of the Saint-poet has an original aim in itself. Accordingly, his language and style, along with his metric-order too, differ from the poetic measures of the other known Hindi epics. In spite of being plain and simple, the language of the Epic poem Mūkamāṭī is not descriptive, but it is generally capable, expressive and lively. The symbolic style is clear, significant and suggestive. The basic ground of the narrative is vast and impressive. Mainly abounding in the qualities of lucidity and grace, it is also full of the virtue of vigour and vitality.

Thus, the easy and natural language and style of the Epic poem Mūkamāṭī, reflects in an effective way the great personality of the Saint-poet. It is also fully capable in hinting at the serious social problems of today, along with expressing the philosophic-spiritual truths and realities of life as well. The sincerity coupled with maturity which is required in dealing with the themes related to the deliverance of soul as well as those of the social welfare – the language and style of the Epic poem Mūkamāṭī duly exhibits the required qualities. While keeping up its poetic grandeur throughout the narrative, the field of the Epic poem Mūkamāṭī has become very large, due to its vastness of background; and within the limits even of that vastness, the unhindered simplicity of language and style is an exceptional characteristic of the Epic poem.

This very simplicity, avoiding poetic obscurity, makes the Epic poem easily understandable to a reader; and leaves upon his heart and mind a feeling and impression of closeness and ownness towards this literary Work. According to a famous romantic poet of English literature, the language of poetry should be almost nearer to the language of prose.

The 'Verse Liberatia' or the 'Blank Verse', in which this Epic poem has been narrated, gets itself positively adorned with eminence due to its usage. In spite of uniformity in the usage of 'Blank Verse' throughout the Epic poem, the style remains charming due to the diversity and vividness of its metric form. According to the waves of feelings and thoughts, the length and shortness of the poetic lines keep up their desired flow, balance, and internal rhythmic motion. However, the Saint -poet– author does not aim at making a show of the artistic aspects of the poetic form, that is, the poetic sentiment, the metre or the figures of speech etc. (Rasa, Chhanda, Alaṅkāra). The Saint-poet wants to communicate his holy thoughts, practices and conduct – re-vitalized by religiousness. But, in Mūkamāṭī, the poetic sentiments, metric usage and figures of speech have been used as only the helping art-skills in this Spiritual Epic poem, which is really thought-oriented, aiming at high ideas and great ideals. It has never been the Saint-poet's objective to lay stress upon the artistic-embellishments. So, the question of their special depiction or display doesn't arise.

Similarly, some historical events or plots or their affiliated hero- heroines. etc., have not been taken as the basic ground of the narrative. Hence, not being fundamentally plot-based or characterisation-based, it is but natural that the element of story-telling remains meagre in the Epic poem. But, with a scanty base of story-telling, the primary aim of the Saint-poet is to give expression to fair or foul emotions and sentiments along with very mature feelings and substantive thought-pattern. And the Saint-poet has performed it all in a thoroughly well manner.

(B) The place of the Poetic sentiments and Figures of Speech– in the Epic poem Mūkamāṭī –

The above-mentioned discussion does not mean that the desired artistic aspect of poetic beauty is not found there in the Epic poem Mūkamāṭī. The Saint-poet has given a proper expression to all the recognized poetic sentiments where and when an occasion arises. Throughout the whole of the Epic poem, there is found the mature depiction of all the nine poetic sentiments (*Kāvya-Rasas*). The unique point is that the accomplishment or ripeness of the poetic sentiments has not been presented as attached to the traditional frame of the heroes and heroines. According to the spiritual view of thinking, the main poetic sentiment, basically established in the Epic poem, may be named as the poetic sentiment of Quietism (*Śānta-rasa*). The permanent feeling behind this poetic sentiment is the freedom from worldly desires-that is, 'Nirveda' (*Vairāgya*), which is depicted as strengthened with the poetic sentiment of 'Compassion' (*karuṇa-rasa*) and sentiment of 'Heroism' (*Vīra-rasa*) that is, 'Dharma Vīratā'.

The great poet-playwright of Sanskrit Literature 'Bhavabhūti' has written in his famous dramatic performance, 'Uttara-rāmacharitam' –

> "एको रसः करुण एव निमित्तभेदात्, भिन्नः पृथक् पृथगिवाश्रयते विवर्तान् ।
> आवर्त्तबुद्बुदतरंगमयान् विकारानम्भो यथा सलिलमेव हि तत्समस्तम् ।।"

That is, the poetic sentiment of compassion is the only main poetic sentiment. Due to the difference of the apparent cause, that very sentiment of compassion holds the different forms or appearances. As, for example, the water changes into the form of a whirlpool, bubbles and waves; but, really, it remains the one and the same."The poetic sentiment of compassion" is the only main poetic sentiment" – to consider from the viewpoint of this saying, the 'feeling of compassion' seems to be pervading throughout the 'life' and the 'world', from the very beginning to end. While making a detailed study of the Epic poem 'Mūkamāṭī,' the supremacy of the poetic sentiment of compassion (*Karuṇa-rasa*) attracts our attention in the various contexts of the narrative. Therefore, from this viewpoint, the 'Epic poem' may also be regarded as pre-eminently 'A Work of the poetic sentiment of Compassion, whose substantive sensibility is 'sorrow' or 'suffering'.

The poetic sentiment of 'Heroism' (*Vīra-rasa*) has been considered in many forms by the learned critics-i.e., bravery in war, bravery in religiousness, bravery in charity or donation, bravery in Compassion and bravery in speech –added humorously by the famous Hindi critic Shri Ram Chandra Shukla, from the modern point of view. In Mūkamāṭī, Epic poem, the references to the bravery of 'religiousness', bravery of 'mercifulness' and the bravery of charity, or donation may be seen into the subordinate contexts of the narrative and the connected dialogues. The references to the heart-touching utterings of bravery of 'religiousness' (*Dharma Vīratā*), and the exemplary conduct are included in the life-story of the devout eminent trader, while he faces terrorism. In the very fourth canto has also been expounded the bravery of charity or donation and the bravery of compassion which give strength to the perfect practice of the accomplishment of asceticism (*Śramaṇa-Sādhanā*). Besides this, the context of the assault-policies of the terrorists, the description of their form, shape and size inspires the poetic sentiment of Wrath or Furiousness (Raudra-rasa) -in the heart of the reader.

In the narration of the devout trader's family being protected by a band of elephants and serpents flavours the poetic sentiment of Marvellousness or Wonder (Adbhut-rasa). But, all these currents of poetic sentiments ultimately, seek their termination into the wide-spread ,deep and cool lake of the basic poetic sentiments of the Epic poem – The poetic sentiment of 'Quietism' (Śānta-rasa) or the poetic sentiment of Compassion (Karuṇa-rasa) .

Figures of Speech –

The brilliance of the figures of speech is also fascinating. The figures of speech enhance the beauty of poetry. Really, the heart-touching sentiments, higher thoughts and deeper experiences are the 'Soul', and language and metres are the body; and the Figures of Speech are the ornaments of a good poetry. From this viewpoint, the figures of speech have as much of the significance, as the decoration of ornaments has upon the body of some fortunate 'Soul'.

In the Epic poem 'Mūkamāṭī,' the figures of speech, depending upon word-usage are : Alliteration (*Anuprās*), Punning-on-words (*Śabda-śleṣa*), Punning-on-sense (*Artha-śleṣa*), repetition of the same syllables or words, at the beginning, middle or end of a verse (*Yamaka*) etc. may also be called an alliteration in different meanings. The figures of speech depending upon meanings, which are charming in the new references of sense-usage, are : Simile (*Upamā*), Metaphor (*Rūpaka*), illustrative comparison of some object, action, feeling or thought (*Utprekṣā*), illustrative explanation of some thought or feeling (*Dṛṣṭānta*), personification (*Mānavīkaraṇa*) and oxymoron (*Virodhābhāsa Alaṅkāra*) etc.

The figurative style is found effective in the wonderful usage of the language, when some person, object or scene is described, or, when the virtues and blemishes; comparing and explaining of the excellence of feelings or sentiments etc., are depicted.

Let us see a good example of alliteration (*Anuprāsa Alaṅkāra*) :

"Jal ko jaḍatva se mukta kar
Muktā-fal banānā hai,
Patan ke gart se nikāl kar,
Uttung utthān par dharanā,
Dhṛti dhāriṇī dharā kā dhyeya hai !"

—*Mūkamāṭī, p. 193*

In the third line of the above-mentioned quotation the repeated pronunciation of the 'consonant'- *'dha'* produces a musical sound-effect. In the same manner, the beauty of an impressive metaphor is noticeable –

"Badle kā bhāva vah Rāhu hai
Jiske/sudīrgha vikrāl gāl mein
Chhotā-sā kaval ban,
Chetanrūpa bhāswat bhānu bhī
Apne astitva ko kho detā hai !"

— *Mūkamāṭī, p. 98*

The feeling of 'retaliation' has been compared here metaphorically' with 'Rāhu', within whose huge and terrible jaws, even the 'Sun of luminous spirit too' loses its existence like that of a tiny morsel.

In another description, how fascinating is the naturally charming scenic view of the morning hour, Personified as follows —

"Now the fickle stars
All like frail ladies
While following at heels
Their husband, the Moon
Like shadows,
Are getting themselves hidden
Somewhere...far away...over the horizon...
Due to the apprehension
Lest they be sighted by the Sun.
The fragrant breeze
Is blowing
In a gentle manner."

—*Mūkamāṭī, p. 2*

It is neither desirable nor perhaps possible to quote from the four different cantos of the Epic poem such fine usages of figures of speech in large number, within the limited space of an 'Essay'.

9. The usage of 'Imagery' in the Epic poem Mūkamāṭī–

The 'imagery' in the Epic poem comes in an easy and natural manner. Really, the creation of due 'imagery' is the main provision of a poetic style. Through the medium of 'imagery' a poet bestows concreteness, sensual perception and communicative acceptability to abstract feelings, thoughts, poetic sentiments, actions and reactions, and objects imperceptible by sense-organs. Just as a painter-artist, while enlivening his sketch-lines with his painting -brush, infuses them with life; so in the same way, the poet's pen becomes his painting-brush, and his management of words turns into the colour-blending. Thus, the provision of 'imagery' in poetry gives clarity, liveliness and impressiveness to some object, event, activity, virtue or blemish etc. by making them picturesque. Please see an example of a terrorist tragedy, encircling a devout trader's family, quoted from the fourth canto of the Epic poem Mūkamāṭī :

"The dense assemblage of clouds
Starts swimming across the firmament,
The empire of darkness seems to be overspread
The glimpse of the earth becomes rare –
Only the foot-steps can sense
Whether the Earth is alive or not,

xx xx xx

The blowing of terrible winds takes a start
In whose clutches is hidden the total annihilation.
The steps of the mountains stumble
And
The turbans of the high hill-tops
Drop down upon the earth,

XX XX XX

The roots of the stronger trees are shaken,
Many of the trees start learning
'*Śīrṣāsana*'–the posture with the head upside down,
The bamboos offer prostrations
And begin to cling to the bosom of the Earth.

—*Mūkamāṭī, p. 438*

In the above-mentioned quotations, the three images are as follows :

(i) The glimpse of the ground becomes rare,
Only the foot-steps can sense
Whether the Earth is alive or not!

(ii) The steps of the mountains stumble, and
The turbans of the high hill-tops
Drop down upon the ground.

(iii) Many of the trees start learning the posture with the head upside down / The bamboos offer prostrations-

The three 'images' indicated above, depict in a picturesque manner, the fierceness created by the totally destructive condition of terrorism. The 'images' are the vivid part of those very natural surroundings. They are neither imposed nor interpolated.

In the third canto of the Epic poem, while-comparing the inclinations contrary to the real 'self' of man with those of the three 'cloudlets', a lady-image has been established. With the help of the usage of that very 'image' the abstract mentality of the 'coloured emotions' (*Leśyāyen*) has been depicted in a concrete and living manner. The extract is as follows –

"Like, frail females in the lane of sky
With a lean and thin waist,
Which have become respectfully alert
Which have pooled a huge store of water
By filling up their pitchers from the sea–
–The three cloudlets have set themselves out
On receiving the signals from the ocean.
Wrapped into a white curd-like *Sāḍī*
That first one cloudlet
In its appearance…
Looks like a devoted nun.

xx xx xx

Which follows the first one, the middle cloudlet,
Like the laughter of a *Palāśa tree* wore a *Sāḍī*
Which diminishes the splendour of a rose,
Which makes blush the loveliness of a lily
Having ruddy feet-soles stained with myrtle;

xx xx xx

And,
Not a false, but genuine
Gold-coloured *Sāḍī* is wrapped
By the rearmost cloudlet."

—Mūkamāṭī, pp. 199-200

The 'coloured emotions' (*Leśyāyen*), are of six types- (1) White (2) Pink (3) Yellow (4) Grey (5) Blue (6) Black.

The first three 'coloured emotions' (*Leśyāyen*), signify the auspicious inclinations; while the last three denote inauspicious inclinations. These first three subtle 'coloured emotions' have been depicted with the picturesque arrangement of images. These fair or foul but emotional inclinations of the mind or heart, speech and body of a living being are called the 'coloured feelings'. At first, through the imagination of the three cloudlets, thereafter with the help of assigning the symbols of three ladies having three types of forms and colours, the Saint-poet has presented the abstract inclinations concretely before the mind's eye. Decorated with such heart-touching 'images', many vivid pen-pictures may be seen in the Epic poem. Such depictions make the poetic style charming, excellent and impressive.

10. The 'symbolism' in the Epic poem Mūkamāṭī –

In the creation of the Epic poem Mūkamāṭī, –basically, there seems to be hidden a great symbolic plan. From this viewpoint, it shall be proper to say the Epic poem to be an excellent 'Allegorical Narration'. By (Late Shri Lakshmi Chandra Jain), Ex-Director of Bharatiya Jnanpith, New Delhi, this incomparable and remarkable 'Creative Work' has aptly been described as an 'Allegory' of the Journey of Emancipation of Soul from the bondage of 'Karmas or Actions'–while going onwards upon the path of perfect purification.'

In other words, the Saint-poet, Rev. Acharya Shri Vidyasagar Maharaj has expressed the mute story of the painfulness of troubled and neglected 'Soul' taken prisoner by the worldly shackles; and its ardent desire for final salvation. The saint-poet, while feeling discontented with only the traditional symbols; wishes to make use of some innovations of symbols. Into the vast arrangement of such symbols, some meaningful 'symbolism' may be investigated thus –

(1) **Mūkamāṭī** – A symbol of the world-wide regular

bodily recurrence of the life-cycle-(The Heroine).

(2) **The Potter-Artisan** – A symbol of the 'Mahāmuni', a great ascetic, who investigates and purifies the existence of Soul into Soil, or a great Saint who is a Spiritual Guide or Gurudeva. He moulds the feelings, thoughts and conduct of a votary house-holder, and inspires him through his own example and precepts (The hero) to advance on the true path of spiritualism.

(3) **The sun** – A symbol of lustrous Super Consciousness or the luminous light of divine knowledge.

(4) **The moon** – A symbol of tranquil and cool innate nature of deep consciousness.

(5) **The ocean** – A symbol of the vast expanse of worldly existence, with its fair or foul depths and waves.

(6) **The river** – A symbol of non-stop life-stream, with its countless waves.

(7) **The mountain** – A symbol of unshaken Faith, renunciation, penance and austerities.

(8) **The lotus** – A symbol of super beauty of Soul, cultural awakening and virtuous course of living.

(9) **The fish** – A symbol of the eagerness of a fortunate soul for 'Emancipation' from the worldly bondages.

(10) **The golden pitcher** – A symbol of illusory infatuation for the power and pelf. The deep-existing sense of I-ness, and My-ness; that is, pride, egotism and vanity. My-ness, that is, the feeling of I-ness and My-ness with worldly objects.

(11) **The earthen pitcher** – A symbol of a dedicated devout house-holder, devoted to high sense of religiousness.

(12) **The clouds** – A symbol of the thick covering of worldly attachments and aversions upon the true nature of the

real 'Self'.

(13) **The pebbles** (stone-pieces) – The symbols of making 'The Image of Soul', rough and blurred through illusive inclinations of attachments, aversions As- (i) The four foul inclinations (ii) The five sins (iii) The six coloured emotions (iv) The seven evil crazes or wrong addictions etc.

(14) **The thorns** – The symbols of the troubles and pains and afflictions (like hunger, thirst, disease, heat, cold etc.)– which can make life better, if they are tolerated with a sense of equanimity.

(15) **The kiln** – It is a means of making the earthen pots perfectly ripe by putting them into fire through a Kiln or Furnace, The symbolic sense which it carries here is that the process of 'Purification of 'Soul' existing in the body and the world, burns away its blemishes and flaws with the help of the fire of religious penance and austerities.

(16) **The different pieces of timber** – Here, the symbolic sense is thus–The efficient causes to burn off the blemishes of our own 'self' as well as those of the others by making the holy-pitcher (*Kumbha*) mature and firm.

(17) **The earthen or sacred pitcher** (*Kumbha*) – It is a symbolic medium of protecting religious rites and practices through self-discipline and forbearance to control one's own passions and emotions as well as those of the others.

(18) **The family of the eminent trader** – A symbol of really dedicated somewhat sceptical devotees.

(19) **An ass** – A symbol of an useful 'being' who carries on the load of worldly 'things' and 'matters' over his back or head.

(20) **The cord-and-bucket event** – A symbolic presentation of the high and holy discussion to throw light upon

the religious routine of a Saint, and a votary house-holder.

(21) **A mosquito or a bug** – A symbol of the helpless but well- wisher critics, who criticize the defects to remove them and to develop perfection.

(22) **Terrorism** – A symbol of the regressive forces of organized crimes against public-good, public-welfare and peace-loving persons. As for example- violence, contrary to non-violence; unrest contrary to peace; and the situations of injustice, contrary to justice; and, misconduct or wickedness, contrary to good conduct in personal or social life.

(23) **A dialogue among the vessels of worship and adoration taken as living characters** – An imaginary symbol of throwing light upon the good or evil conditions of human life, and fair or foul inclinations of human minds.

(24) **Bands of elephants and serpents** – A symbolic presentation of some extra-ordinary situation-condition of protective fearlessness for truly religious, faithful, fortunate house-holder devotees, by supernatural forces.

(25) **Water** – A symbol of the basic need of life. Poetically, it also symbolizes the element of pride and longing in human life. In the form of hailstorm or an ice-pack or devastating floods etc, it is distressing.

(26) **Wind** – A symbol of life-giving internal vital energy. But, in its other painful forms, a symbol of destructive force of External Nature also- like storms, whirlwinds and poisonous gases etc.

(27) **Sky** – A symbol of infinity and purity of all-pervading 'Soul', which is Omnipresent, Omniscient and Omnipotent.

(28) **Changes of seasons** – A strong symbol of affecting continuous change in external Nature and internal Nature, as if it declares-that everything changes except the eternal law of changeableness.

(29) **The holy arrival of Saints and ascetics** – A symbol of accomplishment and adoration by the 'Śramaṇa-Saints', their religious preachings and holy practices and routine observations of asceticism.

(30) **Final salvation or Liberation** – The Eternal, Supreme and Sacred state of human 'Soul', after being liberated from all the 'inward' as well as the 'outward, worldly bondages. Having accomplished such Ultimate Spiritual state of Soul, in the words of the Saint-poet, Rev. Acharya Vidyasagar Maharaj–

"The faith will beget true perception,
Surely it will,
But
At the final destination, not in the way on !"
And,
Rapt into the Supreme Silence
The Saint...
And
As if staring unwinkingly
At the surroundings
...The Silent Earth."

Mūkamāṭī, Last page - 488

The above-mentioned thirty points are some important suggestions of symbols, which attract the eye, while going through the detailed perusal of the Spiritual Epic poem Mūkamāṭī.

On these points, the pen of the Saint-poet, during discussion and analysis, seems to be specially on the move. These points of suggestive thinking have gathered up within its compass the wide-spread symbolism of this 'Creative performance.' The purposeful explanation of this extensive 'symbolism' is possible only through a comprehensive endeavour which can possibly be done separately in a 'Book-form'.

While concluding the essay, I pay my humble homage to the great Poet-author of the spiritual Epic poem 'Mūkamāṭī'-[The Silent Earth] with the following lines, translated from my own poem –

Homage to Rev. Āchārya Shri Vidyasagar Maharaj

(1)

Who soars high upto the Himalayan heights
By whom are fathomed all the oceanic depths,
Each hindrance feels itself bashfully shy
When comes to face the eyelids rapt in 'Muse'!

(2)

The reverend ascetic Shri Vidyasagarji
Who is the Lord of the goddess 'Beatitude',
Whose flag of fair fame flies up high
From Earth beneath to higher bright skies!

(3)

Who truly is a great 'Triveṇī'– confluence
Of right Faith, Knowledge and of right Conduct
The path of 'Liberation', could be perceived –
By you, O our great Spiritual Guide!

Lal Chandra Jain
(Translator)

Eulogium

The creation of the Epic poem –' Mūkamāṭī'– 'The Silent Earth'- is a remarkable achievement of the modern Indian Literature. The first and the foremost thing, indeed, is that the very imagination of making an insignificant down-trodden and poor thing like 'soil', the theme of the Epic poem, is entirely novel. The second thing is that, having visualized the highest splendour into the insignificance of the soil, it is to take the poetry in the state of being one with spiritualism, by moulding its advance towards the greater purity into a metaphor of an auspicious journey to'Final liberation'. Due to this very reason, the Epic poem 'Mūkamāṭī' by Rev. Acharya Shri Vidyasagarji, is not merely a poetic performance, it is the music of the soul of a philosopher-saint– a saint who is a living image of divine devotion and, the divine devotion, which, while treading cautiously upon the destinations of self-purification, accomplishes the universal well-being. This saint wishes to resonate every body's heart with his life-vision acquired through his penance, and mellowed by his own subtle experiences. The serene voice, combined with significant communication, which is manifest in his religious discourses-the Rev. Acharya has given it a poetical form, coupled with the flow of 'verse liberatia', (Blank Verse) and the internal rhythm of poetic sensibility.

At the very outset, it shall not be irrelevant to raise the

question whether 'Mūkamāṭī' should be termed as an epic, a semi-epic or only a 'poetical work'. It is not possible to set it within the framework of the traditional definition of an epic; but, if it is considered that this poetical work, divided into four cantos, is composed within almost 500 pages, it touches the limits of an epic from the point of view of its volume. On opening the very first page, the natural panorama resembling to an epic, unfolds itself :

"In the boundless space
A bedding of bluishness,
And…hither...underneath
Prevails absolute silence,

xx xx xx

The sun is slumbering no more indeed
Yet he is
Still reclining
Into the gentle lap of the mother,
Is changing sides
While drawing the garment over his face.
On the lips of the Eastern horizon…"

–Canto 1, page – 01

–In this very context, the water-lily, she-lotus, moon, stars, fragrance! wind, river-bank…

"Soil of the river-bank
Opens her heart
Before the Mother Earth !"

–Canto 1, page - 04

All this natural panorama, after touching this point, becomes centred upon this fundamental philosophic query :

"When would this life-order

Come to an end ?
When would this embodiment
Be dropped out ?
Tell it to her, O Mother…!

xx xx xx

Give some remedy, O Mother !
Repair the damage Thyself, O Mother !
Listen to me, O Mother !
Make no delay
Show the steps, the path
The provisions too for the journey !"

Canto 1, page – 05

The pain and agony of the soil finds expression in such a piercing and heart-moving quality in the twenty or thirty lines, which come prior to this extract, that the element of compassion assumes a concrete form. The conversation between the Mother and the Daughter goes on taking a sudden new turn every minute, like the current of the river, and the philosophic thinking unfolds itself through it. Every fact seeks its significance into the origination of realizing the 'essential truth'. It is the most special feature of 'Mūkamāṭī' that the philosophic vision of life gets itself defined by this style. The other point is that this philosophic view doesn't seem to be superfluous; it reveals itself through its context and environment.

According to the expectations of an epic, the other aspects of creativity, in addition to the natural surroundings, are also included within the fold of 'Mūkamāṭī'. If one thinks in this context, the question shall arise as to who is the hero of 'Mūkamāṭī', and who the heroine ? The question is very interesting, because it can be answered only with the viewpoint of *Anekānta**.

The Earth indeed, is the heroine; the Artisan–potter may be regarded as the hero...; but this view doesn't bear semblance in its earthly sense. If there is any romance here, it is that of the spiritual type. How much has the Earth stayed in expectation of the Artisan–potter, since ages by gone, that he, having redeemed it, shall bring out the auspicious image of the holy pitcher from within the invisible reality of existence. The significance of the holy pitcher lies there into the holy feet-bathing of the Guru-the Spiritual Guide, who is the basis of the faith of the devotee– eminent trader, a character in the Epic poem :

> " Protect us, your holy feet are
> The ship which floats as well as rescues.
> O compassionate sage of sages !
> Carry us to the shores of the ocean of existence !"
>
> *–Canto 4, page – 325*

The hero of the Epic-poem is this very Gurudeva–the Rev. Spiritual Guide; but for the Guru himself, the supreme adorable hero is *Arihanta Deva***–

"Who live after being liberated from all delusions

---

* *Anekānta* - "An assertion of probability" about the objects or topics, with reference to their different genuine properties. It includes a logical method of judicious thinking under Jain philosophy-*Anekānta*–The doctirne of manifold predications, many-sided view of Logic.

** *Arihant Deva*-This term denotes a perfected Soul/Being who has attained omniscience (*Kevala Jñāna*) and is still associated with the corporeal body. He remains in the world till the end of his life- time, as a lord, having perfect knowledge and twelve unique qualities of religious austerities and penance. Thus he preaches the way to Liberation to worldly beings.

Who are fully free from worldly attachments and aversions
For whom the births and deaths, old age and decay
Can't touch now,

xx xx xx

They are the abode of fearlessness, free from the
*seven fears**
To whom sleep and drowsiness doesn't encircle,

xx xx xx

Who are devoid of sorrow, always in the state of
sorrowlessness

xx xx xx

Those who have neither attachment in belongings nor
any union of saints
Those who are alone–only their own True 'selves'

xx xx xx

They are always fully beyond all worries,
Absolved from the *eighteen blemishes.***

–Canto 4, pages 326 – 327

From the viewpoint of poetry in 'Mūkamāṭī', the beauty of the figures of speech based on word-usage as well as word-meanings is charming under new references. For the poet, the high charm is that of the word, by the usage of which; in the common sense, he bestows a new edge to its structure after sharpening it upon the rub-stone of grammar, unfolds its new

---

* *Seven Fears* - (1) death (2) pains (3) sudden fears (4) Non-safety (5) Non-control of mind speech and body (6) Worldly troubles (7) fears of the other world.

** *Eighteen blemishes* - (1) Birth (2) Old age (3) hunger (4) thirst (5) astonishment (6)discomfort (7) sadness (8) disease (9)distress (10)prides (11) Worldly enchantments (12) fear (13) sleep (14) Worry (15) sweat (16) attachment (17) jealousy (18) death.

layers. The etymology of the word does provide a glimpse of its internal sense; one visualizes the rare and untouched dimensions of meanings through it. At least, fifty examples may be gathered from the Epic poem, if we not only keep in view the sense-exploring eye of the poet, but also this rarity by him, where the sound of the word transforms meaningfully into the various resonances of similarities. As for example–

"Since the prime dawn of the Era
He has been assigned the name–
'*Kumbhakāra !*'– the 'Pot-Maker !'
'*Kum*'..., that is, 'the earth' or 'Soil'
And
'*Bha*'..., that is, 'fortune'–
Here, the one,
Who is a fortunate fortune-maker
is called to be the '*Kumbhakāra* !"

–Canto 1, page -28

xx xx xx

An ass* with a natural course of feelings prays to God That :

" My name should prove its worth, O Lord !
That is to say–
The word *'gada'* signifies 'disease'
The word *'hā'* signifies 'healer'
I should be the healer of everybody's ailments,
...that's all,"

–Canto 1, page – 40

xx xx xx

* Ass– The Hindi word (*gadahā*) – an ass– may be interpreted as (*gada*)- disease (*hā*) – (healer)- that is, the 'healer of disease'.

"To become indeed a path-finder
Is to become a diamond–
The word *'Rāhī'* itself
Is, in its reverse order, indicating–
Rā... hī hī.. rā" *

–Canto 1, page – 57

xx xx xx

"The physical body as well as the desire-body
Will have to be burnt to ashes
Through the fire of penance
By the observance of religious austerities
You will have to undergo severe self-mortification
Then, and then alone,
The Vital Soul
Would come true.
The word *'Kharā'* itself too
Is indicating through its reverse form-
–Without being burnt to ashes,
How can a genuine insight be achieved ?
*"Rā...kha kha...rā**.... ."*

–Canto 1, page - 57

With this very word-discipline, the inner meanings have been manifested as of- *Nārī* (fair-sex), *Sutā* (girl-virgin), *Duhitā* (daughter), *Kumārī* (miss), *Strī* (lady), *Abalā* (fragile woman) etc.

---

* Hindi syllables of the word '*Rāhī*' - the path-finder - put reversely make the word – '*Hīrā*', that is, 'the diamond'.

** Hindi syllables of the word '*Rākha*' - ashes - put reversely make the word - '*Kharā*', that is, 'the genuine'.

Here, it may be indicated that the Acharya-poet* has expressed his feelings of regard and reliance for women. He has appreciated the decorum of their peaceful and disciplined form.

The inner aspect of poetry is reflected in 'Mūkamāṭī', and careful view of the fundamental principles of literature has generally been taken. The quotations, if cited, shall be profusely numerous, because really a major part of the Epic poem is quotable, which constitutes a rare quality of the literary performance. The poet says thus :

> "The word *Sāhitya* [literature] looks as if being cast
> Into the skilful mould of the Artisan !
> "That which is united and co-ordinated with the welfare
> Is regarded to be benevolent,
> And
> The purport of the benevolent
> Is the profession of literature,
> It really means that
> The true literature is only that
> By studying which
> Happiness should be originated and attained
> Otherwise,
> Like a flower devoid of sweet smell
> It is the deprivation of happiness–
> A cluster of words without sum and substance...!"
>
> *–Canto 2, pages - 110-111*

The Epic poem 'Mūkamāṭī' has been divided into four cantos by the saint-poet :

---

* '*Acharya*' represents the organiser of the *Saṅgha*. He is really the chief of a group of ascetics as well as the devoted house- holders. As the head of an order of the saints, he shows the way to the Right Conduct, the Vows and Practices.

Canto : 1. No Admixture, Gain in Category
Canto : 2. The 'Word' is not 'Wisdom':
The 'Wisdom', not 'Purification'
Canto : 3. The Preservation of Virtuousness :
The Purification of Sinfulness
Canto : 4. The Fiery Ordeal : The Silvery Ashes

Canto 1 : The first canto expresses the process of that primary state of purification of soil, where it remains in a mixed stage in the form of a lump mingled with the stone-particles. In the creative imagination of the potmaker Artisan, the auspicious Earthen pitcher has taken its shape. For that significant form, which the potmaker Artisan is keen to assign to soil as an auspicious Earthen Pitcher, it is at first necessary that, after being dugged out, crushed and sifted the soil, should be cleansed fully of the stone-particles. The soil, which is at present, in the form of an admixture due to inharmonious substances - the stone-particles being mixed up with it against its nature, shall only acquire its original gain in category, when it achieves its purified state in the form of softened soil :

"By this reference,
The purport of the word '*Varṇa*'*
Neither indicates a colour
Nor it symbolizes a 'social section'
But,
It means character, conduct, manners.
That is to say–
The one,

---

* *Varṇa* – This Sanskrit word is chiefly used in three senses– (i) colour and form (ii) caste or social section (iii) a letter of an alphabet (in Hindi).

Who is befriended
Will have to adjust
His attributes and functions–
...His image and identity,
According to the other
Who has taken him under his roof.
Otherwise
the blame of caste-admixture
Will have to be born on head…!

xx xx xx

As regards only the colour-tint
The cow-milk too is white
The milk of the swallow-wort too is white
Both of them are outwardly bright
But
As and when they are intermingled
A disorder is produced–
The milk becomes sour
It becomes troublesome !
"The changing of water into milk, indeed,
Is a gain in category,
It's a boon in itself.
And
The becoming of milk sourish
Is the confused mixture of species
It's a curse !"

–Canto 1, pages - 47-49

Canto 2 :

"Lo, now the Artisan
Mingles in due quantity
The filtered pure water
Into the saffron-like Soil,
He is blowing new breath
Into the life of the Soil
Through every gracious particle,

xx xx xx

On entering into the breath of the Soil,
The water
Has attained a new vitality there,
Whereas, the ignorant one
Has acquired new wisdom
At the *feet*, of the wise."

–Canto 2, page – 89

In the process of digging the soil, the Potter–artisan's hoe knocks at the head of a thorn, its head gets torn; it thinks of taking revenge, while the Potter–artisan feels self-aversion at his carelessness. His ejaculations are :

"I pardon, let me be pardoned
I forgive all others,
Hope to be forgiven by all,
Friendliness should prevail naturally
Among all of us for ever !
Why, when and with whom should I
Enter into animosity ?
Here, in the world at large,
There is none to be envisaged as my enemy !"

–Canto 2, page - 105

The effect of this feeling was observed thus–

"Even the Supine sense of fury –
Is being vomited the sense of revenge…
At every moment is taking place the arrival of
The sense of great awakening
Which represents the treasure of virtuous acts"…

–Canto 2, page - 106

XX XX XX

"Without being sprinkled with divine wisdom
These plants of words
Never get flourished,
It's also true that
On the plants of words
Fragrant and pollinated–
The flowers of perfect awakening never smell sweet

XX XX XX

When the flower of perfect awakening
Gets moulded and transformed,
That ripened fruits, therein,
Is, indeed, called purification.
Intellect rears restlessness
Purification bears the fruits of perfect repose,
Not through the flowers, but through the fruits."

–Canto 2, page - 106-107

In this second canto, the saint-poet has depicted literary understanding in its various dimensions. All the nine poetic sentiments (*Rasas*) have been defined here. The inner nature of music has been explained. Exceedingly original exposition of the sentiment of love is presented. The poetical charm in the depiction of seasons is admirable. The philosophic vision as I have mentioned before, is manifested at every step. "All existence abounds in origin, decay and fixedness"*–this aphorism has been translated admirably in conversational language—

" 'In-coming'and 'out-going' is in force
In-coming, that is, birth - is 'production'
Out-going, that is, death -is 'destruction'
In force, that is, fixedness - is 'continuation'
And
'Entity,'that is, the eternal 'Being', is there
This is the 'Truth' indeed, this very the 'Reality'...!"

–Canto 2, page – 185

The sense is that mere utterance is 'word' the perfect interpretation of 'wordings' is 'wisdom' or awakening, and to accomplish it through our sensibility and conduct is 'purification'.

Canto 3 : Due to the piety of mind, speech and body, due to the performance of auspicious deeds, due to aspiring for the public welfare- the virtuousness (*Puṇya*) is accomplished. Anger, pride, deceit, greed–breed the fruits of sinfulness or evil :

"It's a peculiar point, that
The ocean too is the treasure of genuine pearls,
The reason is that

* "उत्पाद–व्यय–ध्रौव्ययुक्तं सत्" – That is, "All existence abounds in origin, decay and fixedness"–an aphorism by–Acharya Umāswāmī's *Tattvārtha sūtra*, Chapter vth, *sutra* 30

The material cause behind a pearl is water,
That is, the water really transforms into a pearl
Nevertheless
It we ponder over it
It is found that
This achievement is obtained mainly due to
 the earth-factor.
In transforming water into the shape of a pearl
The pearl-oyster is an eminent cause,
And
The pearl-oyster in itself is a part of the earth.
Having trained the pearl-oyster, the Earth itself
Has sent it into the ocean.
Having relieved the water of its stupor
And to mould it into a pearl form,
Having taken it out of the pit of decline
And to place it on an elevated position,
Is the objective of the patience-retaining Earth.
This is the real nature of compassion
This is the Kārmic action of the Sentient Being."

–Canto 3, pages 192-193

In this canto 3, the Potter–artisan has depicted, through the story of the development of soil, the auspicious gain which springs up due to the accomplishment of virtuous deeds. The descent of large cloud-pearls from the clouds. The showers of pearls fall down upon the un-ripened pitchers, within the courtyard of the Potter–artisan. The news of the showers of pearls reaches the king. A hint is dropped to the royal retinue to get the heaps of pearls filled into the bags. . . . As soon as the attendants bend down to pick up the pearls, the sky is rocked with a heavy thundering sound–a great misfortune a great misfortune; a great misfortune !– a sin...a sin...a sin !

The king feels that he has been nailed down by some power of spell. Ultimately, the Potter–artisan dedicates the heaps of pearls to the king after considering that he is the real claimant for them.

The ocean agitates on visualizing the glory of the earth/ the submarine fire– an adversary of the anguish of ocean/the surge of the three dense clouds– the symbols of the three coloured emotions (*Leśyās)* – black, blue and brown/the call to the astrological planet Rāhu by the ocean/the solar eclipse/ the assault of Lord Indra by thunderbolt upon the clouds/the hailstorm, the scene of 'universal destruction', –

"High above, the force of atom is at work
Then, hither...downwards
The power of Manu exists !

xx xx xx

The one is a killer
The other a saviour;
The one is Science
Whose subsistence is 'argument',
The other is Faith
Which doesn't worry, for a calling".

–Canto 3, page-249

"Before the deep-insight of the devotee
No difference does remain
Between the water and the inflammable fire.
The journey towards perfect ascetic devotion
Proceeds, all along and ought to proceed, indeed
From diversity to unity
From the perceptible to the imperceptible !"

–Canto 3, page – 267

Canto 4 : The Potter–artisan has moulded the pitcher into due shape and size; now the preparations are on to put it into kiln to get it heated. The whole of the process has been poetized. Amid various methods of performances, the wooden piece of acacia tree relates its pains. The sticks burn and get extinguished inside the kiln; the Potter–artisan constantly tries to keep them burning up. The immature pitcher says to the fire :

"To turn my evils into ashes
Is to make me live indeed
To burn away the faults of our own 'self'
And those of the others
Has been acknowledged by the saints
–As a supreme religious performance.
The faults are inanimate elements,
Are the by-products of some accidental cause,
Arrive somehow from outside;
The virtuous merits belong to Soul,
Such merits deserve reception.
You shall attain the most sublime Truth through this deed,
This life shall be infused with a true purpose by you,
I possess the capability of retaining water
Which is awaiting you,
Your co-operation is inevitable
For its perfect expression."

–Canto 4, page - 277

The frame-work of the fourth canto is so enlarged and the narrative references are so numerous, that it is difficult even to allude them with their sum and substance. The pitcher has been heated for so many days inside the kiln. The Potter–artisan approaches the kiln :

" 'The well-being of the pitcher reflects our own
well-being';
–Having remarked thus, the Potter–artisan
Welcomes joyfully the Kiln,
And
The heap of the dusty ashes,
Which has gathered upon the chest of the kiln
Is removed by him with a spade in hand.
The more the ashes get out of the way,
The more the curiosity of the Potter–artisan
Grows as to
When that proficient pitcher should come in view."

–Canto 4, page – 296

And, he takes out joyfully the mature and heated pitcher. This very pitcher has been placed by the potter–Artisan into the hands of the attendant of the credulous eminent trader of the town , so that the holy feet of the Spiritual Guide–the Guru, –who arrived for the bestowal of foodstuffs, should get washed with the water filled into it, and the thirst be quenched. The attendant beats it seven times before carrying it away-and seven notes of gamut are resonated out of it, which resound their sense within the poets mind thus :

"Sā...re ga...ma, that is,
All types of afflictions
Pa...dha, that is, the essential quality–
And,
Ni, that is, 'not'*, –
–Affliction can never be an essential quality of Soul,

---

* *Sā...re...ga...ma–* The Hindi syllables (Musical notes) -That is *(Sā...re...ga...ma)*, If taken together, mean - All the sorrows-pada – that is, - essential quality (Nature); And '*ni*' –that is , 'not'.

It is only the degenerating after-effect contrary to the real nature
Of the soul, under the bondage of the kārmic
nature of delusion."

–Canto 4, page – 305

In this very context, the notes of -Mṛdaṅga–Timbrel resonate mildly :

"Dhā...dhin...dhin...dhā...
Dhā...dhin...dhin...dhā...
Different are those bodies different the vital con sciousness
Tā...tin...tin...tā...
Tā...tin...tin...tā...
Why worry for the body... why worry for the body...?"

–Canto 4, page – 306

In this canto, the process of the bestowal of food-stuffs to an ascetic has been described in all its details. The sentiment of the devotees, the joy of the bestowal of food-stuffs or the sorrow of its non-bestowal, the insight of the saint, the gist of the religious discourses, and the coming back home of the eminent trader with an unwell mind, after the bestowal of food-stuffs, probably due to the reason that the eminent trader has visualized the final destination of life; but he can't make himself free from bondage at present :

"It is the very significance of a saint's arrival, indeed,
That the end of the worldliness is visualized,
It matters little if
The one, who makes an approach,

May or may not become at once
A saint, or a person with self-restraint–
There is no rule or regulation whatsoever
But,
He is sure to be a man of self-contentment.
A blessing in the right direction, indeed,
Is a temple in the right condition."

–Canto 4, page – 352

This fourth canto is a wonderful beauty-house of references, of assigning a new sense and significance to the off-shoots of thoughts, of visualizing and giving a fair hearing to the lofty points of divine metaphysical thinking, and of the mundane and ultra mundane inquests and inconvenient. Here, the equipments of worship and devotion engage themselves into a living dialogue. The human sensibilities, merits and demerits find an expression through them. This strange dramatic colouring and excellence and the dispersion of the preceding and the following links of the contexts may seem to be Inconvenient to a reviewer, but from the viewpoint of giving relevance to the poetic work, their creative imagination is bold significant and befitting to the modern panorama. This canto is a poetical, narrative, a Semi-epic complete in itself. It is quotable in its full form. The difficulty is that no justice is done to the 'literary work' by giving only some selected quotations. Whatever is left behind is comparatively wide, is significant. Well, let us see the context of the narrative.

The golden pitcher is perplexed and excited as to why the hero of the story, having discarded him, has honoured the earthen pitcher ? To retaliate the insult, the Golden pitcher calls a terrorist gang which, being active, creates panic in the family. What are its misdeeds, through what calamities, the eminent trader, enables himself in protecting his family along with the help of nature-forces and the living beings other than human beings- the band of elephants, and male and female serpents- how all of them are saved by a boat sinking down into the mid-stream, how the sense of forgiveness of the eminent trader affects a change of the terrorist's heart–the narration of all these events is no less interesting than that of a novel. The poetical taste is there indeed, in its abundance. If we do agree, we may take to it that the 'Golden pitcher' and 'terrorism' are the fresh references of the modern life. The solution, in accordance with the contexts of to-day, has been presented through the *analysis* of the modern social set-up with the symbolic and suggestive style of poetry, and not in a plain manner.

The peculiar thing is that we get a sense of social responsibility through the medium of a bug–

> "…It is a pity that
> The greedy and sinful persons
> Turn even the marital hand-taking (ceremony)
> Into the life-taking (formality).
> Generally, the attendants are asked to serve
> In an improper way,
> And
> The disbursement of salaries too, improper indeed.
> –Such persons tell themselves to be
> The progeny of *Manu* !
> The magnanimous human beings !
> On hearing the name of donation
> The symptoms of paralysis come up
> Into their liberal hands,
> Even then, whatever is bestowed
> Or is caused to be bestowed
> In the form of one or a half drop

It is indeed with a sense of ill-will.
The obtainers of which are unable to digest it
properly,
Otherwise
Despite being red, why is our blood
So much bad-smelling ?"

–Canto 4, pages - 386-387

And the bug says to the eminent trader :

"Don't try to confer dry temptations,
A self-dependent life should be lived up,
Offer away the watery libations
To the skill of cunningness !
Pay, homage
To humility which is the mother of eminence !
The sky should be contained
Within the largeness of decorum
And–
The life should become an example of liberality !
Without any pretext–
The troubles of the others should be removed !"

–Canto 4, pages - 387-388

And, in the end, after the adoration of the non-attached ascetic seated on a stone-slab, the terrorism itself speaks out :

"O my Lord !–
The entire world, indeed,
Abounds in sufferings,
There is joy here, but it is sensual–
And that too transitory !
This was...really...felt by us,
But
The genuine faith is lacking

In the eternal happiness;
Yes ! yes !!, if,
After attaining the eternal bliss,
You, yourself
Can make us see that blissfulness,
Or
Can tell us about your own experience,
Relating to that subject,
...Then...
It is possible, that
We too, being fully confident,
May own a perfect dedication
In our lives, similar to that of yours,
Otherwise
The idea approved by the mind shall remain
unfulfilled,
Hence,
'The idea at your inner heart be accomplished'–
Please bless us with such an utterance,
It shall be a great favour done to us."

–Canto 4, pages - 484-485

The Spiritual Guide –the Gurudeva– can deliver only sermons, and can make no promise. The soul can attain salvation really by one's own true spiritual awakening, and the immortal bliss can't be explained through preachings. Penance and austerities must be observed. It is really spiritual self-realization accomplished through perfect devotion and dedication to soul. The sermon of an ascetic is :

"The complete uprooting, indeed,
Of all the shackles
In the form of the body, the mind and the speech
Is *Mokṣa* that is, the Final Salvation,

Within the stainless state of this Final Salvation,
Resides the Eternal Bliss
Which–
On being accomplished,
How it is possible to return
Here, in this world–
–You please tell me yourself !"

–Canto 4, pages 486-487

"The faith will beget true perception,
Surely it will,
But
At the final destination, not in the way on !"
And,
Rapt into the Supreme Silence
The Saint...
And
As if staring unwinkingly
At the surroundings
...The Silent Earth."

–Canto 4, page – 488

These are some hints about the narrative, the poetic grandeur, the spiritual dimensions of the subject-matter, the inspiring flashes of the philosophic visions and reflections of the thought of Mūkamāṭī – 'The Silent Earth'.

Apart from all these, there is so much relevant and incidental in this Epic poem such as the colloquial expressions of public life, the splendours of the mystical seed-syllables, the foundation– base of the science of holy-incantations, the experiments of '*Āyurveda*'*, the wonders of numerical

**Āyurveda– The ancient Indian medical science of medical treatment (in Sanskrit language).*

usages, and produced in modern life by science, some new suppositions which reach up to the 'star-war'.

It is somewhat difficult to say whether this literary work, in its magnitude, is more of an epic-poetry or a Spiritual Performance. But it is, definitely, a fresh sacred Scripture of modern life in poetical form. And, the manner in which a 'sacred book' has to be studied with devotion, a solution has to be sought to our inquests from the Gurudeva–the Spiritual Guide, in the same way, we believe, that self-study and deeper understanding shall, bless with wonderful happiness and contentment.

It is neither an introduction, nor a preface, nor a foreword. It is an eulogium, an invocation to the ascetic Acharya, Saint-poet Vidyasagarji, whose divine wisdom and poetic genius has begot this 'Tree of Paradise'– The wish-fulfilling tree –that is– *Kalpa-vṛkṣa*.

Lakshmi Chandra Jain
Bharatiya Jnanpith

Paryushana Parva
September, 1988
New Delhi -110003

Homage to Jñāna-gurudeva

The Great Seer from whom
I got philosophic visions
The creator of holy incantations–
From whom I got incantations,
Who assigned me a status
Gave a path
Along with its provisions too, for the journey,
By whose tender leaf-like palms
Was cherished this life of mine–
And withered away the majesty of delusions;
–In the blissful lotus -hands
Of that prideless
A treasure of virtues,
Guruvar Śrī Jñānasāgarjī–
–Dedicating 'in absentia,'
The literary creation of Mūkamāṭī–'The Silent Earth'.

–A large-black-bee at the lotus-feet of the Gurudeva

The Silent Earth

Mūkamāṭī

Bharatiya Jnanpith

The Thought Wave
(Mānasa Taraṅga)

Generally, whatever is existent, can't be non-existent, and the origination too of that which is non existent is impossible. Not only the philosophic thinking, but also the new materialistic age has welcomed this fact.

Though, through the nature-born creativity and transmutability of each and every thing, the present-past-future, that is, the triple-timed life is proven; even then, the Creator–Maker of this endless world is some supernaturally powerful *'Puruṣa'*- i.e., some Supreme Being, –and who else can 'He' be, except God Himself ?- generally, all the philosophers extend their acceptability to this recognition. Where are they fully familiar with the settled order of cause and effect ?

Who is the doer of a particular deed and what is the efficient cause behind it? –So long as the mystery related to this point remains unfolded, only till then, this allured mortal being, is engaged, day and night, in the acquisition and protection of suitable things, separate to his own being, and in the removal of unfavourable things.

Yes, well, whether it is an act related to sentient 'being' or insentient 'matter', its origination is not possible without a due cause. And, it is also an irrefutable rule that an effect really resembles its cause. As the seeds are sown, so the harvest is reaped, nothing contrary to it.

Thus, the cause is chiefly of the two types–the first is 'the material cause' *(Upādāna)*, the second 'the efficient cause' *(Nimitta)*. The material cause may be called the internal cause; the efficient cause, the external cause. The material cause is that which moulds itself into the form of the effect, and that which acts as 'helper', in its moulding is called the 'efficient cause'. As for example, a lump of soil changes into the form of a pitcher with the help of a potter-artisan.

On taking a minute view of the above-said example, the related originalities, not only those of the material cause, but also those of the efficient cause become evident. Here, there are few other efficient causes also, in addition to the Potter–artisan who is at work, as an efficient cause– the light, the potter's wheel, the proper rod for the circular motion of the wheel, the string, and the unshakable axle fixed firmly into the earth etc., etc.

Among these efficient causes, some of them are neutral, while some others active. In such a condition, to those who have no faith in the efficient causes, this pen puts questions, that :

–Can even a skilful Potter–artisan make a pitcher in absence of light ?

– Can the lump of soil be moulded into the form of a pitcher without the Potter–artisan's wheel ?

– Is the circular motion of the Potter–artisan's wheel possible, without the rod ?

– Is the circular motion of the wheel possible without the support of the axle ?

– Can all these events take place without the ground, which provides the base to everything ?

– Is the Potter–artisan as neutral or unconcerned as the

axle and the light ?

– Can the lump of soil assume the shape of a pitcher by a mere touch, without being pitcher-like into the hands of the Potter–artisan ?

– Without acquiring functional consciousness in assuming the figure of a pitcher, can the typical pitcher reach the hands of the Potter–artisan ?

– Can a Potter–artisan use his functional consciousness in casting a due pitcher without the desired will for it ?

– Is the wish for casting a pitcher without an aim ?

– What else is that word except 'no', which can provide a solution to all these questions ?

Keeping in view this inevitability of the 'efficient cause', to suppose God as the 'Creator of the Universe' too, is to deny the independent competence of the reality of substance, and to put a question-mark upon the venerability of the status of God.

Not only within the sects if the explores of the true nature of substance, and those of the enjoyers of the real state of substance, but also among the true devotees of God too, that doubt may arise as to where did God reside before the 'Creation of the Universe' ? Was He an Incorporeal Being or a Corporeal One ?

In the form of an 'Incorporeal Being', the creation of an endless universe is indeed, something of a distant affair; even the petty worldly activities can't be performed. Yes, it is also not proper to say that God, having forsaken his state of 'Beatitude', re-takes an embodiment-and disposes off the worldly affairs; because the formation of a body depends upon the past life-Karmas, the bondage of Karmas depends upon the fair or foul innate feelings, thoughts and sentiments; and the incidence of these innate feelings thoughts and sentiments is based upon the sense-organs and the craving for mental inclinations; and it is universally accepted that

God remains entirely above all these things.

Having renounced all sensualities and unclean emotions, after being triumphant over the slavery of senses, and foul emotions-and thus becoming a winner of his own mind; the ascetic, who has dedicated himself with full faith for 'self-accomplishment' and has attained 'eternal happiness' after revealing the hidden Godly powers from within his soul– that God can't incarnate Himself now into the world. After churning out clarified butter from the milk, can the clarified butter turn back into the form of milk again?

The second option too, in the form of supposing God as a 'Corporeal Being', is not proper; because, the body in itself is that bondage, which is the root of all the other fetters. If the body is there, the world is there; what else is there in the world except sufferings ? Therefore, 'Godliness' cannot accept or tolerate any bondage in the form of afflictions. Thus, the accomplishment of 'Godliness' is not possible under 'worldliness'. Yes, worldly one may become God on the basis of perfect divine dedication, after eliminating all worldly bondages.

It can also not be said that, when the attractive cities etc. are erected even by the 'Vidyādharas' and the celestial deities through the strength of their occult or magical arts and super powers of alterations of body, then, what hindrance is there in the creation of universe by Corporeal God? Because, the cities etc. constructed by the celestial deities etc., are instantaneously improvised, and not triple-timed, i.e. related to the past, the present and the future. Even these constructions too are limited and not world-wide. Moreover, there is no purpose of beneficence there, but the purpose is that of satisfying a mind thirsty for sensuous pleasures. The real thing, indeed, is that the occult arts and super powers of alterations of body too bear fruit in accordance with the rise of the pre-accomplished auspicious Karmas, otherwise not.

According to Jain philosophy, the corporeal Supreme Soul too, regarded as the piercer of the mountains of exploits of past Karmas, the Knower of the true state of things of the universe and acknowledged as the 'Supreme Guide' for the path of 'Salvation', is corporeally existent. As he acts like a benefactor for all worldly beings through religious preachings, similarly, it is not reasonable to say that God obliges us all through the creation of this universe. Because,firstly, Jain philosophy has only formally accepted the corporeal Supreme Soul as God. Really, they have been assigned the status of an ascetic–well-versed in Holy Scriptures, and only such *Snātaka-Muni* in natural (naked) form, who are free from all worldly attachments, bless with religious preachings unselfishly.

Having adopted as basis the religious preaching of Jainism, to support one's own view, the very acceptance of God in the form of the 'Creator of the world', is to prove God an image of partiality, having a feeling of attachment to one and aversion to others; because, why His worldly beings created by 'Him', are some poor and some rich, some full of demerits some meritorious; some of them humble, inferior; some pitiable and slaves, while the others free, independent and prosperous; some of them men, while the others monkeys, animals and birds; some the deceitful, the cunning the knave, and the heartless ones, while the others virtuous and pious; some having well-shaped bodies and looking beautiful, while others ugly and distorted etc., etc. why ? Why that God won't have made all of them at par with one another ? Or, 'He', should have made them all similar to himself after 'His'own image? The personality of a God, merciful to the poor, a treasure of compassion, can't be as such. To save God from this great defect, it is also improper if one says that God allots the worldly beings their due heavens or hells etc., indeed, to let them undergo pleasures or pains according to their own merits or demerits; because, what purpose remains to be served by God when all the diversities and disparities of these living beings are the resultant of their own auspicious-inauspicious Karmas? Not because of the police, but due to theft, a thief gets himself into the jail; not because of the celestials, but due to her good moral character, Sita's fame has spread far and wide.

In this context, one more thing deserves to be added that, "Some schools of philosophy, take Jain philosophy, to be an atheist one (*Nāstika*) and propagate that those, who don't have faith in God are 'atheists', who do not accept God". This estimation by them really shows their little knowledge about philosophy. It should be known that 'Jain', philosophy, which is the sustainer of the '*Śramaṇa Sanskṛti*'*, has affirmed its deepest faith in God as supremely revered and venerable, not as an Architect of the Universe. Hence, Jain philosophy is an ideal theist (*Āstika*) philosophy, which shows the right direction to the Atheistic philosophies. Really, to recognize, God as the 'Creator of the World', is the very negation of 'His' existence, and it is; indeed, 'Atheism'– a falsehood. In due confirmation of this relevant topic, the Fourteenth and the Fifteenth memorable couplets (aphorisms) from the fifth Chapter of the Hṛidaya Sthānīya Gītā, in the great epic Mahābhārata, may also be quoted here–

---

* *Śramaṇa Sanskṛti – that is, the great ancient culture, propagated by the Jain ascetics in India.*

"न कर्तृत्वं न कर्माणि लोकस्य सृजति प्रभुः ।
न कर्मफलसंयोगं स्वभावस्तु प्रवर्तते ।। 14 ।।
नादत्ते कस्यचित् पापं न चैव सुकृतं विभुः ।
अज्ञानेनावृतं ज्ञानं तेन मुह्यन्ति जन्तवः ।। 15 ।।"

– That is, The Lord or the Supreme Being doesn't prepare the creativeness of the World-[doesn't make Himself the 'Doer' of the World]-doesn't really create the Kārmic actions and the work of joining their resultants. The very nature of the world makes the world take its own course.

– Couplet,14

– That Lord or the Supreme Being neither owns one's sinfulness nor auspiciousness as well. The worldly creatures feel infatuated due to their vision being clouded with delusions.

–Couplet, 15

– This very sense is very clearly expressed through the following memorable verse in the *Tejovindu Upanisad* (5/51-52) –

"रक्षको विष्णुरित्यादि ब्रह्मा स्रष्टेस्तु कारणम् ।
संहारे रुद्र इत्येवं सर्वं मिथ्येति निश्चिनु ।।"

– To suppose *'Brahmā'* as the 'creator' of the world, *'Visṇu'* as the 'protector' and *'Maheśa'* as its 'destroyer' is untrue. To set this supposition aside is, indeed, 'Theism'. So be it.

For unravelling some such fundamental doctrines, this Literary Work has been done, and it is such creative work, due to whose holy contact, there appears an uprise in the feelings of detachment, even in a life enveloped with the sentiments of love full of excessive attachment to worldly pursuits, in which, the earthly figures of speech have been adorned with unearthly fineries; the figure of speech is now feeling itself as enough; in which, the word-usage acquires its true meaning and the meaning gets filled with the ultimate sublime truth; which has, under the pretext of criticism, bestowed eyes to the new way of investigation; which has affected and influenced the Hindi-world with its splendour even prior to its complete appearance like the sun hidden within the lap of the East at the day-break; during the perusal of which, even the poets skilled in the art of poesy, would find themselves far away from the creation of spiritual poetry; whose adorable deity is the perfectly pure consciousness; from whose every line of each reference, soul gets inspired to awaken its dormant powers of consciousness; which hasn't denied the settled order of the race, caste., high family etc. but has affirmed in accordance with the conduct after birth, the high or low forms of changes in them. Therefore, along with avoiding the blemish of 'caste-admixture', which has recognized the 'gain in category', as the nobility and success of human life; which has declared a life full of the sentiments of purity and goodness as truly 'religious', whose real purpose is to keep up alive that perfectly passion-free and calm '*Śramaṇa Sanskṛti*'– that is, the 'Culture of Asceticism', which aims at uprooting the corrupt customs and practices, pervading the social, educational, political and religious fields of life; and thus moulding the Age from (Bhoga) that is , the enjoyments of the materialistic world to (Yoga), that is, the religious and abstract meditations of the Spiritual Bliss (Yoga), by initiating the auspicious purificatory rites; and thus which has been given the name –'*Mūkamāṭī*'– The Silent Earth.

At the... '*Maḍhiyājī*[1] in Jabalpur
It was the occasion for the second reading
Of the Holy Scriptures,
When this 'Work' at first came into being
And, at the sight-gladdening Naināgiri[2]
The literary-journey came to its completion
–The *Samavasarana Temple*[3] came into existence
When took place the *Gajaratha*[4] ceremony.

– The large-black-bee at Shri Guru's lotus-feet

(Vidyasagar)

---

1. 'Maḍhiyājī – A famous place of pilgrimage at Jabalpur, M.P., India.

2. Naināgiri– A sacred place of pilgrimage in Chhatarapur District in M.P.

3. Samavasaraṇa Temple– The holy and grand place, where the great gathering meets to hear the religious preachings of Tirthankaras–a symbolic temple of it.

4. Gajaratha Mahotsava– A great religious ceremony, with a large three storeyed Chariot-carrying the image of 'Jinadeva'. The chariot is driven around by two elephants through a track crowded by general public.

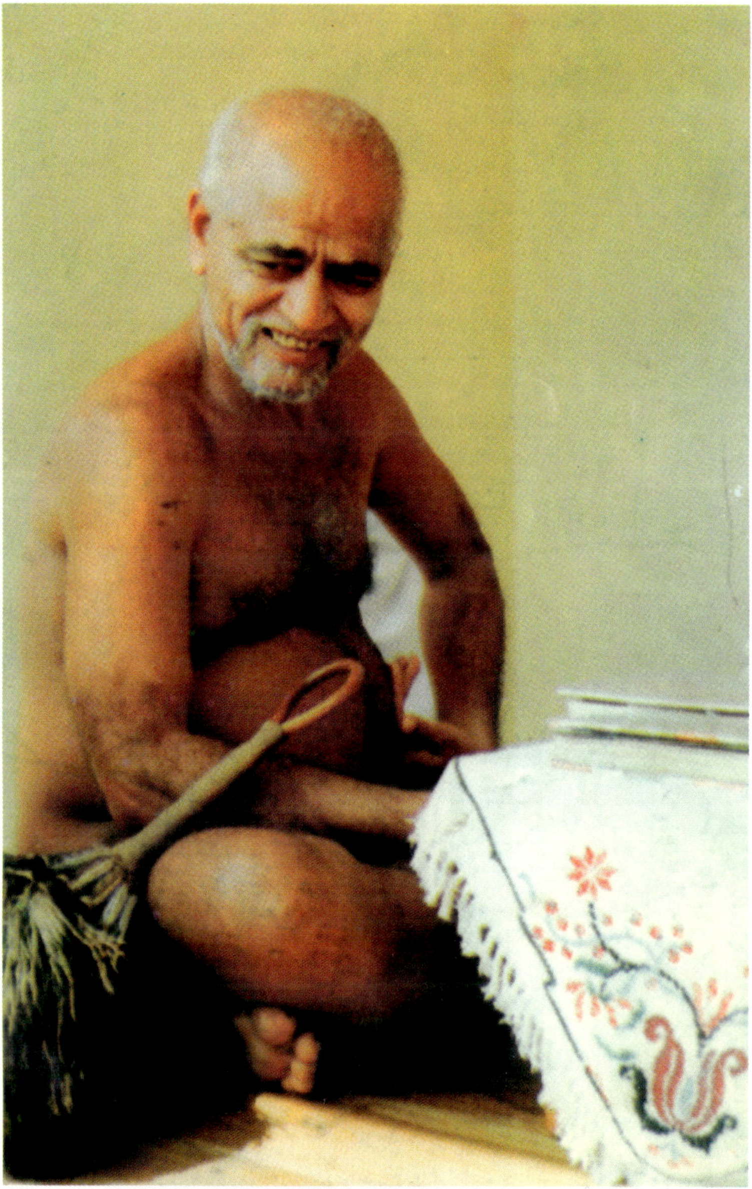

The Poet-author of the Epic poem 'Mūkamāṭī'
Rev. Acharya Vidyasagar Maharaj

CANTO : FIRST

No Admixture, Gain in Category

The Silent Earth
(Mūkamāṭī)

In the boundless space
A bedding of bluishness,
And…hither...underneath
Prevails absolute silence,

The night is touching its termination
The dawn is now attaining its arrival

The sun is slumbering no more indeed
Yet he is
Still reclining
Into the gentle lap of the mother,
Is changing sides
While drawing the garment over his face.

On the lips of the Eastern horizon
There lurks a light graceful smile
No hem on the head is there
And
Like the scattered scarlet dust
The splendour of the colourful tint–
Appears agreeable, dear brother...!

The water-lily as if sinking
Behind the veil of shyness
Wishes to evade
The finger-touch of the Sun;
She tries to give a covering of the petals
To her pollen–
To her emotional countenance.

Lo !... hither...!
The half-blossomed she-lotus
Doesn't look even at the moonbeam
Of the waning moon
With her eye-lids opened.
It's not under everybody's thumb
To conquer envy,
And...that…too...
In the life-cycle of a woman–
An event...almost impossible !

Now the fickle stars
All like frail ladies
While following at heels
Their husband, the Moon
Like shadows,
Are getting themselves hidden
Somewhere...far away...over the horizon...
Due to the apprehension
Lest they be sighted by the Sun.
The fragrant breeze
Is blowing
In a gentle manner;
Life is-to keep going

With its onward motion
It is telling :

Lo!
It is indeed the twilight-hour of dawning !
The fragrance is perfuming
All around, upto the distant limit.

For me
What juncture…
Can be more auspicious
Than this one !

There is neither the moon, nor the night
Neither the sun, nor the day
All the directions too are at present blind;
The odour of this confidential discourse
..Can't even reach–
The nose of others !
In such a situation
How can arise
Into their minds
That crafty contrivance…!

And...hither...before me
The river...
Which is gliding fast
Towards the vast sea
Can't hear this discourse
Because!
The wayfarer of a virtuous path
While treading his way onwards
Doesn't turn back to see
Even by the body, or by the mind too.

And, the bashful
Modest and lovely–
Soil of the river-bank
Opens her heart
Before the Mother Earth !

"I myself am fallen
And am demoralized by the others,
...By the wretched sinners
I am trodden away, Mother !

I am devoid of happiness
And afflicted with grief
Mother, I am damned and deserted !

Its woe is invisible
To whom should I express it !

I am out of order
And, without heroic deeds
Its fate-line is hostile in itself.

These tortures and sufferings !
How many types of agonies
How many, more...in future
For how long...is not known
Whether they shall come to an end or not !

At every breathing,
Keeping the nostrils hushed up
I do go on swallowing
Only
The grief-mingled draughts
And
With this event

To let the others not feel troubled
I draw the veil over my face
Having suppressed the suffocation,
...The draughts
I do go on sipping,
And, am living up nominally only
The so-called life !

When would this life-order
Come to an end ?
When would this embodiment
Be dropped out ?
Tell it to her, O Mother...!

This life of hers
Would evolve, or not
Having unfolded so many virtues
Would decline, or not
Give some remedy, O Mother !
Repair the damage Thyself, O Mother !

Listen to me, O Mother !
Make no delay
Show the steps, the path
The provisions too for the journey !"

Then,
For some moments
The silence prevails–
Both of them, unwinkingly
Stare at each other
The eye of the Earth into the Soil
The eye of the Soil into the Earth

Penetrating...very...farther
Fills inside…deeply !
Now,
By and by
The silence is broken
From the side of the Mother !

Whose eyes are growing
More candid–
More tearful,
Through which
Is being mirrored forth
A hearty consciousness,

On whose
Broad forehead
Without a trace of piercing cunningness
There appears an exaltation
Of spiritual gravity,

On whose
Both the cheeks
Flushed with the lustre of roses,
A continuous flow of tears
Is rolling down
Due to the increased delight,

Separation-emptiness, want–
And that of a sense of rupture too
By and by
The degradation is taking place,

Say it a mission or an experiment
In a natural easy manner

A touch of unique intimacy
Is being felt.

And that
Patience-sustaining Earth
Tends to utter a few words,
Due to the charm of the Soil
Being before Her.

Lo !
With dewy feelings
Thus begins the address :

"The existence is eternal, dear Child !
Pro-existence is filled with
Countless possibilities
Of rising and falling,
That seed of the Banyan tree
Is too tiny
Like a poppy-grain !

Should it be sowed into a proper field
Should it be nursed
With timely manure, air and water
It gets sprouted within a few days,
Having assumed a huge form
Is incarnated as a Banyan tree.

And there lies its true glory
The existence is perpetual
The existence is luminous, dear Child !

This odour covered with mystery
Will have to be inhaled properly

Primarily with the nose of Faith,
Do you grasp the point...!

And pay heed to this also !
What a manifest phenomena is it that
The shining showers,
Which pour down from the clouds,
On being smoky, after mingling with the dusty ground,
Are converted into a morass.

That very current of water
When mingles with the roots of Margosa
Is moulded into bitterness;

That very stream, dear Child,
When merges into a sea
Is called a 'mine of salt' !

While dropping into the mouth of a snake
It is moulded into a venomous wine;

While falling into an oceanic oyster
If it is the period of *Swāti* [1]
That very watery existence...
After turning into a pearl,
Dazzles, dear Child !

The intellect holds good
According to the company we keep
The advancing course of action unfolds itself...
According to our line of thinking
And that is what has happened
Since the ages long-departed
Since the births by-gone !

Hence, for a life,
On being imbibed with faith,
The path itself, becoming the preceptor,
And hailing the devotee
Provides company as the one to his co-traveller.
On the strings of Faith, indeed,
Play the fingers of devotion
Of an accomplisher,
In a purposeful life, then,
Flow the transcendental musical notes...!
Do you comprehend, dear Child ?

And,
As thou
Hast taken thyself
To be a fallen fellow
Thought to be a most trivial one,
It is an uncommon happening
More so, because,
Thou
Certainly
Hast recognized
The Supreme Lord,
The Almighty !
Into thine far-sightedness
Has reflected undoubtedly
The image of His Sacred Soul !

A genuine reckoning of falsehood
Is the affirmation of Truth, dear Child !

The experience of the infernal downfall
Is to adore,
Re-surrection and loftiness !

But, dear Child !
Only so much is not enough.
If you have to assimilate
The sum and substance of Faith
And have to perceive it,
...Then
You must cast yourself joyfully
Into the mould of devotion !

From the foot of the mountain too
We find that
The lofty peak
Is visible,
But
Without utilizing the feet
The touch of the summit
Is not possible !

Yes ! O yes !!
It is true that,
There is no way out without Faith
There is no top without root,
But
Do the flowers blossom
Ever at the root ?
That bunch of fruits
Swings upon
The crest, at last !

Yes ! Yes !!...
Don't take it to be a sport
It is the outcome, dear Child,
Of a much prolonged endeavour !

It doesn't matter
If that Faith is lasting
Is firm, and even firmer too
Even then
At the primary stage
In the field of accomplishment
The probability of stumbling
Remains always there, dear Child !
Despite a person being healthy and mature too
The step does slip
Over a mossy stone !

Not only this much,
Even after the ceaseless practice
The staggering is probable;
Daily-for years,
The one would have been cooking and taking his bread
Even then
Why the first bread of the expert cook
Goes stiff, dear Child !
Therefore, listen to me !
Don't be afraid of diligence
Don't be a prey to indolence !

Now and then
In the course of attainment
Such ravines too

May come across that,
Under a little of adverseness,
The one, whose equanimity,
Kissed the skies–
Even he too
May be sniffed...
By the female-serpent of inequality
And that way-farer
May get distracted from the path;
He may heave
A sigh of pain, then.
In such a state
Why that 'Bird of Enlightenment'
Won't flutter away ?
Why that Old Woman of Anger
Won't grumble away ?
What else except mishap would occur
In a life of faltering devotion ?

Hence,
The refreshment of retaliation
Will have to be given up, dear Child !
The retention of irreligious conduct
Will have to be revoked, dear Child !
Otherwise
After a gap of time, certainly,
Both of these
Shall prove to be an annoyance
In the adoration of Faith !

One thing more to say,
That

While bringing some task to perfection
To wait for convenience
Is not the true Supreme Manhood
Because
All that, at present,
Is happening as a prelude to attachment,
And due to this reason
The slackness affects improvement.
In the same way
The retaliation against adverseness too
In a different manner
Is to invite malice,
And due to it
The intellect gets blemished.

Very often,
Due to lack of advancement or progress
The Feet of Hope get frigid,
Even endurance, courage, fervour
Heave a sigh,
The mind feels depressed
But
For a man of faith, all these
Aren't a curse,–
On the contrary,
Prove to be a boon
For the one who is self-disciplined, self-restrained
And always hard-working.

Listen to me further!
Not only by the sweet curd,
By the sour curd too

If it is properly churned,
The benefit of butter accrues certainly.

From this, it is indeed inferred
That
The conclusion
Of a life full of struggles
As a rule
Is filled with happiness, how blissful !
That is really why
I make you remember once and again
That
Not in evading
But in obeying
The preachings of the chaste female and male ascetics
The proverb–
'The coming events cast their shadows before'
-Accomplishes its real meaning, dear Child !"
And,
For some moments
The silence prevails.

□

Now ! The silence is broken
From the side of the Soil–
The expression of the vibrant feelings :
"This life should be awakened
Through this address,
I felt subdued, Mother !
I found myself somewhat refreshed.

I experienced, Mother,
Some sort of illumination !

Something almost untouched
By the external view
And
With the outward universe
Almost touched
The inner world,
This vital utterance, O Mother,
Is singular and unheard-of before !

With the union of...
Kārmic Nature and mundane soul [2]
With the involution of...
Deformation and profanity
In an inward manner
The subtlest
Creation of a third object
Which comes into being,
Can't be discerned
Through a microscope,
But reflects into
A right far-sighted view–
It's an action-based acute observation, Mother !

The synthesis of actions,
Then their analysis
In relation to the Soul
For differentiating the True Self with the False Self–
Both these endeavours
Depend upon...

The ripeness of attachment and equanimity
Of the Soul.
So, you exhorted thus
And she gave her ear to it,
This is, O Mother, religious churning !

Who has the perception
Of this creativity
Of the consciousness ?
Who has the cognition
Of this compassion
Of the Animated Being ?
Who even talks
Of it agreeably ?
Who even hears about it mindfully ?
And
For its adoration
Who is at leisure ?–
A life without Faith, O Mother,
Is a field of flesh and skin !".

"Excellent ! thank you, dear Child !
My purport, my sentiments
Have gone deep…into your conscience.
Now, I am not worried at all !
And
On your journey
You have to set out
Since tomorrow morning !
The potter–Artisan will come at morn
To get yourself sanctified from being degraded,

With a sense of dedication
You have to prostrate
At his blissful feet,

You have to make
A start for your journey !

Under his auspices, indeed,
Your advancing life
Would glitter like gold.
You need not take pains
He would exert himself;
In his hermitage
You have to keep up
A firm-eyed look
On his service-craftsmanship,

You have to initiate
Your journey onwards !

Due to their own inherent reasons
The dormant powers
The wave-like manifestations
You have only to find out
Day-in and day-out,

On your journey
You have to make a beginning !"

□

The day-time
Somehow passed over
In thinking and discussing
But !

The...night...
Is growing longer.
The earth has been
Surrounded by sleep
And
The drowsiness doesn't
Even touch the Soil.

She is changing sides
While awaiting the dawn.
Nevertheless,
To the soil, the night
Looks like a morn :
"When the agony of unhappiness
Is lessened
Even the suffering seems to be a delight
And this
Is the result of sensibility
A point of suitableness...!"

At last, the appointed hour
Indeed, arrived
On which
The eye was affixed
Constantly...unwinkingly...!
And
The Soil
Hailed the chance,
At once spoke out that

"I saw so many dawns
But

Couldn't find in the days gone by
The one like that of to-day
And
The Morn of to-day
On the back of the dark Night
With the light red ink
Seems to inscribe something, that,–
This is the Last Night,
And
This–the First Morn;
This is the Ultimate Body
And
This–the Primeval Supreme Being !"

And, with a sense of ecstasy
Presents to the Night
In the form of a gift
A greenish *Sāḍī*
Dipped into a light brilliance
Of the tender tendrils.
Having clothed herself with it
She, while departing,
Pays her homage to Morn
With a gentle smile...!
As does a sister to her brother.

□

Hither...into the river
There is an upsurge of waves,
Winning over the splendour of silver

As if mocking at it,
The countless garlands
Of innumerable flowers
Directed by the river,
On being waved off...
Upto the river-banks,
Are being offered
At the feet of the Earth.

It, too, is a rare
Spectacular scene
That
Inside the river-shores
Under the guise of foam
The curd gets spilled about,
Those river-banks...
Are standing
With an auspicious
Jovial jar
Into their hands !

And look here, please !
In the guise of grass-points,
Like a mirthful river
There is a gush of compassion
Amid the soft centre of the ground,
And
All her limbs
Are plunging
Into natural dancing
With a peculiar thrill of joy !

To-day !
Among the dew-drops
There appears to be
A merriment and rapture
Joy and dignity
With a sense of alertness.

To-day !
In the moments of zeal
The detached illumination
The eternal blossoming
Deep contentment is being visible.

To-day !
In the heart of Passions
The dejected Cupid
With the colours of doom
Is appearing to be senseless.

To-day!
In the grains of failings
The horror of vexed restlessness
The occasion of downfall
And a treasure of merits
Is being perceived !

□

It is the beginning of the journey,
To-day...!
The first step drops
Of this way-farer
Upon the very start of the path
And

At the finish of the course
Occurs something like a throbbing
A turmoil takes place there !

Simultaneously, a communication
Flows, like a flash of lightning,
From the non-violent foot-sole
Of the way-farer,
And that
Lakshmi, the goddess of success herself,
Who, having drunk deep the despair,
Was passing her time sleeping
Since ages gone by…
Stands erect
On the end of the path-
With a sense of respect and humility
In expectation of the wayfarer.

Due to the harmony of thoughts
Due to the similarity of conduct
There appears an elegance
In communication,
Otherwise
It gets spoiled !

Without being scattered,
The expansion to the current of appliance
Towards its objective,
Like an effluent river
Controlled by its strong banks,
Is the proper form of communication !

Yes ! yes !! in this context
The remarkable thing is that
Even by mistake,
To foster a sense of dominance
Towards the missionary
Is the misuse of the mission
It doesn't bear fruit also !
And,
Then advent of a sense of partnership
Is to make good use of it, is fruitful.

Communication is that fertilizer
Through which
The seedling of congeniality
Gets strong and stout
And reaches its full bloom;
Communication is that taste
Through which
The perfect knowledge of *'the True Reality'*[3]
Gets contented and gratified
Gets enlightened.

Yes ! yes !!
It should also be accepted that
At the preliminary stage
The medium of communication
Seems somewhat of a burden
Seems to be as if worthless
And,
There is some feeling of tension
Within the mind

But,
The posterior position
Is contrary to it all.
Even by a skilful writer too,
Who writes with a pen
Embedded with a new nib,
A sense of roughness
Is felt
At the very outset of his writings,
But,
While writing proceeds
The nib gets rubbed off
The writings are gradually
Imbibed with more clarity than before,
Then...the pen, indeed,
Having assumed the rank of a maid of thoughts
Becomes the madam of thoughts…
At the last...stages...really
The tip of pen
As if swimming fast through the waters
Gathers perceptions.
Better, we put it thus, that
It is but a natural way.

□

Hark !
What ?
A hint of an auspicious event...!

On returning to wakefulness from
senselessness
A deer
With expanded eyes,
Leaping on and on
From field to field
With a speed and understanding,
Crosses over the path
And, having reached…far ahead,
Disappears beyond sight…!

'If a deer, keeping to the left,
Crosses over to the right–
Lord Rām returns home
After gaining victory over Laṅka'
The memory of this saying
Got refreshed,
And
Far...very far away…
The Soil sighted–
Treading into the valley,
Who were those ones ?
They are familiar or unfamiliar !
Indeed, towards us all,
Advancing continuously
Are approaching
Those toilsome feet...!
And
This innocent Soil,
Is puffed up with joy,
While gazing towards the valley, indeed,
With her unwinking eyes,

In the early morning
Her mind
Felt exulted, and

Presently, those feet
Have come nearer, at close quarters !
The expansion is subsiding
Gradually, the scene,
Having shrunk itself
Is becoming compact
And
The skyey vast panorama too
For this very reason
Is growing vacant,–
The insight being fixed
On the adored deity near-at-hand
Everything else, really, disappears.

Lo ! how fortunate !
A face
In all its completeness,
Which is filled with
Unique sentiments
Unyielding enthusiasm,
Has risen
Up, yonder !

Whose very forehead
Is not immature
Is veteran and vast
A treasure of fortune !
Listen ! in which

The burden and disorder of tension
Never finds recourse !

He is doubtless
A man of firm resolve
Who never likes
Even an iota of
Futile talkativeness !

He is an expert Artisan !
His craft
Bestows various forms
To the soil scattered
In the shape of particles.

The government doesn't
Ask for taxes from him
Because
Due to this Art
He always remains absolved
From the charge of stealing.

The wastage of money
Is something uncalled-for
Even the spending of money
Is not availed under this Art,
It makes the Artisan
Wealthy
Without wealth;
Since the commencement of an epoch
Till to day,
He hasn't
Deformed his culture,

Unstinted is this Art
And skilful is this Artisan.

Since the prime dawn of the Era
He has been assigned the name–
'*Kumbhakāra !*'– the 'Pot-Maker !'
'*Kum*'[4a]..., that is, 'the earth' or 'Soil'
And
'*Bha*'[4a]..., that is, 'fortune'–
Here, the one,
Who is a fortunate fortune-maker
Is called to be the 'Kumbhakāra !'
Really
Each and every substance
Being actively self-existent in itself,
This has been an usage–
The 'creator' has been assigned
The name of Kumbhakāra.

□

Yes ! now the Artisan
While commencing his task
Offered his salutation to '*Omkāra*'[4b]
And he
At the very outset
Has vomited his egotism !

He has turned away
From the doer-mindedness
And

He has joined hands
With the duty-mindedness.
Yes ! yes !!
This activity of turning away and joining with,
O Ārya – thou noble one !
Remains inevitable
Till the completion of the task ahead...!

□

Ahem ! what this ?
What duty is it ?
By whom has it been ordered ?
What is the motif behind it
To be fulfilled ?
The forehead of the Soil
Is being beaten
At its frontal part–
The soil is being dug out
With a cruel hard hoe.
The hoe is getting lost
Into the softness of the soil !
Has the tenderness of the Soil
Called upon the hard-heartedness of the hoe ?
Is there fast friendship
Between mercy and cruelty ?
If it is not so...then
Why a sigh of tears
Didn't pass through the lips of the Soil ?
And

Why wasn't the face of the Soil
Clouded with a flush of anger?
Isn't it the mystery, indeed,
Of the greed of gain?
It seems, that,
Barring some exceptions,–
Through the external activity
A true intuitive perception
Of the innermost soul
Can not be accomplished.
And
One can't live
By passing a wrong judgment.
Thus, this life itself,
Lingering between doubts and counter-doubts
And answering according to its own vigour,
Is going ahead, on and on
Unhampered and unwearied,
...When

Hither...
The innocent Soil
Kept her mouth closed;–
And
Is being filled into the bags...
Both the ends of the bags are tied up,
Right in the middle is the opening!
And
Like a nicely-clad and embellished,
Bearing a look of shyness,
Newly-wedded lean-waisted bride
As if peeping through her veil...

The simple Soil
Once and again,
Is only peeping through the bags !
This very ancient convention
Is dearer to chaste women
As well as to ascetics.
In comparison to it,
The new and ultra-modern
Life-style of our present Age,
Which prefers uncontrolled wantonness,
Finds itself de-valuated.

That is why…
The sensitive Artisan
Has asked the Soil
That
"On thy pious cheeks–
Away…from sinfulness,
There appear to be some boils,
Some pores look like rising up,
I wish to get into the mystery–
Some doubt is being felt,–
Would you tell me, please ?
If you…feel no…hesitation…indeed !"

For some moments
The past flashes back
Before the Soil
And
In answer to it
Nothing else
But a...deep…sigh !

That deep sigh alone
Rendered immaterial
The doubts of the Artisan
And
The Faith, to take a breath,
Found an embodiment.
Even then,
The proper concentration didn't prevail
The right remedy wasn't found.
The inquest of the Artisan remained alive.
While keeping this in view
...The Soil
Expresses her confidential feelings
With the help of these words :

"Not to mention an aristocrat,
It's the thing of the poor;
Not to talk of a mansion,
It's the reference to a hut

Which, under some scanty rainfall
In the rainy season
Makes a dripping sound,
And
Due to that drizzling
Holes are formed upon the ground,
Afterwards...
Throughout the life-time
A flood of tears is seen
Into these poor frail eyes,
An unending...
Shedding of tears

Has rolled down upon these cheeks,
In such a condition
It's but natural that
The cheeks bear boils
And
There remains some difference too
Between the sores of love and those
of the sufferings !
Are the sentiments of
Amorousness and renunciation uniform?"

On hearing the history of Soil
From the mouth of the Soil Herself
The Artisan simply spoke out
That

It is the real life, indeed,
It is the pious life, indeed
How fortunate !

And,
This too is an unfailing rule
That
Without the culmination point
There is no access to the finis
And
Without the end
It is impossible to visualize the beginning !
The sum and substance is that
The climax of suffering, indeed,
Is the conclusion of suffering
And
The conclusion of suffering
Is the commencement of happiness... .

While solacing the Soil thus,
In a protective posture
Some moments
Of the Artisan passed away
And
His own comrade and helper
An honorary 'ass'
Was called out,
Who also gets somewhat
Of a salary for his labours,
And, being free from all shackles,
Who was wandering into the ravine.
None of the restraints
Are up to whose liking,
He is simply tied up
On the behest of his master.
The feetless Soil
Is being carried
Upon his strong back
Upto the hermitage of his master.

□

While going mid-way
The eye of the Soil falls
Upon the back of the ass.

His back is being skinned off
Due to the friction of the rough baggage
And
Having entered through the Soil

And piercing down upon him
An agony is being begotten.

The fragile existence of the Soil,
On being awe-inspired by compassion,
Is jolting about every second.
The affection is blossoming
Inside and outside
As a true friend;
Not only the nearness of a holy place
But the affinity of feelings also
Is very inevitable
For this conviction.
Here at
Not the unconscious
But the rational observance–
Of the consciousness is being embraced !

The intimacy of feelings
As if wiping out fully
The distance of the body.

And,
The Soil, from inside the bags,
Every second
Getting itself filtered,
On entering the holes of scratches,
Is turning into
A most mild ointment;
Is being kneaded further
With the sentiment of pathos.
Not only so,

In that place
Even the crude touch of the baggage
Is getting drowned
Into a thick mildness.
But
Despite it,
On the face of the Soil
There dwells the fairy of the sway of melancholy
Who is forbidding
To migrate elsewhere.

For this condition of the Soil
The reason is that

Behind this scratching
Behind this inflammation
'I myself am' the prime cause–
–On realizing thus,
The Soil almost getting scorched
Into the fire of repentance.
And
On beholding her,
Where was a sense of relief
For the inner Compassion
Which was nourished there
And was lying helpless ?
She couldn't bear it
She couldn't live upto it
And sobbing and lamenting
In the guise of tears
In the guise of sweat-drops

As if drenching
The full baggage,
Gushing out that Compassion !

In this matter, any how,
There can be no room for doubt, that
An Epicurean[5] always,
Adopts worldly pleasures and passions
As his subject.
And
Into the inner eyes of heart,–
Whether it is day or night–
The very life of inner consciousness
Is reflected,
It matters little if that life
Is devoid of kindness
Or accompanied by mercy.

And
The existence of mercy
Is the right introduction
To metaphysics.

But, to take pity on others
Often seems
Like being an extrovert...
Like having a delusive misconception...
Like being shunned from self-acquaintance...
-Away from spirituality...

By such an exclusive notion
The spiritualism is injured.

Because, hark !
One comprehends
The 'Self' with the 'Non-self'
And
The 'Non-self' with the 'Self'
Well, either of the two
May carry a primary or secondary importance.
We cast a look at the Moon's halo
The entire firmament too comes within the purview.
While taking pity on others,
One recollects his own 'Self'
And
The very remembrance of the 'Self'
Is to observe self-pity,
The syllables, when arranged reversely,
Make out the same sense–
Yā...da da...yā...[6]

Along with it,
This point should also be kept in mind
That
The amorousness of passionate inclinations…
…Is allurement,
The evolution of mercy…
…Is emancipation–
The one reduces the life badly…
To ashes,
Is horrible, is like ambers !
The other fosters the life
With perfection…
Is benedictory, is an ornament.

Yes ! yes !!
The mercy-pathos, bestowed by halves,
Is not a part of allurement
But
The destruction of partial allurement.

The life-span of amorousness
Is insensient...is corporeal
The kindness-mercy isn't time-bound,
The axis of that mercy
Is the sensitive…consciousness
Which is the home of the nectar.

From the stalk of compassion
Falls off constantly
The fragrant odour of equanimity;
In such a condition
Who says
That
Compassion is related to wantonness ?

He would, indeed, be the blind
A slave to his passions,
A servant of his sense-organs,
And
A slave to baser 'self'–
He would possibly be frenzied !

It's granted
Every object
Acts as an agent
To itself
But

It can also be benevolent
To another one.
And
It acts to itself
As an instrumental cause
But
It can also be a means
For some different one;
That is...why
That ass is neither blind
Nor haughty too,
His inner conscience
Is entirely sensitive–
He comes forth
With a natural course of feelings
Prays to God
That

My name should prove its worth, O Lord !
That is to say–
The word '*gada*' signifies 'disease'
The word '*hā*' signifies 'healer'
I should be the healer of everybody's ailments,
…that's all,
Nothing else is desired–
The healer of ailments... *gada…hā…gadahā*[7] !

And what a wonder ?
The Soil comes to realize
Something which seems to be impossible
The surprise goes beyond limits,

The gist of the miracle remained only
That
The buds of feelings blossomed
All the blooming flowers bore fruits;
The cheeks of the Soil
Being soreless,
Being poreless,
...Were smoothened bright !
Today the name acquired its significance
–'*Gada-hā*'...*Gadahā*...how fortunate !

The sympathies of both of them are innate,
Both of these appear to be
Like twin-sisters...
Not like younger...elder ones !

"*Parasparopagraho Jīvānām*"[8]–That is
'All the living beings have a sense of mutual
favour'
–This pithy maxim
Is gratified between these two !
Every thing is lively here,
The life ! the life-cycle !! the life-fostering !!!

Besides it,
Expressing her own insignificance
The tenderness of the Soil–
That
Whether on foot or without them,
To travel onward
While making the consciousness one's
vehicle–
Is only a state
Of imperfect compassion, which
Is disagreeable to this life.

And the Soil
Having pacified her breathing
As if minimizing her burden...
Stares at the hermitage
In a posture of expectation;
Like a King's better half, at the time of journey
Beholding her harem,
While seated in a silver palanquin,
But, feeling tedious...
With a sense of modesty and diffidence !

Here one finds
The pond of virtuousness
Fully elevated.
And
The Soil has achieved
A first chance for her !

□

It
Is the campus of the hermitage
Here, the exertions are undertaken
With full force
Day in and day out !
Here,
There is an apartment for *'Yoga'* [9a, 9b]
The laboratory too is vigorous !
Where one gets
From the Artisan
The disciplines and training
At every minute,

Which impresses the internal life
In an upright manner !

Here at
Life doesn't mean simply 'maintenance'
But it is 're-constructed'
The history itself is an eye-witness to it.

The degenerated life,
Being regenerated,
Becomes sublime;
Even a downcast
And helpless life
Itself becomes a helper.
Those, who were mere onlookers,
Get at some ideals here.
The problems belonging to history
Entangled since centuries ago
Stand unravelled easily
Through its association for a short while.
And
Despite being unsolicited
Those desiring purificatory rites
Through a homely and excellent culture
Get at good counselling here.
Some such aphorisms are found
For the 'Sword', for the 'Ink' too
For the 'Farming' and even for a 'Sage' too
That those selfless ones also
Get here at the 'Texts of the Ṛṣīs'
'that is '*Ārṣa*'.[10]

□

Lo, as the Soil is unloaded
Now, at the hermitage
When, at once,
A sieve, woven with thin wires,
Is brought
And
The soil is being sifted.
The Artisan himself
Is the conductor of the Sieve.

He
With his merciful eyes
Inspects
In a congenial manner
The bare Soil
Brought down there.
Extends a touch
To the purified Soil
With eagerness
Through his holy hands.
And
Being unhurt,
Feels gratified
Within his mind and body.
Then, all of a sudden,
The delightful words are
Expressed through his lips, that

"This is the supreme state
of candidness
And

The tender-heartedness
Reaches here the climax of glory
...How fortunate !"

The Soil was purified,
The Soil was hailed,
But,
Among the outcast pebbles
There appeared a feeling of anger
Which seemed to be proper.
Even then, those pebbles,
Entreat the Artisan
In a sober language, that,
"Why are we being separated
From the Mother-Soil ?
Causelessly !
Is there any reason behind it ?"
On hearing this, at once,
The Artisan replies in gentle words–

"This art of mine
Attains elegance
With the soft Soil,
With the trivial sections of people,
And
By the saddle of a mule
By an eminent breed
It gets scattered
Without delay.

The other point is
That

I had to ward off
The blame of admixture
Hence
I repelled
The storage of pebbles."

On hearing these words
The pebbles become
A bit more warmed up
There lurks a typical vibration
Around the lips of the pebbles,
And
There appears some extra expression
Of warmth into their utterings,
...That

"Whether it is concerned with body or caste,
Only the one thing is clear–
There is equality and similarity
Between us and the Earth
No sign of dissimilarity is visible !
Is it discerned by you, Mr. Artisan ?
Have your eyes under-gone
A surgical operation ?

And
Now remains the point of a man's caste !
How to describe it in words ?
That, too, is similar between both of us;–
Which is obvious
The hue of Lord Krishna is dark-blue
But it is not a colour to be pulled off.

Do you hear ?
Are your 'ears' in order !
Who should then talk about
The admixture of castes ?
We should adore silently
Śaṅkara, full of the hue of equanimity !"
And…
The pebbles become quiet.

Hereupon too, the mood of the Artisan
Doesn't get heated
Even for a short while.
Through it is reflected thus
The natural sense
Of earth-like equilibrium
…That

By this reference,
The purport of the word '*Varṇa*'
Neither indicates a colour
Nor it symbolizes a 'Social section'
But,
It means character, conduct, manners.
That is to say–
The one,
Who is befriended
Will have to adjust
His attributes and functions–
...His image and identity,
According to the other
Who has taken him under his roof.

Otherwise
The blame of caste-admixture
Will have to be born on head...!
And
It will be unavoidable.

By this mention
The caste-advantage would have been denied
–Such is not the case,
The tribe of water is separate
The tribe of milk is distinct,
The senses of touch, taste and tint too
Of both of them
Differ with each other–
And
It's known to all,
Even then
In due way and in due quantity
As and when water is mingled with milk
The water turns into milk.

And, listen !
As regards only the colour-tint
The cow-milk too is white
The milk of the swallow-wort too is white
Both of them are outwardly bright
But
As and when they are intermingled
A disorder is produced–
The milk becomes sour
It becomes troublesome !

"The changing of water into milk, indeed,
Is a gain in category,
It's a boon in itself.
And
The becoming of milk sourish
Is the confused mixture of species
It's a curse !
It's the very outcome of this all."
Enough of the elaboration !

□

"O thou pebbles !
You, indeed, mixed up with the Soil
But
You did not become one with the Soil !
You came in touch with the Soil
But,
You did not get dissolved into the Soil !
Not only this,
You do not forget
Your attributes and characteristics
In spite of you being powdered
Into a grinding mill !
It doesn't matter if
You are broken to pieces, turn sandy;
Still you do not become Soil !

You get drenched also
With the sprinkling of waters,

But, even by mistake,
You don't get bloomed up !
You don't catch dampness
As the Soil does,
Isn't it
Your deficiency ?
Tell me, O thou mean fellow !

Where is there within you
That capacity of sustaining water ?
While staying into a water-tank
You can't become
Yourself a drift to water,
For centuries !
I won't tell you, really,
To be heartless;
But
You are surely stone-hearted,
Your chest holds likeness…
To that of the one
Who can never
Sweat itself out
In spite of beholding
Others in trouble and pain !

Even then,
The preachings and precepts
Of Sages and Saints always
Communicated us, indeed, that–
Hate the sin
But, not the sinner,
Hate the mire
But, not the lotus

O thou Nobleman !
From Manhood
Rise to Divinity
By doing just and opportune deeds."

Thus, having taken
As if a bitter draught through the Artisan,
The pebbles, now,
With pitiable looks
Stare at the soil.
And, the Soil
With freedom-blended eyes,
Looks on, while turned towards the pebbles,–

The decorum of the soil
As if imparting some holy instruction...!
That
"You ought to do
The investigation of the 'Absolute Mother-Existence'
The expedient 'Will'
And
The purgation of the 'Vile Existence'!
That is to say–
The abandonment of frivolity
The oblation to excellence
Is the creation of blissfulness.
The boat reaches
Across the boundless ocean
If it's only
Without a leakage !

Nevertheless
That boat, now and then,
Gets confused,
And that confusion
Is caused neither by water
Nor by the depth of water,
But
It is due to the bad sense of liquid sway
of water,
Which
Having set aside the depth of water,
And, on being caught into the rolling waves,
Remaining afloat...!
Half-sunk,
Is a lump of Snow–
A measuring-rod of pride....

It is a sharp deterrent to candidness
An awakener of poisoning,
Not only this much,
A hard exploiter of humidity
And
A cherisher of density!

Neither does it know swimming
And
Nor does it wish to swim,
It's a matter of grief, that
It is desirous of drowning
The boat as well as the saviour.
It wishes to float upon the surface
But,

Without being mixed up with the water,
Having drowned the world
Up to the bottom of the water,
Tries to live
Up and above it
Not mingling with the water...!
O thou arrogant being !
Do have a look at the water,
And, even now,
Be much ashamed of thyself...!
O Lord, the Umpire !
When is the pride to go disrespected ?"

And, by the Soil,
The flow of precepts was not yet broken,
Because, now,
Having departed from the literal meaning
She moves towards suggesting the sense, that

The seed has been sown
The rain has fallen
The seeds have sprouted
And
Within a few days
The harvest stands blooming –
With awns,...like a frail woman...!
But,
Not only the frost
The cold wave too,
Within some minutes –
To that ripened harvest –

Burns like a blaze.
The water bestows life
The snow takes the life away,
This is the only difference
Between the higher nature and the contrary nature,
This, indeed, is said by the sages
Who
Are well-versed in universal life.

The outcome of this all is
That
It matters little
If the outer layer of the snow
Is chilly-natured
But, from within,
The snow is now devoid of coolness !
There has risen, certainly,
A sense of inflammation into it !

Otherwise,
He,
Who is feeling thirsty
Whose throat is getting dried up,
And due to which
Whose eyes are burning,
Takes a slice of snow,
In place of water,
To make himself free from those tortures
As soon as possible,
But, on the contrary,
Why does the thirst take a sharp rise ?
Why does the mucus drop out of the nose ?

This indeed is the success of the false nature
And
The confusion of the true-natured state of mind !

Despite so much of it,
The watery sway of the ocean
The Absolute Mother Existence
Doesn't drown the ice-berg-
What is the secret behind it ?

Seemingly,
It's the motherly affection
Towards her off-spring,
Towards the part and parcel of her family
She can take no such step
...Ever, even by mistake,
All the burden of troubles
Is borne herself by her
And,
within herself,
She keeps mum.

"Granted !
The manifestation of separatism
Is the fruitage of pride,
Along with it
The point can't be denied
That,
The utter dwarfing of pride
Seems to be the termination of pride
But,
For the future respectability

It may also be the sowing of
The pride itself!"

Thus meanwhile,
An ironical wave surged up
From the side of the pebbles
And
Having moved straight onward,
That ripple of pebbles,
Untouched by the attachment of relationship,
Not only touches the limbs of Soil
But also meddles with her heart!
When
At once,
"Nay... not so! it's impudence,
The mistake be pardoned, Mother!
This occurrence
Doesn't happen in your case!"
And...
The band of pebbles started shedding tears.
Then, in the form of a prayer–
"O Thou an image of mildness, above
arrogance,
Mother Earth!
Bless it with a '*Mantra*'– incantation –
So that it may become
A diamond
And should make itself like pure gold!"

On Hearing the request of the pebbles
The smile of Earth resounded;
That
"Take to the path of self-restraint

To become indeed a path-finder
Is to become a diamond –
The word *'Rāhī'* itself
Is, in its reverse order, indicating –
Rā...hī...hī...rā[11a]
And
You will have to become so hard
That
The physical body as well as the desire-body
Will have to be burnt to ashes
Through the fire of penance
By the observance of religious austerities
You will have to undergo severe self-mortification
Then, and then alone,
The Vital Soul
Would come true.
The word *'Kharā'* itself too
Is indicating through its reverse form –
–Without being burnt to ashes,
How can a genuine insight be achieved ?
"Rā...Kha...kha...rā..."[11b]
and,
As if raising up her hands of blessing
The posture of the Earth –
Like a sea of benevolence.
□

Today, the Soil
Has to be swelled
Through the vessel, but

Having mixed proportionately with water
It has to be got dissolved.

At present, the soil
Has only to be swollen !

Step by step
Having lessened
The bye-gone moments,
The old turmoil
Has merely to be forgotten,

Today, the Soil
Has only to be swollen !

And, into her every particle
At every minute
A new freshness
Has merely to be called in

Today, the Soil
Has only to be swollen !

With this very purpose in view
There is a well inside the courtyard
Standing over it, is the Potter- artisan
In his hand there was a bucket –
Full of swivel and fitted with chains,
And,
Having put it down,
He is trying to unravel
The entangled cord.
It gets unravelled also, almost quickly,
But,
While trying to get it disentangled

There dropped a knot...
At the mid-point of the cord,
It's a tight knot.

It is inevitable to untie it
And
The effort of the Artisan began.
Between both of his thumbs,
Between both of his fore-fingers,
Having applied his full strength
He concentrates himself,
The breath stops –
The breathing in and breathing out stands still !

Lo ! The *'Kumbhaka Prāṇāyāma'* [12]
Taking its decreasing course itself.
The posture as that of eschewing the lips,
The network of nerves
Within both the arms,
Is gathering tension,
There appears some uprise into the skin
But,
The knot is not getting unravelled.
The force of the thumbs
Has decreased,
Both the fore-fingers
Are getting almost numb,
And the nails
Have become blood-red
Still the knot is not getting untied !

In the mean time
"Oblige the attendant, O Lord !
By permitting him to serve."
Thus spoke out the team of teeth
To the Artisan,
And
"It is opportune, O Lord !
We have heard only the ethics
That

When the dignity of our say
Falls flat
The usage of hand, then,
Comes into action.
And
When the usage of hand
Turns ineffective
The Ārya – a nobleman – then
Brings some weapon into operation.
Therefore
Give him the cord, O Lord,
Without having any suspicion !"
And
As the cord was lifted upto the row of teeth
When

At once
The tooth, acutely-sharp
Spoke out thus to all the teeth –
"O brother !
Inside this knot –

The investigation of the joint-hole
Can't be done by you !"

And,
The lower sharp-tooth
Of the right side
Inspects the knot
Thoroughly from all sides,
And, without delay,
Immerses himself
Into the depth of that joint-hole,
With the co-operation
Of the upper sharp tooth
On the right side.
The pivots of both the sharp teeth
Come together at a close,
And
The strong roots of those sharp teeth
Gather strength from each other.

Even then ! despite this all !!
The unravelling of the knot was a far cry,
It doesn't even get shaken
On the contrary,
The very roots of the sharp-teeth
Are about to move
And
The hinges of the sharp-teeth
Are at the brink of being
Broken, fractured.

Lo ! the soft gums, indeed,
Have got erased and inflammed
During this scuffle

The flesh
Is about to peep through them.

On seeing this occurrence happening
The tongue also,
On being excited, spoke out
That

"O thou damned cord !
The name-roll of mine as well as thine
Is one and the same,
But
Today, thou art
Appearing to be dull and dry
Almost without flavour,
Thou wert, till now
Simple and upright,
Regarded like
A grand-mother or elder-sister,
Large-hearted and slender-bodied,
Now thou hast not remained candid !
Hast become heavily knotty
And
Hast become solidly tough.

Keeping thy obstinacy away
Let the knot be left loose !
Otherwise
Thou wilt obtain only repentance
Within moments, when,
The indivisible life of thine
Shalt get bifurcated...!"

And
For this culpable deed
The tongue, as if cursing,
While saying...tush...tut...
Fie...Pish...
Drops its saliva
At the juncture-point of the knot.
The result was that
The cord was frightened
For its fearful future !
And, within moments,
The knot got moistened
It softened,
It looked loose.
Then, what to say !
The teeth were warmed up
On seeing the success !
The upper as well as the lower
And all the frontal teeth
Untie the knot at once.

□

Now the cord asks the tongue
With a sense of curiosity –
That
"What was the obstruction for your lord
By this knot ?"
Hence, the tongue reveals the mystery :
"listen to me, O cord !

My Lord owns self-control
He is afraid of violence,
And
Non-violence is his very life.
He observes
That
A man is not a genuine one, without temperance
That is to say
A man is truly the one
Who is suitably
Filled with…self-restraint.

Non-violence
Is our venerable deity
And
Where there is the *crooked knot* [13a]
The violence certainly
Hoodwinks us all.
It means that
The knotty distortion
Is the motive-force behind violence
And

The non-violence is fully cherished
In the state of *perfect asceticism*,[13b]
Every minute, it flourishes,
...Is invigorated.

We are the wayfarers of the path of asceticism
Amongst us
We always discuss, adore and admire
This very religious order.
This very life, in this very from,

Should go on and on in future too
It's enough !
Nothing else is desired.
And you
Had preserved
The hard and tough knot,
Without it being disentangled;
At the time when the filled up bucket
Is being pulled out of the well-bottom,
If that knot
Falls upon the reel,
The balance of the bucket,
As a rule,
Would be spoiled.
And, then –
The cord would get entangled with the reel.

As a result of it
A lot of the bucket-water
Would leap down
Into the well again,
Many watery organisms living in that water
Would face an untimely death
Due to the injury thus inflicted,
How can my Lord
Be the owner of such a blemish ?
Hence, the unbinding of the knot,
Became not only necessary
But also inevitable.
Do you grasp the point !

O thou cord !!
What a crazy one !
A friend of mine !

□

What did this happen here ?
The shadow of the Artisan's body
Having a smooth-smiling intellect,
Fell upon a fish
Swimming at its sweet will
Into the clean water
Of a distant well.
The head of the fish
Thrust itself upwards,
And
Its mental state too
Attained some elevation,
But
The fish is really worried
As to how its body
Would raise itself
Upto the person high above ?
The body is after all non-sentient' indeed
The non-sentient expects support,
And that too of the sentient being.

And listen !
Illusion has been fostered by the corporeal existence
This intellect of mine is
Mixed up and affected
With illusion, that is 'Māyā'....

The intellect may be righteous
If illusion is discarded...really...

I am lying there into a dark deep pit
Due to the feeling of ugliness
My condition is similar to
That of a frog-in-the-well.
The actions, the thoughts and the status –
All have been distorted
How can the true form and natural character
Of my own 'self' be perceived ?
On being communicated from the top
Even a single ray of hope
Doesn't descend upon me.
And,
Through the jaws of the fish
Sprang out a distress-dripped sound
That
"Let some one pull it out
of this dark deep pit,
Let some one get it united,
With that 'Swan-Soul',

None is there indeed
Even to hear this bewailing
O thou listeners !...
Have all of you turned deaf ?"

This lamentation has
Remained only a cry in wilderness –
Thinking thus, once again,
The fish sinks into various options,
And through that dip –

She obtains a ray of light
That
"Due to worthless alternatives
The hope to live
Gets only poison
To swallow up
And,
The fruitful capacity to work
Which remains slumbering for long,
– That patience and steadiness
Unfolds its eye
Into the very lap of firm resolve."
Enough !
The fish took a solemn vow,
To move out upon the earth.

The hope of the transient breath of life
Took to escaping away,
The thirst for the Supreme Spirit
Took to awakening up
Within the personified body of the fish !

Then
What then ?
How far would stay ungrounded
The affection of the insentient water ?
That too faded away within moments
Vanished...somewhere.
The fish in its life
Got a shelter-house of safety
The frightfulness disappeared.

The triumph
Came about henceforth,
How blessed...!

□

Now !
The relevant function proceeds,
Each of the limbs was cultured
Hence...
Both the hands of the Artisan,
Which were disciplined
With the training of self-control,
Were filled up with restraint !
Instantly, that Artisan,
After bending up the bucket with the cord,
Drops it down into the well
With a slow motion,
So that
The destruction of
The various living organisms
Like fish etc.
Might be warded off,
And
Here or there
Now or then
Our true nature of the 'Supreme Spirit'
Should not be cheated
By our own actions
Or...by the consequences thereof !

Lo ! hastily
The resolve seeming to bear fruit,
The calm eyes of the fish
Expecting to see
The dreams being materialized
Cast a look upwards.
An aerial car, landing downwards , was sighted,
Which carried an inscription over it;
' Dhammo dayā -visuddho' –
– " The religion consists in true compassion "
And
'Dhammaṁ Saraṇaṁ Gacchāmi' –
– " I seek the shelter of *Dharma.*" [14]
The more the bucket
Moved down into the well,
In the like manner
The frogs etc.
Numerous watery creatures
Fathomed quickly
The depths of the water
To save their lives.

But,
Being free from any act of motion or commotion
With unwinkingly fixed eyes,
The tongue-tied and taste-greedy
All those fish
Stare at the descending bucket,
With the hope
They would get some food grains from it !

But, what wonder ? deception ...!
On seeing the hollow bucket

And assuming it
To be a new bondage of some pitfall
All the fish run away out of fear.
Only that dedicated fish
Still stands there
Having only one female companion with it
And
She whispers something to her thus :
" Come, O friend, come...!
We should take refuge herewith.
' *Dhammo dayā-visuddho* '
– " The religion consists in true compassion "
– This is the only
Harbour for the forlorn
This is a great shelter-house
Here only we get protection
Otherwise,
Certainly, today or tomorrow,
We shall become a morsel into the jaws of mortality !

Don't thou know ?
A tiny fish is swallowed up entire
By a bigger one, here,
Moreover,

The feelings of hostility and malice
Are found against each other amongst those
Who are co-related through religion or caste !
A dog growls fiercely,
While scratching the ground with its nails,
At the very sight of the other dog. "

Now, on hearing this,
Its helpmate says –
“Somehow it is true what you say,
But
By eating us up
If our own caste
Is nourished and gratified
Then...it is desirable,
Because,
at the ultimate hour
Our own caste proves to be of avail
The remaining others stay as onlookers
Posing themselves as philosophers !
And
How can the different caste be trustworthy ?
Today, the breath of Faith
Is seen being suffocated evidently
At every round of respiration...!

And listen !
According to the external writing
The internal inscription,
If the goods are grabbed
How pleasant of it !
Here...we do find...
‘A honey tongue
A heart of gall’ –
– Hypocrisy plays tricks.

The preaching of Compassion is excellent,
And
The practice of Compassion is strange –

There is inherent life in the one
There is melodrama of life in the other.
At present...
Upon the arms, weapons, clothes –
And even upon the swords
It's found inscribed –
'Mercy is the root of all religions'
But,
The sword is not merciful,
Thus they declare themselves :
We are the swords,
We don't mind mercy !

How far we should go to describe now !
The banner of creed too
Changes into a rod
The Holy Scriptures turn into weapons,
Whenever a chance avails.
And
Even a melodious flute too
Engrossed in eulogizing the Lord,
Can beat, on assuming the form of a cane,
Those who tread the path of the Lord,
Thanks to the twists of times ! "

On hearing the words of its companion
The fish further adds:
"If thou does not wish to come, don't
come , but
Don't waste the time
By bestowing preachings...! "

And, departing with its companion,
The fish starts off all alone,
Leaving behind the timely wise sayings :

To face every obstruction
With due precautions
Is to achieve fresh concentration,
Or it should be re-told thus –
It is to find out the final solution.

Along with the virtues
It's absolutely necessary
To understand the vices also,
But
To breed ill-will against vices
Is to help grow the vices
And
It's to destroy the virtues;
To foster malice for the thorns
And to miss
The fragrance and pollen of the flowers
Is regarded only ignorance,
And
Having secured ourselves against the thorns,
To make good use of the fragrance and saffron
Is a symbol of wisdom –
That…
Which is found rarely amongst us !

□

Hither...descending through the space,
The bucket filled with water
And the water encircling the bucket.
Both of them get fully
Immersed into each other,
The fish finds
Entrance inside it
'*Dhammaṁ saraṇaṁ pavvajjāmi,*[15] that is,
' I'm seeking the shelter of '*Dharma*'
–While assimilating this incantation– *Mantra*–
Its faith
Is getting gradually assured,
Its soul
Is getting more and more healed up.
On seeing this height of steadiness
On seeing this fidelity of intellect
All the fish
Felt astonished
And
For some moments
Their fears
Were faded away.

One of them felt inclined
And made up its mind...
To do virtuous deeds
And
All the rest of them
Extended their approval.

The one was inspired
The rest of them were impressed
The one was imbibed with insight
The direction was obtained by the remaining
others.

They got the shelter of compassion
The beam was blossomed in the heart
And
All of them
Were brightened with brilliant lustre
Were bathed and washed
At once
Not only inwardly but also outwardly !

□

On this occasion
The whole of the family
With cheerful faces
Seeks its presence.
Caused by the swimming fish
The surging fluid waves,
The fish encircled with the waves,
Appear as if
Each one of them all
Holds a garland into its hand
And
The great fish
Is being greeted,
The slogans are being raised –
" The journey towards Final Liberation
...Should be a success,

The dose of delusion
...Should become null and void
The *'Dharma'*–'Righteousness'–should come out
triumphant
The *bondage of 'Karma'*[16] – Actions–be blotted out,
Be victorious, be victorious
Hail, a thousand cheers !"

Lo ! the time has approached nearer,
That bucket, like an aerial car,
Is just to rise upwards
And
The well-wishing is uttered –
Through the lips of the fish :
"My ambition is
That
In the ensuing endless eras
This earthen vessel of mine
Should have no 'Desire' at all !"

The only purpose
Of this auspicious journey is, –
The equilibrium and equanimity alone
Should be my food-stuff
My sensibility should be
Ever – bright and ever – radiant
Having acquired even a devilish body,
My human heart,
Shouldn't be affected by violence,

In the heavens, on the earth
Down into the underneath worlds

The religion of Spirituality
The religion of Compassion
Should achieve supremacy...!

□

Brimming with water
The bucket gains momentum
Upwards, through the well-pit,
Now !
From its downfall into the underworld
Towards its lofty upliftment.
The fish is only looking on,
There is no lack of water
There is no want of strength
Even then
The fish is not swimming.
It has almost forgotten gliding into water,
It has attained the stability of mind
No sooner does it visualize its real 'self'
Than, it appears now that,
All activity stands still...!
It begets a state of inner strength !

That bucket was lifted up
Unhindered, upon the ground
The fish was freed
From the bondage of the well-pit ;
The greeting to the sun-light
Was golden and mirthful...!

That heavenly garden of beauty
After being filled up with the sun-shine
Became a pool of pleasure.
That heap of dust
Turned into the vermilion on the face,
The eyes of the fish
Now run straight
Towards the hermitage...!
The Sun has sent His graceful lady
For all day long
In the service of the hermitage,
The every nook and corner of the hermitage
Along with the courtyard
Seems to be kissed by the sunlight...
Absorbed in service thereof...!

It is thick
It appears like a charming heap of beauty
But it escapes capturing.
It is beyond the touch of others
Leaving the sun aside,
Bearing similarity with the Lord,
Who has assumed that beauty
Which evades the minute touch ?
...It is that of the sunshine,
It should be accepted
This sense and sensibility
Is caused by the shadow of the hermitage
And

The demolition…
Of the error of the fish
The afflictions were shattered.

A scene manifests itself
Inside the courtyard of the hermitage :
There is a heavy vessel,
Whose mouth
Is tightened
With a neat and clean
Doubled piece of hand-woven cloth
And
The Artisan proceeds towards it
Holding a bucket in hand.

Observing utmost care, keeping up the flow,
He filters the water
The water is filtered slowly,
In the mean time
The sight of the Artisan
Slips a bit in some different direction.

Persisting in jumping up,
This fish
Takes a leap from inside the bucket
And
Gets itself thrown
Upon the holy feet of the Earth...!
Then
Weeps bitterly,
Her eyes
Are filled with compassion

And
Are clouded with pain
Altogether, at the same time,
They have a thirst for singularity
Like a maid-of-honour to the Lord
Have attained excellence,
Those eyes, from which
The bright and white drops of tears,
On being dripped down,
Bathe the feet of the Earth...!

The drops, which
Have captured basically
The holiness of the Milky Ocean,
The abundance of the sea of compassion
Has flowed from whose crown of the head.

□

Here, to this Age,
This writer's pen puts the question
That
Is humanity, in these times,
Totally dead ?
Has the devilishness
Prevailed here throughout...?
It seems that
The true charity
Has departed away from humanity ?
Moreover –

When has the demonocracy
Cherished that charity ?

" *Vasudhaiva kuṭumbakam* ", that is,
'The whole of the world is like a family' –
The vision and taste-sense
Of such individuality
Has not remained feasible, now,
To these eyes...!
If it's easily obtainable at all
Then, not in *Bharat – India* –
Seek it through the '*Mahābhārata !*'[17a]
In India, selfishness visibly prevails.

Yes, O yes !
This much of change has surely occurred
That
" *Vasudhaiva kuṭumbakam* ", That is,
'The whole of the world is like a family'–
This maxim has been modernized;
'*Vasu*',[17b] that is, the 'money-matter',
'*Dha*', that is 'to hold'
The money, chiefly, has become
the family-affair to-day-
The wealth has really become the crown of
life.

Now, the fish addresses the Earth –
" You too, Mother ! tell something,
Let this topic be elucidated
By you, O Mother ! "

So, on request by the fish,
The Earth utters something as a gist –

" Listen, my child !
This very thing
Is the true identity of *Kaliyuga*– the Modern Age

To whom
The true and the genuine
Has always been disagreeable
And
The Golden Age be regarded by thee
Where even the evil
Has appeared always like clarified sugar."

Again, breaking the continuity
The fish entreats
That
The subject is taking a profound turn,
Deal it, please, with a bit of simplicity !
So, the Mother adjoins :
"Try to understand the point, dear child ! "
Whether a Golden Age or an Iron Age
It's not an external
But an internal event,
The vision really devoted in search of Truth,
Is the Golden Age, dear child !
And
Sunk deep into the false objectives
From top to bottom
The view, which regards the Truth as falsehood,
Is, in itself, '*Kaliyuga*'–the Modern Age–dear child !

The Sin is like *Yama*– the Death
It has been a house of mercilessness,
It has been so cruel,
And, the 'Virtue'
Is like a creeper of buds
Which has ever remained kind

Is filled with mildness.
In the eyes of *Kali* – the Sin –
The gloom of error really
Deepens always,
And
In the eyes of 'Truth'
The thought of peace really
Beckons always.

The vision of the one
Is taking recourse to
The individuality,
The vision of the other
Is an awakening
Towards entirety,
The creation of the one
Is transient as lightning
The creation of the other
Is an art everlasting,

The life of the one
Appears to be lifeless
Is a charmless corpse,
The life of the other
Seems to be nectar-like
Is the glorious '*Śiva*',
The corpse will have to be put on fire,
And
The devotion will have to be awakened in *Śiva.*
Do you grasp the point, dear child !"

"O Mother ! I was ignorant, I grasp the point,
I was entangled, am unravelled Mother ! now,
I don't need the water-element
Now to drink;
I don't expect vigour and vitality
For sustaining life now,
Worn and torn
Tattered and scattered this life
Should only be united somehow
With the Supreme Being,
...With the Divine Knowledge,
Should become patchless, nothing more !
No needle-and-thread is required
Now, for stitching.

In spite of being born in water
This fish went on burning
From water or from the watery creatures,
Where is the coolness at root, O Mother ?
Which has been achieved, within moments,
At thy feet !

The sandalwood of the *Mount Malaya* [18]
And
The heart-stealing
Brilliant radiance of the moon too
Went off somewhere, with a jump,
from the mind
On my contact-today.
Thy tranquillity
Has showered happiness.
Mother ! Thou art a creeper of coolness !
An Embodiment of Final Emancipation !

Only in thy lap
She
Would gain more wisdom, Mother !
Only in thy lap
Then would commence the investigation
Of the multitude of countless merits.

And listen, Mother !
She is not afraid of *ailments*[19] as much
As she fears *mental agony,*[19]
And
She has no fear of the mental distress
As much as she is afraid of *possessions.*[19]
She needs *means of subsistence*[19],
And not property or belongings, O Mother !
She should only achieve *Samādhi*, that is means of exhaltation –
Samādhi – the 'Absolute Serenity'
And not a negligent intellect.
'Upadhi' – that is –
The means of subsistence - aren't they helping !
'Upādhi' – that is –
Possessions – aren't they injurious ! "

And the fish adds,
"Hence, confer upon me, O Mother !
'Sallekhanā' – the Supreme Renunciation ,
The seeds of Divine or Right Knowlege, –
Bestow upon me such Holy Sermons, Mother !
Let me be the seer...of Right Faith !
I should only visualize – the *Samādhi* –
The Absolute Serenity ! "

On hearing this, with a budding smile,
The Earth says :

'Sallekhanā', [20a] that is,
One has to reduce, dear child !
The body as well as the foul passions,
By weakening the body
The foul passions stop breathing,
...It ought to be so.
And,
Not by making the body perish,
But in the withering away of body
In the gaining of worldly objects
Neither getting saddened
Nor getting gladdened
Is the genuine '*Sallekhanā*'–
Supreme Renunciation - otherwise,
The wealth of Soul is plundered, dear child !

Whether air-comfort is at hand or not
Whether regard to discourse is observed or not,
There is found some goodness hidden
Into the gain of pleasure or pain
It can be seen, if desired, through the eyes
of equanimity
The word '*Lābha*' [20b] in itself
Is signifying in an inverse manner –
Lā...bha...bha...lā...,

Ultimately,
I have to say only this thing, dear child !
That
You shouldn't be the victim of any fraud
Like the fish
Who were deceived in their life-time,
Even by mistake
You shouldn't be swept away
Into the waves of sensuous pleasures.

And listen to me, dear child,
To be an innocent fish,
This is the mother of '*Samādhi*', [21] that is,
'Absolute Serenity'
Furthermore,
The Earth drops a hint to the Artisan
That
" Rehabilitate this fortunate soul
Again into the well
With protection, and without delay !
Otherwise
She shall perish
You will be an accomplice to it,
An unbearable agony
Shall follow as its outcome !"

The water has been filtered
And
The watery organisms have remained within the cloth,
Keeping into the pure water inside the bucket
Those organisms along with the fish,
Are caused to enter safe into the well
With utmost care by the Artisan.

Once again , inside the well,
The acclamation resounds
'The religion consists in True Compassion'
And
Sound to sound, the echo,
Emerging out of the walls,
Continually clashing about, reaching upwards
Immersing within the hermitage,
As if...sinking...down...!

□

CANTO : SECOND

The 'Word' is not 'Wisdom'
'Wisdom', not 'Purification'

Lo, now the Artisan
Mingles in due quantity
The filtered pure water
Into the saffron-like soil.
He is blowing new breath
Into the life of the Soil
Through every gracious particle,

From separation towards close relationship
The unfolding of unification
And
The Soil is swelling up.
That flow
Was the nature of the water-element –
It's experiencing
Pause at this time.
On entering into the breath of the Soil,
The water
Has attained a new vitality there,
Whereas, the ignorant one
Has acquired new wisdom
At the *feet,*[22] of the wise.
The unsteady achieved steadiness
The undurable found durability
A new fresh transformation...!

It's an eternal dancing
Of the consciousness into the body
Which of the eyes are those,
Whose are they, and where they are ?
– For whom it's possible
To visualize this dancing ?

□

Yes ! now here comes
Some reference to the winter season,
Certainly, some deformity
Plays a role through it,
There is snowfall
On each of the branches
Of trees and plants
At every leaf there-of.
And making an humble submission
Flattering to it
Along with Nature,
With a melancholy heart, ornamented body,
Is the wind holding conversation.
Fine, soft, skyey
These vines and creepers,
Getting pale
With the touch of winter
Are appearing to be fully within watery mould.

The bodies of each one are acquainted
With the experience of shivering
But where is the heart
Filled with compassion ?
Who and where is such a being ?

When does he show his grace ? –
The showers of superior compassion
Fall upon the ground.

In the hour of singing a song
When were they initiated disciples too,
When were they educated and trained also,
Even then, like an experienced one,
The teeth of every one appear dancing.
The day manifests shrinkage
The fury of the Sun too
Seems to be alarmed and diffused,
And
Despite being at apex in the sky
The Sun is there with an inclined forehead.

Where-ever the eye flashed around
The dignity of snow was fragrant on earth,
And today !
The dense, dark-hued as a large black bee,
Like the shelter-house of Saturn...
The mother of fear, pride and sin –
The night has lengthened two-fold.
At last, this winter
Is appearing troublesome to all,
But ! but what ?
One note-worthy point is, that

With the Artisan
That night passes in a light way !
Only a single one
Thin-looking sheet of cotton

Covers his limbs !
And it's enough for him,
The option of winter is closed.

Even then, as the public practice prevails,
The Soil says something to the Artisan
From outside the courtyard –
" The body is only body
A shadow and a phantasm of the matter
Which seems to be our better-half...
So...
Please draw at least a blanket, indeed,
Over your body !
So that...and..."
The Soil keeps quiet
Soon...then...
Hears some discourse, from the Artisan –

" Those who possess little strength
Keep a blanket with them
And
Play a slave to their passions.
We are full of strength
Are the devotees of Rām
And
We sleep beside Rām.
The support of the blanket
Isn't necessary for us
We have a regard
For a cheap cotton-sheet only !
The additional point is that

Those who are warm-skinned
Are, indeed, afraid of
The functioning of cold weather,
And
Go against
The right conduct.
My nature is cool-tempered
And
The quality of the weather too is cool–
laked
Both of them strike similarity,
That is why our friendliness
Is going on unobstructed.

We really have affection for
Our own true self
And
We see our well-being
Within our own true self.
If the Soul
Deviates from its 'Nature', that is, 'True Self'
It shall surely be
A pool of deformities,
The oneness of the 'Soul'
With the 'Nature'– that is the own true self
Is 'Salvation', is the 'True Essence'
And
To feel delighted elsewhere
Is to be caught into the whirlpool
Is delusion, is worldliness...!

And listen !
From the highly self-disciplined ascetics

We have found a maxim that –
Not only the external idleness,
But
The lustful leanings
Ill-will and sensuousness
Of the one who is a slave to his passions
Is the internal cowardice
In the true sense of the word !

Listen, hear the truth !
With a concentrated mind !
Be immersed into the incorporeal !
The bodily existence and hopelessness –
Both of these
Should vanish into the lap of the last breath
For the ensuing eternity !

□

The soil is fully expanded
Like the petals of a flower,
This very blooming of the soil
Is the primeval root formation
Of smoothness-of the sense of affection.
And
It's the uprooting
Of the roughness of the malicious feelings –
By making them non-existent.

The motion thus attained by the Soil
Is caused by what the Soil has done –

– Is the result of the drinking of water,
But
When will the capability of holding the water
Manifest itself through it ? –
When, within the Soil
The smoothness increases
And
When it shall absorb the fire.
The advent of the Artisan is meant
For making the smoothness of the Soil
Reach its crest.

> The joy of the Soil knows no bounds
> On the auspicious occasion of the day-break,
> And
> Lying aside thereat
> A thorn, viewing this scene,
> Peeps through the garment-tip of night
> Like an astonished thief !

At the time of digging the Soil –
On being struck with a hoe,
Whose head is half-torn
Whose hand is chopped off,
Almost lean and thin...
Whose back and waist appeared
That very portion now more cut off,
The side of which the leg is broken
The eye of that very side is blinded,
And
The transient fragile age too

Has been affected by knocking about,
It too, has almost decreased.
It goes without saying
That the prickly body of the thorn
Now appears to be disorderly.
It is beyond doubt, that
It may breathe its last at any moment
The life-breath now can not be relied upon,
Even then
The sky, indeed, hangs upon hope !
The strength of the body
Appears like that of a grain
And
The power of the mind
Appears like that of forty 'seras', that is a '*mana*'
It is a rule fit for ever.

Yes ! it is, what is happening here,
The physical body of the thorn
Is entirely encircled with fever –
Even then it's not perishing
It is living its life,
And its desire-body, the mind,
Is relishing the flavour
Filled with sweet tides,
At this point
Whose heart shalln't feel astonished ?
Hear the cause too, of this surprise !
The mind has been supported by deception–
The mind is playful by nature,
Even then

The fraudulence of this mind is stable
The mind is really the mine of '*Māyā*'- Phantasm !
It has resolved to take revenge
With the Artisan.
This mind shall feel relieved
By inflicting a heart-rending sorrow
Upon the Artisan –
So to say,
The mind is an abode of hostility, indeed.

The arrogance is reared up really
Under the shadow of the mind,
The fore-head of the mind is not bowed,
If non-mindedness is there, then alone
The homage is paid to an 'ascetic',
Therefore the 'Desire body', the mind,
Always tells –
No bowing ! no bending !! no nodding !!!

The band of clouds should get melted,
The revengeful attitude of the thorn
Should somehow get softened,
With this very intention
The soil tells it thus :

" The revengeful attitude is that morass
In which...
What to talk of the bulky bullocks,
Even the mighty bands of elephants
Are badly entrapped
And
Run deep into it
Upto neck-and-cheeks.

The feeling of revenge is that fire
Which
Burns the body, even the spirit also
Upto the future births and re-births !

> The revengeful attitude is that *Rāhu*[23a]
> Within whose
> Huge and horrible jaws
> Even the Sun of luminous Spirit too
> Finds its existence lost
> Like that of a tiny morsel.

Hear a bit more !
The ten-mouthed Rāvaṇa had firmly resolved
To take avenge upon Bālī [23b]
What was the outcome then ?
The physical strength was squeezed
The vitality of the mind was distressed
And
The brilliance of the fame faded away,
Isn't it what happened !
Guard me ! Protect me !! Save me !!! –
Shouting aloud thus
He started weeping in the tone of a demon,
Then was he nick-named
As 'Rāvaṇa'

> "Yea ! indeed ! sufficient ! enough !
> Lay at rest more preachings, Mother !
> Only the view shouldn't represent a name,
> Mother !
> Now, Mother, there should also be some expansion !
> Towards some meritorious work as well !

Here, where a raid is storming
A sapling of rose stands
There, near by
Emitting its fragrance.
And
From the band of thorns...
A spirited voice resounds
That

" We acknowledge the point
That
We are certainly an 'apparent cause'– a '*Nimitta*'
Behind the woe and worry of others
Hence we are thorns;
Even then
It's a blunder
To see us barely in the form of a thorn,
At times, even the thorns
Are found softer
...Than flowers too
And
At times, even the flowers
Are found harder
...Than thorns too.

That blooming bunch of flowers
Touches us
With its tender fleshy cheeks
Due to this tough pricking
Every bud of that mildness
Takes flowering

A rare joy and tranquillity
Plays therein with a touching sense.

Then, it should be told by you, that
How do we remain thorns ?
How do they remain flowers ?

That lustful play
Has attacked us,
Has immensely
Put our adoration to troubles
Isn't that flower
A thorn, even then ?
It seems that
There lurks some dust into the eye !

These charming creepers...
Try to distract us
From our righteous disposition
Come forth to cling to us,
Get freely embraced –
Even then
The splendour of righteousness
Of the thorns, which we are,
Isn't melted or deviated,

They come to diffuse our prickly faces
With their pollen of affections
Nevertheless
They fail to make us impassioned
They aren't able to put
Blemish upon us.

Upto this nose, beyond expectation,
Their sweet-smelling

Is communicated by them,
But, but do they
Succeed in awakening hope
Within these nostrils ?

Having wonder-struck eyes,
Having smiling lips,
They push on rapidly
Some fascination, some deliciousness
Upto these eyes,
They keep on dancing sportively
In front of us, always
In coquettish manner, with graceful motions !

Generally it has been found
That
Those, having lovely skins,
Are used to show crooked moves,
Appear from outside
Having some clean and soft bristles
And
Appear from inside
Bearing some impure rough tribe.

Indeed, the universal opinion goes
That
The weapon of the Cupid is Flower
And
The weapon of Lord Śiva is Trident.
There is pollen in the one
The dense passion is there –
The fruit of which is worldliness.

There is renunciation in the other–
The sinless resignation
The fruit of which is Emancipation.

The first one almost takes away the breath of others
And, in return,
Fills only with arrogance,
The second fills others with self-restraint
Then, instantly,
Makes them pridelessly sensible.

Self-restraint is joy, the source of happiness
Arrogance is pain, the death of joy !
Even then,
What a mockery is it
That
Only flowers are lauded
By every lip,
And
The thorns are crushed
Is it not
An assault against the Truth ?

The Western culture
Is not a prohibitor of aggression,
But !
It is largely aggressive
In whose eyes
Stares the sport of destruction, a terrible sight,
Always staging a show of itself,
And –
The direction towards which,
the magnanimous ones
Moved their renunciatory steps.

Having renounced all belongings,
Took to the track towards forest –
Being immersed deep within themselves –
Adopted nakedness;
– Towards that very direction...
Is found Indian Culture –
An indication of their following
Which provides entrance for
happiness and peace.

The thorns are revered,
Hence
The flowers are talked-of.
Certainly, the flowers are the articles for adoration
They are dedicated upon the feet of gods,
But
The God doesn't touch the flowers
Despite being the bearer of the Trident.
The Lord has reduced the Cupid to ashes
That is...why...
These flowers, being shelterless,
Come to the feet of the Lord
With a hope for protection;

And, listen !
On getting the holy contact with the Lord
The thorns have transmuted
Contrary to the flowers,
From where upto here
And
From here upto where ?
From what time upto this hour
And
From this hour upto what futurity ?

Some on, and so forth...
The subtlest and minutest
Indication of place and time
Is communicated
Through the thorns easily.
Otherwise,
Why do the needles exist
Within the mariner's compass
And
The time-indicators – the watches ?

This point too shouldn't be forgotten by us
That
To alleviate the impertinence of those
Who are filled with hot pride,
A penal code is adopted
And
The royal throne of the rulers shouldn't be
flowery
It should rather be thorny,
Otherwise,
That royal majesty shall become
The 'queen'– the kingdom of ornamentation !

That is...why...
In such a bent of mind of the Artisan,
A change-move is desirable
Towards the right direction...!
And
That wounded thorn
Adds again –
The Artisan should, at least,

For this error
Tender his apology with the thorn, O mother !"

□

Now, thus addresses the Soil :
" Hark, listen !
Whence do you know
The nature and morality of the Artisan ?
An embodiment of forgiveness
An incarnation of forbearance is he,
Who has reached across the other side
Of the unbounded, the infinite
Sea of forgiveness. "

Meanwhile, the utterances,
Which were digestive of the fire of
anger,
And which were full of the nectar of
compassion,
Dropped out of the Artisan's lips,
Wherein
There was a flow of patience
and earnestness too –

"*Khammāmi, Khamaṁtu me* [24] – that is,
I pardon, let me be pardoned
I forgive all others,
Hope to be forgiven by all,
Friendliness should prevail naturally
Among all of us for ever !
Why, when and with whom should I
Enter into animosity ?
Here, in the world at large,
There is none to be envisaged as my enemy !"

Subsisted by humility, that covering, –
Which seemed like a highly fluxed mica,
Having passed through the expanse of body,
Effected
The eternal consciousness of the thorn.

Even the supine sense of fury–
Which soared to prominent heights
Coming down, in a contrary manner,
Is getting pacified
Like a very chilly fire
Due to the absence of fuel.
At every moment
Is being vomited the sense of revenge
Which is the agent of the store of sins.
At every moment is taking place the arrival of
The sense of great awakening
Which represents the treasure of virtuous acts,
And
Here, naturally and easily !
The salutation is being extended
To the sense of purgation,
Which represents deeper perception !

Manifesting more lucidly what is above-mentioned
This pen too makes its enterprising effort, that
Without being sprinkled with divine wisdom
These plants of words
Never get flourished,
It's also true that
On the plants of words
Fragrant and pollinated –

The flowers of perfect awakening never smell
sweet
Then !
Where and when shall swing
The sensitive and delicious bunches of fruits...? "

Come, listen attentively !
The pen relates, that
When the flower of perfect awakening
Gets moulded and transformed,
That ripened fruit, therein,
Is, indeed, called purification.
Intellect rears restlessness
Purification bears the fruit of perfect
repose,
Not through the flowers, but through the
fruits.
Contentment is felt,
The flower ought to be protected
And
The fruit should be eaten;
Yes ! O yes !!
The flower may well bear fragrance
But, where is the juice in it !
The fruit is verily full of flavour,
It's perfumed as well !
With sweet smell too...!

The heart of the wounded thorn
Was shaken about,
Its hardness melted away –
With this craftsmanship of the Artisan
With the conversation unheard-of before.

The thorn adds with a sense of remorse
That
" It seemingly felt
The useful hidden into the harmful
And
The detrimental hidden into the beneficial,
The approach couldn't reach the root
The crest didn't appear to it pleasant,
It committed a blunder.

The adverse steps covered up,
A long distance...backward...
The favourable path remained behind,
The fragrance was said to be filthy
The moon was declared blind,

It seemingly felt
The nectar to be poison,
The error be pardoned, my Lord !
Let it be blessed with an excellent *Mantra*-incantation,
As a result of which
Its life, from top to bottom,
Should be pacified and blissful
Then, gradually, that period
Should come in the life-span –
Which should be an abode of shelter
Fear-free for the fugitives
It should be also highly venerable. "

On hearing this, the Artisan says that :
"A *Mantra* – incantation – is neither good
Nor bad
Good or bad, indeed,
Is our own mind.

A serene mind is truly
A *Mahā-mantra* – an efficacious incantation–
And
A fickle mind is really
A realm of sin, full of wantonness,
The one is a stair for happiness
The other is, hence, a drink of sufferings. "

Again the thorn expresses its curiosity
That
" What calamity the 'delusion' is
And
What art is the 'Supreme Salvation' ?
The true indications of these are required, not
explanations,
The genuine attributes win over the award.
By the lengthy and Sky-touching elucidation
The value of the 'fundamental' decreases,
The true evaluation is found missing.

It doesn't matter if you mix-up
The milk with water in due quantity –
The sweetness of the milk surely decreases !
The smartness of the water is frozen over the
tongue ! "

The inquest of the thorn is rectified
In the addressing of the Artisan –
" Leaving behind our own 'Self '
To be infatuated with alien objects, indeed,
Is the result of 'delusion'
And
Abandoning entirely everything else
To contemplate within our own True 'Self ', indeed

Is the Abode of Final Liberation."
On hearing this, at once !
Well ! well indeed !
Exclaimed the thorn again.

" Today, it [the thorn] has
Found itself
Under the true shade of literature,

These rows of words
Emerging from your mouth
Appear like pearls,
Having a glimmering lustre,
The usage and application
Of this suggestive metaphor is uncommon
I heard from many persons, but
It came rarely as such to my hearing.

And
Your subtle expression too, seems to be
faultless,
The different tasteful eatables get into
oblivion.
If it's convenient,
It will be so kind of you –
By becoming large-hearted,
Let me amend my style of literal expression –
Kindly relate…so that...I may hear, my Lord !
If it is related to the word 'Literature'
Then, it is so good,
– The contemporary shall be the best !"

The word *Sāhitya* [Literature] looked as
if being cast
Into the skilful mould of the Artisan !

" That which is united and co-ordinated with
the welfare
Is regarded to be benevolent,
And
The purport of the benevolent
Is the profession of literature,
It really means that
The true literature is only that
By studying which
Happiness should be originated and attained
Otherwise,
Like a flower devoid of sweet smell
It is the deprivation of happiness –
A cluster of words without sum and
substance...!

This point may also be put thus
That
A fruitful life, indeed,
Breathing peacefulness,
Is the creator of immortal literature,
Such a literature
May be read also by the eyes
May also be heard by the ears
The hands may also serve it,
Indeed, such a literature is alive ! "

Well...this time...the thorn
Feels indeed much delighted
Even many times more
Than that of the re-union with one's better-half,
Despite having its forehead crumbled, –

While stirring the literature
Its forehead…
Obtained the form of Cupid's churning-stick !
Absorbed into the taste of literature.
Being deeply charmed
The single-legged one, yet
Engaged into dancing, the thorn !

Smiling gracefully
Its individual soul
Makes the Artisan feel
That
The *Haṁsā*,[25a] that is–Soul–lives everlastingly
Sustaining no blemish at all,
But that body of everybody
Causes pains to one and all
Hence, it seems that this dead body
Is put to burning ceremony in the end.
O Body ![25b] being burnt once and again into flames,
Turning into ashes and dust even several times –
Thou still inflameth the 'Spirit' frequently
By taking births once and again.

□

Hither, this pen too started saying something
About the topic of literature, under reference, that

More than the writer rich in penmanship
And
More than an eloquent propounder of sacred texts even,

The hearer, who is subdued with faith,
Assimilates the literary essence
In a largely multiplied quality.
He is an expert in the art of sermon-hearing;
Like a swan-flamingo-
Discerning the milk from water !
It is quite proper that
The tongue of a butler
Can take only a little of relish
From the tasteful foodstuffs.
Because
The preacher at the time of preaching,
The author at the time of his writing-period
Both of them return back into the past.

In that period of conviction
There remains neither the taste
Nor the sense of tastelessness,
Only a bare clash looms large
Upon a non-attached past, indeed !

□

The Artisan's arrival is taking place
Towards the Soil !
The swollen soil is to be trampled,
Having trampled it
It has to be kneaded into lumps,
That process of trampling too –

Isn't possible with the palms,
The affluence of smoothness
Is to be added to the Soil, indeed !
It has to be made into gum
It's possible only through the soles
Due to the reason that,
In the field of duty
The hand generally appears to be timid,
And
The hand asks for hand,
And that too, in a frank manner !
Not only this much,
It is surrounded with arrogance
It falls down from humanity;

On the contrary, there is the conduct of the foot,
Being fully convinced with diligence
It, in its completeness, by taking pains,
Is generally injured
And
The foot bends upon humility
Delights in purification.

Lo ! all of a sudden, what is it going to happen !
That sun of breathing
Crawling down the Western horizon...
The right foot of the Artisan
Is getting benumbed,
Where-in there was circulation of blood
Now, therein
The accumulation of blood is appearing.

And
The other foot-step utters some songs of devotion
At every pace, it prays to God
That
On being desirous of an office
I shouldn't kick the others,
I should create no disturbances,
I should never crush, O Lord !
The life of any living being…
And, O my Lord !
How can it be possible ?
It's like a blow with a foot...
On the forehead of the Mother Earth
Who is the virtuous 'Woman-existence' of Peace !
It is like a torrent of annihilation
Over the fields of bliss and well-being.
It is like the fall of a thunderbolt of cruelty
Over the mountain-top tender with love.
This Age should not be separated
From happiness and peace
And
It should not be reduced to pieces
By sufferings and vexations.

□

A wave of eagerness
Runs through the Soil
The position of ups and downs of life too
Leaves behind the emitted poison
That –

What happens henceforth
Is not known !
The component of that happening
Would manifest itself in what form
And
The uprise in that very shape
Shall stay on how long ?
Shall its outcome be proper or constructive ?
– All this is hidden into the lap of future
But,
The knower of the present, the past and the future
Is uniformly radiant in omniscience.

The understanding of the Soil
Becoming faintly, immerses into silence,
The faded mind too of the Artisan
Bows before the silence,
It found itself fully incompetent
In ordering the foot-steps
And what can indeed the lips communicate
Without getting hints from the heart ?

On hearing this, the tongue interrupted that
" Being the follower of improper indications
The very tongue itself
Has been the way to hell "
That is to say, the living being
Who overcomes his tongue
The pains of that very being are emptied out
A happy life is led by him
That very being becomes long-lived –

And
There is found sense in that person's utterances
Which redress the pains of his own 'self' and those of the others
Like life-giving pills...!

> To go on, to move on wrongfully,
> And to trample –
> There are these three ways.
> The point under reference is that of trampling
> The Mother-Earth shall be crushed under foot...!
> Well, then,
> What should be said and why ?
> How should the feet be addressed to ?
> And, the tongue assumes graveness.

The nose of the Artisan too
Took this spreading bad smell
As its foodstuff
That is...why...
It doesn't allow the Soil
To be trampled under foot,
It only condemns this hateful deed,
And
Twisting itself a little,
Getting the nostrils puffed up, the nose
Fully supports the footsteps
That
The abstaining of the footsteps from this work
Is justified and according to their dignity also !

> The golden lustre of the broad fore-head
> Like that of the rising sun –

– On seeing as losing freshness and
getting faded
Both the eyes of the Artisan
Send very far off...within
Their lustrous flame
And close the doors.
Through it, the result was that
The refraining of the eyes
On such an occasion
Means the disapproval of an impending
misfortune.
These eyes too !
Are very far-sighted;
In brief, I should say that
All the parts and limbs of the Artisan's body,
Upto the head
Became the travellers of the same path
On which the feet tread as wayfarers.

The Earth as well as the Artisan
Both of them are staring at Him
Who is standing as 'Silence' between them,
Who is the One greater than Silence ?
Who renders secondary the taciturnity of Silence
And
The taciturnity sings with a hum
The One, who hears it, is greater than Silence.

That body of the speech
Is made of time-limit, indeed !
The charms of the drum
Have really escaped due to its circumference !
But, listen !

Where is the time-limit
Of the shadow of hollow space ?
It
Is the treasure of all the treasures
Like the spouse of enlightenment
Is sacred since centuries, indeed !
At first, the reticence turns towards the Soil,
Like wax
The reticence trickles and melts away
And
The lips on the face bearing a smile get opened.
Like soft and tasteful sweet-balls
The utterances full of equanimity
Drop out from his mouth :

" O mother Earth !
Thine faith too about the Artisan
Seems to be dubious.
This thing is certain that –

That which glides and slides
Is called a river
Hence it remains transient.
And
The sea doesn't glide
Hence it remains constant
But,
The river, indeed, slides towards the Sea !
Otherwise,
Neither the river nor the sea would exist !
This very gliding is *the eminent conduct* [26]
of the river

This viewing, indeed, is the accurate conception
of the river
Really this is what we call Faith.
The Faith feels agitated
Unless it gets foot-steps to move onwards,
And
Delight is not felt, can't be gained
In the conduct without Faith.
Then,
The activity abounding in Faith only
Is called fidelity,
This fact should be kept in mind !

That which springs up from deepest fidelity
Like the pure fragrance of a night jessamine,
That which sweet-smells
The external as well as the internal atmosphere
That very fruitful dignity
Of devotion is called consecration,
It is agreeable and soothing
To the hearts of one and all, of the fortunate ones.

Gradually, the object of honour
Gains reputation,
When and where the glory
While flowing on and on
Reaches climax and holds good
That very ground is called
a *proper establishment of conduct* [27a]
Thus, step by step.
Promoting its 'grade'
That very genuine Faith –
Passing through devotions and dedications
Attains the '*Eternal State*,' [27b] Mother !

Of the establishment of 'Supreme Soul'
– Of entity, knowledge and joy –
Free from buying and selling for ever.
And
The Silence immerses within itself.

" O Silence ! give a bit of thy ear to me
Don't thou talk of blank faith
Hold some discourse with Right Faith ! "
Thus challenges the Faith of the Soil
To Silence, which stands face to face.

"I am mum due to sin
Thou art mum due to Faith,
Except sin –
Thou art vacant from everything else !
The hope may come within the reach of the eyes
But
– Only Faith begets Faith –
The true vision of Faith is possible
Neither through the eyes nor through the expectations.

That fundamental formation
Can be perceived
Not through the corporeal eye
Based on meritorious or sinful deeds
But
Through the Spiritual eye of Faith."

Out came that Faith of the Soil
Retreating into a deeper understanding,
Her eyes looked a bit reddish too
While turning round, as if staring at the Silence !

Brow-beating at once the taciturnity
Upon its reddish eyes
The bluish eyes of the Artisan
Sprinkle bluishness for a moment !

Visualizing the bodily aspects
In the form of an opponent,
The Artisan cautioned the other side –
The Soul, by telling
That

"The body, the mind, the speech-all these
Have been obtained once and again, for
many a times,
And
Having completed their destined existence,
Have melted away as trails of liquids,
Under the subjection of the folly of
delusion
We folded them into arms,
But, alas !
In spite of being with the Supreme 'Spirit'
They don't keep company with the
Supreme 'Soul'.

The Functional kārmic world[28] has offered nothing
To the Soul uptil now,
If something has been given... too...then
It has bestowed mere outer covering without substance,
Has played a plain fraud.

Has cheated ! let it be so –
Telling thus repeatedly,
The Soul swallowed it up
After cleansing it with the water of the eyes
And even to-day –

The mundane or worldly soul is awaiting
a chance
Of gaining something rare from the
corporeal existence…! ”

The Spirit now tells
Her import to the Artisan :

“ The salaried classes are able
To pay scant attention towards the nation
And
How far the Spiritualists can remain
Attentive towards the bodies ?
That is why...
The King’s demise
Takes place in the battle
While protecting his subjects,
And
The great saints see their mortality
Amid the forests
While defending the religious banner,
Under whose broad shade
The entire earth is alive
Acknowledging the happy breath joyfully !”

□

Some deformity sprang up at once
Upon the features of *the Functional kārmic nature* [29]
On hearing her bitter criticism,
And her iron-clad eye-sight
Appeared to be more reddish distressed !

The light from which
Her surface of the fore-head is enlightened
From which emanates a sharp row of rays
On that are written some lines :

“ Not the Real or True Nature, but
the mundane soul
Is the heap of sins,
The culture-tradition of the Real or True Nature
Has never been defeated by the alien elements,
But
Has ever been alert in itself. ”

In the form of right manly conduct,
Some more discourse to the mundane soul !
“ Never take hold of the alien nature
Which is a filler of the attitudes adverse to our real
own self ”
Examine it in its true form, O thou mundane soul !

Breed no sins
Within your heart, in any way,
But, losing into it for a moment
Put the sin to a test too,
Then, whatever is ascertained,
Is yours, lo, make it your own !

Then
The grappling with the minute, nay, the minutest flaw
The rolling of the *Knowledge* [30a]
Towards the worldly objects, indeed,
Is the sharp pain of sickness,
And
The reflection of the objects truly
Within the '*Absolute Knowledge*' [30b]
Is the play of the most Sublime Truth –

The one is in the guise of humility –
Is ashamed of its reversal,
The other dwells in the land of liberty –
Is adorned with the fruitfulness.

The mundane soul has been beaten up by the
Real or True Nature,
The consciousness too, in a different manner,
Came within its thrust.

On hurting a meritorious person
The merits too are affected, indeed,

" When the root is struck
The tree withers away,
If the root is watered…then....
It flourishes to its full. "
Hence ! on being awakened
The consciousness of the Artisan
As if throwing light upon his own duty
And that of the others also !

The mundane soul shouldn't have its effective control
Over the Real or True Nature, but over the
consciousness,
– The consciousness should not exercise
Her control over the 'Sense-organs of knowledge',
But over the conscience–the Mind,
–The 'Mind' shouldn't exercise control over the body,
But upon the 'sense-organs of actions', and
The flock of all the sense-organs shouldn't
Exercise its control or rule over the alien elements
But always upon the body itself.
So to say, the body should be controlled as a rule
It should be allowed to be the ruler or controller of
none else,
Due to it being enjoyable itself !

And
The Real Self or Soul should be all in all, the Controller
The 'Meritorious', the flock of merits, the Knower,
the Experiencer
Due to He being the enjoyer Himself !

The creative force of the consciousness
Which is not stipendiary
Becomes active,
Extending its approval
To this state of consciousness –
A smile rises upon
The lips of the Artisan… .

The very core of the functional consciousness
That very bright manner
Fills the '*Yoga*'[31]– the means of salvation – with
brilliance
Each and every limb of the Artisan
Moves like a machine mobilized by a driver
And, at first,
The right foot of the Artisan
Gradually stepping upwards
Poses a benediction,
Then,
Descends upon the forehead of the Soil.
Like a clever ruddy she-goose
Longing for the moon-light,
The Soil, moving up her fore-head,
While welcoming the process of craftsmanship.

The upside downwards
The downside upwards –

The soil is shuffled
Swiftly and speedily !

The steps of the Artisan felt –
Made possible, that, which was impossible-found it so,
It seemed as if that tender touch
Is, somewhere at the farthest end,
Testing, the Supreme Being
Who is beyond the grasp of the touch;

Here at,
The self-prestige of the delicacy of velvet
Seemed to be half-dead.
The charming mango sprouts
The softness and smoothness of the delicate
tendrils
Has forgotten its self-prestige, here,
Is getting itself concealed behind the veil of
shyness
While not putting up with its mockery,
And
Has looked somewhat fretful,
Otherwise
Its external thin skin
Is why slightly blood-reddish ?

The mildness of the Soil,
The mother of wax,
Couldn't keep quiet
The mystery couldn't remain concealed
She spoke out thus –
" If desirable, listen, I tell you
Something to be heard and to be told :

How should I tell you
About the pre-eminence
The recognizable address
Of that Supreme Spirit ?

The eyes where-in
With black collyrium
Has over-brimmed
That compassion,
Which makes us learn something –
You identify
Your Spirit...!
The lips where-in
With crystal-clear redness
Has reflected
That true flush,
Which confers upon us, something,
– Cherish equanimity always
Like a supplemental drink…!
The cheeks where-in
With plumpiness
Has rolled down
That youthfulness,
Which hints at something –
Let the proper vigour
Be offered as sacrifice...!

The locks of hair where-in
That curliness
Which degrades the merit of the black-bee
Has come forth
Into telling thus –

Don't bow in respect
Before *the body...!* [32a]
Saluting those feet
With the venerable assembly,
Has joined joyfully
That fast stepping
Which is 'humming'
Having accomplished a perfect journey
Stay in rest...! [32b]

And listen !
Where is the beginning and the end of that
'Supreme Spirit'
Where is the brink and bank of the
'Supreme Soul' ?
Whatever is there is manifest –
A particle of an Infinite vastness
A libation of a drop to the ocean –
And that too while staying into the ocean
indeed !"
Uttering in this way
The mildness of the glad Soil
Draws the veil of silence over her face !

□

'Having accomplished a perfect journey stay in rest !'
This saying
Awakened the Spirit of the Artisan
And
Stirred up his conscience
With full agility was flushed the body
Which had become languidly slow.

The process of trampling gains momentum
Into the depth of the Soil
The feet of the Artisan sink upto the knee !
Coiling round the strong shins
Of the *'Puruṣa',*[33] *the Nature*, the Soil
Felt thirsty of the fragrance
Like a female-serpent embracing a
sandalwood tree...!

Through this act of adherence
The sentiment of heroism is oozing out
From the arms of the great existence–the Earth*
And
It is asking the Artisan
That
" Why has it been remembered ?
Why has it been called out ?
The sentiment of heroism is produced
Which is lauded by the brave,
It has bestowed valour from age to age
...For centuries !

Have it ! drink it in cupfuls
Let your ambition for victory be fulfilled !
Be the hero of the Age ! be the most
valiant one !
Be thou the one, having indelible valour ! "

Now the valour of the Artisan speaks
...To the sentiment of heroism, that
" You are talking under intoxication !
At this point, our belief
Has gained firmer roots –
That –

It is never possible
To reach the shores through the sentiment of heroism
And
Through the mere brave heroic sentiments
The cessation of woes
Is impossible in all the three times-the present, the
past and the future !

Even the cool water
Comes in contact with the fire,
Little by little,
Being heated up,
Gets boiled, indeed.

But listen !
It can extinguish even the blazing fire
By bringing it under control.

But,
By the usage of *the sentiment of heroism* [34]
The human blood instantly
Begins to boil extremely
It goes beyond the control,
To bring others into the fold of peace is a far cry,
Even the peaceful atmosphere starts
boiling
Like a volcano,
And
By the usage of it
The excess of increased rudeness
Takes rise in life,
The hunger of subjugating others
Is the outcome hereof.
The root of pride is as hard
As the stump of an acacia tree –

And stands up denying others
Tramples under its feet the value of others,
The pride being jostled
The heroic sentiment raises a bogus cry,
Losing self-control, on being infuriated,
Holds in disgust the tradition of the ancient sages.

The ethics of Manu was inherited by mankind
Was it forgotten, or did it fade away entirely ?
The first wording should mean that –
– Which is the contemplation of pride,
The next wording should correctly mean that
– The ego should be beaten off,
And that too at the very root of it ! no mistake
about it ! ”

On seeing the unsuitableness of the
sentiment of heroism,
And
Keeping in view its disregard
The sentiment of humour,
Cracking and slipping
From the lips of the great existence of the Earth
Bursts into a laughter towards the Artisan :

“ The sentiment of heroism has its history,
The brave heroes understand it, but
You don't dare make it a laughing-stock!
Those who aren't brave, are the brave-nots,
What to talk of them, even on their pictures,
The auspicious red-powder isn't sprinkled !
Yes, it's something peculiar, – that,
While carrying them on a bier in eternal sleep
It might be sprinkled, indeed...!

At their history
It seems befitting neither to weep nor to laugh ! "
Uttering thus, the sentiment of humour,
Added a proverb with a boisterous laughter –
'Take the food at half of the due quantity
Drink the water in the double amount
Work hard in a three-fold measure,
and laugh in a fourfold quantum

That is how one can live for quarter past hundred years
!'Delightfulness is a friend to the near-lucky
one to salvation,

Delightfulness is a shelter, a divine branch
Upon which...
The tufts of flowers and fruits of virtues
Swing for ever and ever.

" O Thou the jester !
Don't enter into argument laughingly
Don't value the sentiment of humour so much !
We do not approve of thy idea,
We can't agree upon the jocular view
Like true reality, at any cost ! "

The Artisan again adds thus –
"For uprooting the sense of sorrow
The liking for humour may be necessary indeed,
But for the development of the sense of
divine knowledge
The abandoning of joking is inevitable,
Joking is really a foul emotion (*Kaṣāya*) [35] !

A jolly fellow
Is generally a rash fellow
Is the power to discriminate between good or bad actions,

Is seriousness and patience found there in him ?
He looks as crazy as a young boy

That is…why...!
When do they cut jokes who are
equanimous in wisdom ?
When are the spiritualists caught into
The snare of infatuation and illusion? "

Finding itself not being effective
Seeing its move going meaningless,
The humour changed its side.
And
Remembered its companion, which
Very far inside the great existence of Soil,
Boiling into the mysterious inner hell
Is awakened –
The terrifying black 'Sentiment of Terror'
Which is inflammable, heartless
And with the seal of cruelty,

The chanced event became known to him
His billious humour became fretful
His heart felt enraged,
The eyebrows looked stretched in a bent
The pupils of the eye
Were filled up with acid-redness.

Within a short gaze, the balloon-like –
His fluttering long nose
Went on swelling.
If the incence-stick had not come
Into contact with the wick…then...

The Matter was different...was incomplete,
But the matter was completed,
The gunpowder was, indeed, adequately
filled inside
Then, what remained !
Towards outside, through the nose,
The flames of fury full of dense smoke
The brandishing mucus started flowing –
Now that nose appeared to be dangerous.
It seems, due to it, that
'The very nose is the treasury of wrath
No one feels any doubt in the saying –
The vital breath fully rests within the nose .'

'The end of the existence of goodness
Was manifested here
The excess of avarice and ignorance
Was talked about now.'

"Don't give too much of introduction – "
The Artisan fearlessly told the Sentiment
of Wrath
In the polite posture of the moon :

" Vehement anger is deformity and defect
Which is full of destructiveness,
Welfare is a mode of Nature
Which turns into indelible wonderful performance.

And listen !
Hasn't this maxim reached thy ears ?
'Little income with extra expenses
Is a sign of being destroyed,
Little strength with violent anger
Is a sign of being beaten off,'

Sure enough, meanwhile
Somewhat contrary situation arises
The understanding of the Artisan goes astray,

Of the Great Existence,
The most terrible mouth is gaped wide
As huge as a cave, that,
Even the seven elephants
Having a height of seven cubit each,
Can pace it in and out together !
In the jowl and jaw of which
The scarlet-eyed horror
Is staring outside once and again,
The half-projected reddish tongue
Through the mouth of which is hanging down,
And
The saliva, like the red blood-drops
Is dripping down from it,

Into that mouth…
Like the fathomless and bottomless underworld
My sight, having slipped away, disappeared
My feet, having slipped off gradually,
...Stopped at the shores
And
My life-breath, on brink of being faded away,
Was held back upon my intense pain...!
The eyes whirled around
It gazed upon me
…I too beheld something with a blurred sight
That fear ! O yes, horror !! dreadful terror !!!

Thus ! crying aloud chirr chirr
Save...save...save...!
Protect him, what !...no ?
Tell me, my Lord !"
And
Clinging to the chest of the Artisan
The very Intellect of the Artisan, trembling
with fear.
Very soon,
The palm of assurance of safety by the Artisan
Turns upon the head of the Intellect,
Surely, it was enough !

A light consciousness awakens
Into the eyelids of the Intellect,
And,
A momentary wavering touches through
The curly locks of the Intellect
Inclosing over the surface of the forehead.

The assurance of protection stands on one side
The fear makes its haltage on the other
And
In the very middle
Is staying itself the double-headed Intellect…
Which is imbued with fear and fearlessness both
Let us see...whereto does it incline...so
Whether it falls into the snare of fear
Or…
Comes to dwell within the benediction of
fearlessness ?
A few moments pass over when
The Intellect attains fearlessness

It was influenced by the *'Puruṣa'*,[36] the Soul
...Profusely!
The influence of the *Kārmic nature (Prakṛti)* itself gave way
...Extra-ordinarily.

□

Lo ! it is fleeing from the battlefield –
The Brave in the form of a coward –
The Terror in the form of the diseased and the
distressed
And
The Fear in the form of the afraid
was found !
The Wonder itself wondered
Over this wonderful event.
On its broad fore-head
Rising upwards,
Appeared the serpentine streaks of surprise,
For a few moments the eyelids of Surprise
Remained asunder !
Its voice became speechless
And
The hunger slacked downwards.

On seeing such a condition of surprise
Even the prestige of the sentiment of love
Is just about to dry up
And
The sweet story of the admirers of lustful pleasures
Appeared to be light-blinded !

O God ! when shall the blind and the
lust-blind
Get the fragrance of the divine flame ?
– The Artisan, thus taking a deep breath !

– Appeared again the words of discourse –
" The one who has been the lover of the
tasteless – Soul –
How shall he relish the passions or
(sensual pleasures)?

The one who touches the 'Untouchable'
Shall he like to desire a pleasant touch ?

And
The One who avoided good or bad smell–
What fragrance would be adored
By his nose ?

One thing more, that
An embodiment attains a body
Whether it is elegant or ugly,
The elegant tries to bring added brilliance to its beauty
While the grotesque tries to reform its deformity
Through adornments, ornaments and decorations.
But
For the one who is not thirsty for beauty,
Who is hopeful for the incorporeal,
What concern does prevail upon him
For the senseless material decorations !

This longing for and the tasting of
The flavour and chemicals,
This testing and seeing
Through dependence upon the alien elements
Since what a time by-gone is going on
This adoration of lustfulness ?

This consciousness of mine
Wishes to bear
A change in view
No dictates of desire, now,
...*Rām*[37] should be attained !

How hard heat it is !
Inside as well as outside
These volcanic tempests !
Almost scorched-up
My body desires
A change in the sense of touch,
No basking now,
...The final abode be gained !
In these days, the inner dimension too
Has furthered itself much ahead,

That splendour of the Cupid
Has indeed lessened
The chewing and churning of the divine
knowledge
Has been done deeply, is still going on.
Now
The conscience seems to be wearied
The body appears to be inactive
No bubbles of foam now,
...Mellowed maturity be accomplished !
I acknowledge, in this bud,
There are countless possibilities
But, upto what point of time
Would this bud remain unblossomed ?

When will the fragrance
Flow out from its inner joint ?
This veil creates obstruction
In beholding that divine revelation
No attachment now,
...The subtlest pollen be achieved !"

Lo, the Sentiment of Love gets some more
Wealth, in the form of address from the Artisan–
"O thou sentiment of love !
Whether thou conform to it or not,
It is a fact that,
Every living being is thirsty for happiness
But,
The aim of an impassioned one has been money
And that of an ascetic has been
The most Sublime Truth !
This subtle impenetrable line of difference
Is not based
On external give-and-take *(Nimitta Kāraṇa)*,
It is an internal self-dependant occurrence –
A contribution of its own *'eminent cause'*
(Upādāna Kāraṇa)![38]

The genuine ornaments , the true decoration–
Peep into your own self, evaluate it,
O Sentiment of Love !"

Puts a question to the tenderness of the Sentiment
of Love :
"In what rhythm do these sprouts
Sing a song, and for what reason ?
From which circuit do they come forth,
To which ring are they procured and are lost ?
And
Their breathings ultimately –

Fall vacant into what cadence ?
In what rhythm do these sprouts
Sing a song, and for what reason…? ”

Some more light is thrown on
The fineness of the wealth and the most Sublime Truth :

“ The balance in which the last particle,
Even the weight of a hair is weighed
Is not an ordinary balance for coal,
It is called an extra-ordinary balance for gold !
The gold indeed is weighed
Hence...it is not inestimable
And
The balance itself is never weighed
So…it has been matchless,
And
The most Sublime Truth can never be weighed
Upon the scale of money !
The usage of wealth as a balance
Is to deny the very meaning of economics
And
It really means to push the Age
Into the blind-pit of all the absurdities.
Does an economist know this purport ? ”

In this context, even the recollection
Of the 'voice' couldn't take place,
Thus, some notes of the Sentiment of Love
Issued forth from the pressed lips !
The 'voice' has been compared to the radiant God.
“ Even the God Himself owned the 'voice.'

How the reception of the eternal luminous happiness
Is possible without voice !

Voice is the vital life-breath of music
Music is the back-bone of delight
And
To attain happiness is the aim of all beings
Where is any room for doubt in this matter ?
It can be asserted, beyond doubt–
To attain the incorporeal existence…indeed
The embodiment of voice has to be recognized
O Thou incarnate Soul ! O Thou Artisan ! "

On hearing this, utters in clear terms
Artisan's neat and clean turban
Made of hand-spun cloth–
Due to the friction of the Mundane Soul–
with *the Functional (kārmic) nature* [39a]
The gamut arises
Through the pungent-transient *Functional nature*!
But, not from the *'Supreme Being'-(Puruṣa)*. [39b]

Whether harsh or melodious
All the sounds are perishable.

These Divine Powers and Almighty
Might well be immortal
But,
Their voices, indeed, are transient !

Why not that joy of hearing…
Should be treasured up within the voice,
In the primary condition – upto a limit –
'The voice' might have been
The external means for the eternal happiness

Even then,
The gamut is neither the aim, nor beneficial
The voice is neither boundless nor a nectar-like
drinkable
The devotee should know it very well ! "
And
The Artisan sinks into the posture of thinking–

"O, thou strength of hearing !
How many times
The voice was heard,
O thou heart-winner !
How many times
The voice was recollected
Since how long has been going on
This music and song ?
What period in the past
Has been spent, if known to thee, please tell...!
The innermost heart has not yet been drenched
Both the organs remained deaf
Where were they found verdant ?
O thou passionlessly green !
No set speeches now, real environment is needed !

Don't indulge in self-praise
By saying music the back-bone of delight,
Don't crush the genuine music
O thou Sentiment of love !

The music of my regard is that
Which plays beyond worldly attachments or possessiveness
And
Accepted as love is it...

Which is beyond the bodily limits
My companion is the music
Which transgresses the limits of gamut...!

All these organs of embellishment
Are destructible by the sword
The age is going on hoodwinking
And
All these hues of ornamentation
Are inflammable,
The age is going constantly on fire,
A preventive measure to this injury
...Has been found by it to-day
In the form of this uncommon drink !

The bodily afflictions, on being deferred,
Are broken to pieces within seconds,
On being cleansed, the riddles of mind,
Are eliminated within seconds
By taking it as a drink.

My companion is the music
Which is dispassionate, colourless-cool.

It is not possible for me to live
While binding myself within some age-limits !
And
It is not possible for me to say
While taming myself within some limited
musical measure!

My companion is the music
Which is '*a bondage-free naked observance*'. [40]

If we deploy our insight
Towards an ocean,
The ocean seems grave and grim-looking
With a time-span extending upto universal destruction;
If we keep our eye
Upon a wave,
The ocean seems to bear a short time-span.
The one and the same object
Is interpreted in various modes of thinking
Is multi-coloured and wavy !

My companion is the music –
'*The usage of seven-moded deliberations*'.[41]

He was fed up
With the drop of delight,
He was drowned
Into the sea of sufferings,
At times, with garlands
He was honoured,
At times, by defeats
He was insulted.
He was lured
For obtaining something somewhere
He felt agitated
Over the destroying of something somewhere,
Somewhere he met with his Kinsman
Elsewhere with deception !
This unfortunate one went on roaming about !
But today,
All these miseries have almost faded away
Since...when it was found...

My companion is the music
Which is a healthy brave triumph."

□

On hearing about the mortality
And worthlessness of the 'voice'
Started flowing the nose of nature,
Which gushes out under the spill of the Sentiment of love.
A bit dense, and somewhat flimsy
Some greenish with yellowish mingled –
Secretion was issued forth
Which looked hateful at its very sight !

Over it, the flies
Which are mothers of passions,
Which are the admirers of sensuousness
Started making a buzzing sound...so...
It appears that even the Sentiment of Disgust
Has dishonoured the Sentiment of Love –
Hasn't selected it !
Otherwise
Why does a nasal...
Only a negative syllable
Turns out from everybody's nose ?

Having clung to the upper lip
Came descending to the lower lip too
That filthy secretion !
And
The tongue of the Sentiment of Love tasted it
...With too much of eagerness,

On seeing which
The original mother– river of all the sentiments
The Mother-Nature fretted and fumed
Over the ignorance of the Sentiment of Love,
And
Struck the cheeks of the love-sentiment
With a few slaps,
The cheeks of the hero of the youngsters
Appeared reddish like coral.

Having given birth to a son
By barely presenting him before the world,
The chastity of the mother
Doesn't become renowned and fruitful
Contrary to it,
The latent power of sons or offspring
Has to be awakened, and
Has to be rendered cent-per-cent capable
And concrete, through the true refinements.
–These very holy words have been heard from the sages.
In the downfall of the offspring
Mother's hand of restraint is raised
And
In the progress of the offspring
Mother's head of favour is held high –
And that is what happened –
In the eyes of the Mother-Nature
The tearful compassion,

Drop-by-drop,
In the form of eye-drops...

The compassion addresses
Something to each and every particle :

" A strife broke out amongst you
It transgressed the limits, it was wrong.

Why have you poised yourself to destroy and
to be destroyed

You are so wise !
You have sharply engaged yourself in bringing
extensive destruction

You are washed with poison !

The mother has been deeply injured
By this incident

Don't make life a battle
Get the wound of the Mother-Nature healed up !

Be kind–hearted !
Take pity on the hard-hearted
Be fearless !
Let a nectarial drizzle of humane amnesty
Be dropped upon the terror-stricken,
Always keep up a well-intentioned viewpoint,
O my heart, make thyself live in sociability !

Don't make life a battle
Pay off the debt of the Mother-Nature !

Only your 'own self' shouldn't get recorded
The others should also be evaluated,
But, keep this point too in your mind
The alien should never be desired
The alien should never be blamed !

Don't make life a battle
Don't agonize the heart of the Mother-Nature !

What is the life and the world ?
Grasp the purpose, win over the wishes !
Realize the desire to be the snare !"

Then, something more is added gravely
By the Mother-Compassion–

" If my tears
Cause your face to bloom
May confer happiness upon you
Lo ! I..am...weeping...
And may go on bewailing,
And
Due to my presence
If your heart quivers with timidity
Palpitates, is pained with perplexity
Lo, I would like to lose my presence,
Would wish to go to eternal sleep,
I pray to God, that,
As soon as possible,
I should cease to exist
My existence should get itself merged
Entirely with the void, that's all !"

At this, the Lord rejoins that
The annulment of the 'Being' is not possible, dear child !
'To exist' indeed is an ally in the struggling battle !
'To be' is the everlasting song of joy.

I beg your pardon
Your wish remained unfulfilled
O thou pleasure-seeking man !

Hence, it blocks up with emotion the throat of this writing pen
While supporting the Mother –

> "At times, for some condition
> Compassion overbrims into her eyes
> And
> At times, for some condition
> Rosiness sparkles into her eyes
> What should I do ?
> Should I…weep...or laugh...
> On the strangeness of the world ?

The world does look at
This bewailing pen
Puts it to test to the best of its ability
Keeps faith too in God
And
It carries also a deep imprint of God on itself.
But, the only shortcoming remains
That the impression has been limited merely upto the head,
Otherwise
Why does the man of to-day
Is proceeding with his *'head up-side-down'* ?[42a]
His feet have become stand-still, O Mother !
The holy path showed by *the Prime Brahmā,*[42b]
The very first Tīrthaṅkara, Ādinātha,
Is not non-existent today, O Mother !
But,
On that sacred path

The grass has sprung up in abundance !
Not due to rains,
But due to the crowds of those
Who, showing indifference towards right conduct,
Cause the nectar of religion to rain
Only by melting the essence of compassion into
their speeches !

Today, the guides themselves
Have lost the vision of the true path, Mother !
The reason is well-known –
The one, for whom the true path is being shown,
Doesn't want to tread the path himself,
He wants to make others follow the track
And
The number of these cunning conductors is
countless.

What should I do ?
I put into black and white…
Whatever is happening,
I taste the flavour thereof
Then…I go on…bewailing...
Try to transcribe it ...Mother !
I...do am a pen... ."

□

On seeing the Artisan motionless
Did the pan of Compassion weaken ?
Don't indulge in so much of hair-splitting –
Uttering such words, the Compassion started
shedding tears !

At this, the Artisan Says :
"Bewailing is not the nature of Compassion,
Without weeping, the application too
Of compassion is not possible.
The compassion in feeling
And
The compassion in action –
There is difference between both of them,
Nevertheless
So much of excess doesn't seem befitting !

I acknowledge the point,
That
In comparison to an unmanured field
The harvest of the manured field
Is more flourishing,
But
On sowing the seeds into the manure...
The crop gets scorched and emits flames.
Yes, O yes !!
The field is filled with manure and water in due proportion
The seeds are scattered over the farm
Even then they don't get sprouted
Without the hand of the Soil caressing them.
Not only this much,
Those seeds,
Upon which the pressure-weight of the Soil is too heavy
Don't appear out of the soil –
On getting sprouted –
Inside the very layers, they get themselves suffocated.

Compassion is not worthless,
Compassion has its own beneficence
Its own limits...!
Even then,
The true place of compassion has to be
understood.

The one who shows mercy
May not well be a cherisher of self-conceit,
But
He takes himself to be
Surely an eminent disciple
And
The one who is being favoured for compassion
Thinks himself to be
Certainly a younger disciple.
The heart of the both of them is compassionate
The disciple by obtaining shelter
The spiritual guide by granting shelter
Experience something unique.
But
We can't say it to be the true happiness.
The door of the cessation of sufferings
And
The attainment of happiness was surely opened,
Even then the both of these two
Forget the woes at this occasion !

The one who is compassionate
Is not indeed a lower man
But
The one, with a downcast face, that is –

– He is certainly an extrovert.
And
The one on whom the mercy is being shown,
...Isn't really a downcast man,
– Is definitely the one with his face upcast.
Nevertheless,
There is no set rule about attaining the 'higher self'.

There are two states of compassion –
The one which is greedy towards sensuousness
The other which eliminates sensuousness, indicates
the right way.
The first one is not under mention here
The second one is being referred to and adored !
"In what words should I describe
The flavour of this compassion !
If you believe
It is the taste
Of the saline tears !"

That is why
It is erroneous
To recognize the inclusion of the Sentiment
of peace
Within the Sentiment of Compassion.

The earnest inclination leaping forward for
promoting its application
Like a canal
Is compassion !
And
The bright bent of mind devoted to 'Self'
Like a silent river !
Is the Sentiment of Quietism !
A canal enters a field,

Having effaced the inflammation
It gets dried up, and
The river flows towards the sea
Having erased the way
It attains happiness.

I would like to go into more details of the topic –
That
As soon as the water drops down upon the dust
It changes into the marsh
But,
That fragment of snow
Even if it is confined within the dust
There is no probability of change in it
The receptive-sense doesn't exist therein.
And
As soon as the water comes in contact with fire
Its coolness disappears
And it
Not only burns itself but also inflames others !
But,
The piece of snow
On being placed upon fire
Doesn't lose its coolness
And
Neither it burns itself, nor scorches others.

Almost this is the state
Of compassion and the Sentiment of Quietism.

The compassion is fluid, flows on
It gets influenced instantly by external factors.

The Sentiment of Quietism
Doesn't flow under any drive
Even when the era alters
It stands firm on its very spot.
It also implies that
The admixture of Parental Affection
Is not possible with Compassion
And
The Parental Affection
Can neither be declared as baseless
Nor can it be asserted as mere imaginary.

Upon the surface of the circular cheeks
Of the grand existence of Mother-Nature
This Sentiment of Parental Affection rejoices.
The Sentiment of Parental Affection, like
compassion,
Is bipartite indeed
But, along with fondness, it is merry-making,
With it
The external give and take plays an
important role,
The internal factors are subsidiary
That is why the sense of non-duality
Remains inert in it.

Like an associate member of a religion
It is applied only
On behaviour and thoughts
The expression of it
Is surely not possible
Without a sweet smile.
In the tasting of the Sentiment of Affection,

A glimpse of sweetness…then
The sense of transience reflects.

With the dew-drops
Neither quenches the thirst, nor the hope
– Extinguishes only that lamp of breathings !
Then you please tell yourself,
How is the Sentiment of Quietism
Included into the Sentiment of Affection ?

If there be a child into mother's lap
If the mother is making him suck her breasts –
The child, while sucking the milk,
Certainly gazes upwards towards the mother,
At her lips, into her eyes
And
At the pair of her cheeks.
The position of action and reaction
Is reflected in what form –
The observation goes on,
If the compassion or harshness
– Would peep through her eyes
He would turn towards weeping
After being somewhat serious,
If the cheeks would appear playful and vibrant
Due to a faint smile upon her lips
He would give out a dash !
It is the only reason that
Mostly, the mother, while making the baby suck her milk –
Gets the face of the child hidden
Under the border of her *sāḍī*.

That is to say,
That experiencing of the Sentiment of Quietism
Should take place at a pleasant lonely spot
And at that time
That experience should be all alone...!

> The confluence of our colourless or coloured limbs
> With the colourless and waveless
> Conscience of a pond
> Is appropriate, indeed
> It is the only attachment of the Sentiment of Quietism
> ...It is really its limb !

The Sentiment of Compassion is the vital breath of life
It's like a sweeping wind with sharp sound.
The Sentiment of Affection is the deliverance of life
It is like a bright current of water.
But, this point
Is related to the world of duality,
The Sentiment of Quietism is the lyric of life
It is melodious like the merits of milk.

> The Sentiment of Compassion is acknowledged only that –
> Which transforms into the soft wax –
> Even the hardest of the stones,
> The manner of the Sentiment of Affection,
> Changes even the worst stupids
> Into the form of a moon !
> But, it conveys the point
> Related to worldly wonder.
> What should be mentioned about the Sentiment of Quietism,

It makes a self-disciplined prudent person
A devotee to '*Om.*'[43]
So far as the Sentiment of Quietism is
regarded
It is concerned with the sense of assimilation
In a few words
I should say, in the style of negation,
The Sentiment of Quietism is
The tranquillization of all the other Sentiments.
Thus goes on enchanting
The innermost conscience of the sages.
...How blissful !

□

On the other side, the process of trampling the Soil too
Reaches its completion while stressing upon
The beneficiality of the Supreme
And mellowed Sentiment of Quietism.
And
Like a mountain-top,
Upon the wooden rod – buried into the earth,
The Artisan revolves his wheel
With a two-cubit long stick in his hand.
Then Upon the spinning wheel
Puts a lump of the Soil,
The lump too starts whirling round –
With the same fastness as that of the wheel, when
The Soil tells something to the Artisan,

" The root '*Sṛ*' is used in the sense of motion,
'*Saṁ*', that is, 'proper'
'*Sāra*', that is, to 'proceed'...
That which proceeds properly
Is called 'the world' [that is, *saṁsāra*].
The time itself is not the wheel
It is the motive-force behind the wheel of the world,
That is the reason why
In conventional usage, the 'Time' is called the 'Wheel'
The outcome of it, indeed, is that
I have been whirling round into
'*The four life-cycles' of births and deaths*[44a]
And, the eighty four lacs forms of existence.

Lo, you have placed it now
Over the potter's wheel too!
What a swirling motion,
Its head is reeling !
Bring it down...let it...be saved ! "

Again, in the form of a reply,
Awakening the understanding of the Soil,
The posture of the Artisan :

" The wheels represent various types
'*The wheel of the world'* [44b] is the one which
Is the cause of passions and anger etc. –
– The exertions of the ill-sentiments ; due to
ignorance
An emperor's disc-weapon is that which
Is the cause of destruction'
Of the physical life,
But –

This potter's wheel is that whet-stone
On being placed upon which, the life
Gets purified in most excellent aspects,
It is an instrument of dignity of holy life.

Yes ! yes ! the giddiness which you are feeling
Is not caused by the potter's wheel,
But
It is the fault of your vision
Because
On keeping the eye upon the circumference
The spirit gets degraded
And
On keeping one's view fixed upon the Supreme One
The spirit gets salvaged.
One roams about within the circumference –
The life is whiled away aimlessly,
The genuine joy is felt within the Supreme One
The life is found to be happy.

And, listen,
It is an ordinary thing that
The winding ways, indeed,
Ultimately kiss the skies –
Make the pilgrims reach
The unattainable mountain-top
Undoubtedly, without hindrance !"

□

Now, naturally, at first
The Artisan makes a resolve,

Into his functional consciousness
The figure of the holy pitcher (*Kumbha*) takes shape.
The incidental became the natural,
The cognizance merged into the form of the cognizable,
The meditation merged into the form of the
meditative !

The body too imitates the mind,
Both the hands of the pitcher-maker
Turned into the pitcher-like shape,
The preliminary touch took place
An unforeseen thrill, the beginning of intimacy
Was perceived within the Soil.
Lo, gradually
Little by little, in a wave-like serial,
Making their appearance in various forms,
Sprang up the charming beauties of the Soil
Which were hidden behind a veil of mystery
...Since long !

The opening of the veil of mystery
Is in the hands of the supreme manhood (*puruṣārtha*)
The stern thirst to smell a secret
Pinches only that very experienced one
Who is sensitive,
It is not an act of the Time,

The one, who doesn't possess
A hand, that is, an instrument of action
Neither acts upon the other, nor does get it
actuated.
The one who doesn't possess
A traveling foot
Neither moves on himself even a step

Nor does he make the other move on.
– The Time is inactive, indeed !
It is beyond the reach of buying and selling.
Since time immemorial, the Time
Is seated on one and the same place
Neutral to everything remote...!
Even then
In this manner, the presence of Time
Here-at
Is inevitable for every affair; mutually
It represents the relationship of the efficient
cause and effect !

Untouched by prestige and pride, the Soil
Getting itself rescued from the roundish lump
Is moulded into the form of a holy pitcher
Assumes the pitcher-shaped appearance,
Is rising up above the earth with steadiness.

Like that,
In an ordinary manner, for ever,
The journey of things goes on
With its uninterrupted motion
Despite it, in special manner,
The dimensions of development arise
When goes hand in hand with them
The intellect, which is opposed to pride,
And
The phases of destruction confront us
When is extended the hand of sensuousness
Which is outstanding in exciting pride,
This is indeed a prelude to rise and fall.

Like a pot filled with clarified butter, that is, *Ghī*,
The Artisan, with utmost care,
Brought the holy pitcher (*Kumbha*) down the wheel,
Upon the ground !
An interval was found
For two or three days
So...the humidity of the pitcher
Was almost withered away...
Hence, the laxity of the pitcher…
Was almost contracted.
Today, the Artisan is highly delighted –
The holy pitcher has been picked up in hand.
He has taken up a wand in one hand
Has provided a cover with the other one,
And
The flaw of the holy pitcher has been hit with it.

On keeping in view the covering of hand
The sense of compassion is perceived,
While keeping an eye upon the strokes only
The sense of cruelty seems to be boiling over,
But,
The strokes are really confined to the flaw !
The precaution is being observed;
The eyes of Artisan do not wink
That is…why...
Having bestowed an excellent form to
the holy pitcher
He has polished and smoothened it,
The throat of the holy pitcher has not been
choked!

□

The marking of some numbers
Which exhibit the essential truth
The depiction of some strange diagrams
And
The creation of some poems has been done upon
the pitcher !
The digits of 99 and the 9
Which look like an embellishment
Are marked upon the ear-spot of the pitcher,
Are making themselves their acquaintance known.

The one provides an indication of the salty world
The other that of the milk-essence.
The one provides the deepening of delusion,
The other opens the door to final Liberation,
The digits of 99
On being multiplied by the digit 'two' etc.
The number may well grow successively,
But
The obtained digits, being summed up
The digit, which remains is that of 9 only.

For example :
99 x 2 = 198, 1+9+8 = 18, 1+8 = 9
99 x 3 = 297, 2+9+7 = 18, 1+8 = 9
99 x 4 = 396, 3+9+6 = 18, 1+8 = 9
In the same way, the series of multiplication
May be carried upto the digit of 9
And
The digit of 9
On being multiplied by the digit 'two' etc.
The number progressively growing too

On being added with each other
Precisely the same, the digit of only 9 remains,
For example :
9 x 2 = 18, 1 + 8= 9
9 x 3 = 27, 2 + 7= 9
9 x 4= 36, 3 + 6= 9
Thus, let the order of multiplication
Be carried upto the *figure of 9* [45a]
And the number obtained, retained and sighted shall only be 9,

That is the reason, why
That 99
Is a hindrance, illusion, hoodwinking,
Is a perishable by nature
And
Is the enhancer of the non-spiritual element;
And this digit of 9
Is a dense shade
Is a cradle, where in life is nourished
Is imperishable by nature
Ever-young, immortal, eternal –
Is the awakener of the spiritual self
Enough of details...!

The world is *'merry-go-round' of 99* [45b]
This proverb has accomplished its sense
Therefore
In view of the fortunate ones , desirous of final Liberation,
The 99 should be despicable and
Attainable by meditation should be the 9 –
The source of a new life !

One more number is also marked,
Upon the throat of the pitcher,
That is 63 [46]
Which makes us remember
The personages among the holy scriptures.
It carries a speciality that

The digit three
Is facing the digit six
And
The digit six is in the frontal view of the digit three!
The sharing of pleasures and pains
Mutually with each other
Is the recognition of gentility,
And
To be jealous of the happiness of others
To feel delight in the sufferings of others
Is the true symptom of wickedness.
When
The ideal personalities are forgotten
Then
The reverse of 63 holds ground
That is
The advent of 36 takes place.

Three and six – the direction of the both of them
Is contrary to each other.
The perversion of thoughts
Makes the true nature of our conduct
Take an evil turn.
A strife, a conflict starts with one another.

What next is to be told !
Ahead of 36
One more digit of three is added,
In sum total
Three hundred and sixty three creeds are originated[47]
Which are at daggers drawn
With each other,
Whose views are commonplace
Around this earth to-day !

□

The depiction of lion and dog too
Is marked upon that pitcher
It is imparting its message without giving its
tongue indeed –
The life-style and daily routine of the both of them
Is opposite to each other.
The lion doesn't make an assault
On anybody stealthily,
He doesn't roar without his concern too,
And
Without a gnarl
Doesn't browbeat too in anger upon anybody –
That is
The lion keeps himself away from any
fraudulence.

But the dog often pounces upon
To bite from behind,
Every now and then, even barks uncalled-for.

For life-stuff
The adoration of poorliness

Is never adopted by the lion !
When
While swinging the tail behind his owner
The dog trails for a loaf of bread.
A belt can't be tied around a lion's neck,
Due to some reason
A lion, put behind the bars,
Keeps loitering without a belt, indeed,
Even inside the cage
In that period, his tail
Remains straightened up, backwards
He never allows his liberty and self-respect
To be injured
In any way !
And a dog
Doesn't know the value of freedom,
The slavery and humiliation
Doesn't ever pinch a dog,
Even the chain around the throat of the dog
Holds the form of an embellishment.

Moreover, the special point is that
The dog when stoned at
Bites the very stone on seizing upon it
And not the stone-pelter !
But
The lion applies his commonsense,
The lion's insight always
Catches at the genuine cause…indeed…
He hits back upon the killer.

The dog-civilization and culture
Is condemned due to the reason
That
On seeing his own tribe
He paws the earth and growls.

The lion loves cordially mixing himself
with his clan,
The tendency of a king is found similar indeed,
It ought to be likewise.

Some of the dogs
Go mad also
And the person too
When they bite,
Running amuck like a dog
Dies barking as a rule
Within some period,
But
It has never been heard
That a lion went insane !

There is one more entirely absurd action
Of the tribe of dogs, that
At times, while suffering from hunger,
When the eatables are not available,
He feeds himself even upon the sewage,
And
When even the sewage is not found...then…
Eats up really his own offspring,

But, listen !
To pacify his hunger
The lion doesn't treat the sewage as food

Nor does he eat up
His newly-born cub...!

Exactly there...upon the pitcher
The depiction of the tortoise and the hare
Is serving a note of caution
By telling the method of devotion to the devotee.
The tortoise moving on with its slow gait
Has attained its goal within time,
And
The hare – despite taking a run,
Legged much behind;
The reason is well-known indeed –
The gait of the one was without any hindrance
The other one had slumbered on its way,
Negligence is the formidable foe of the wayfarer.

Now the on-looker beholds –
Upon the facial disc of the pitcher

The two syllables-'*Hī*', i. e., 'only' and '*bhī*'
i.e., 'also'
Both of these are the prime syllables or code
characters –
They represent their own respective philosophies.

'*Hī*',[48a] that is, 'only' is the vindicator of the doctrine of
absolutism,
'Bhī', that is, 'also' *is symbolic of 'Anekānta' and*
'Syādvāda'-[48b]

That is, Relative 'Pluralism' and 'Assertion of Probability,'
'*Hī*', that is, 'only' always advocates thus –
We, and only we alone are all in all,
You are insignificant, nothing !
And '*bhī*' that is, 'also' asserts that
We, too, are there

You do exist as well
Every thing exists !

'*Hī*', that is, 'only' beholds the other with an inferior viewpoint
'*Bhī*', that is, 'also' looks at all with a proper insight,
'*Hī*', i.e.,'only' seizes upon the shape of a thing
'*Bhī*', i.e.,[49a] 'also' touches the inner core too of a thing,

'*Hī*',[49a] i.e., 'only' is the Western culture
'*Bhī*' i.e., 'also' is the Indian culture, the fortune-maker.
Rāvaṇa [49b] was the worshipper of '*hī*' , i.e., 'only'
'*Bhī*', i.e., 'also' was seated within Rām.
That is the reason, why
Rām has been and shall be in future an object of adoration.

Around the '*Bhī*', i.e., 'also' –
A crowd certainly seems to be grown,
But it is not really a crowd
'*Bhī*', i.e., 'also' is the back-bone of democracy.

The nest of democracy in the world
Shall remain secure, so long as
The '*bhī*,' i.e., 'also' shall go on breathing.
Wantonness and passion-blindness is pacified
– Through the '*bhī*' i.e., 'also' –
The dreams of liberty are materialized,
The seeds of right thinking and right conduct
Pulsate within '*bhī*', i.e., 'also'; and not in '*hī*', i.e., 'only'.

We pray to God that
This world should be freed from '*hī*,' i.e., 'only'
'*Bhī*', i.e., 'also' should be embraced by all,
It be so whether just now or in distant future.

"Place the right upward palm upon the left one" –
This line inscribed upon the pitcher shows that –

For our bright future
The Lord commands that :
'Where do you sit while losing your breaths
Take up the genuinely true endeavour,
Being free from sin and hypocrisy
Adopt the posture of sainthood
You shall be saved.
Otherwise
Being blinded by the jumble
Being put into prison
You shall be consumed...!'

□

" Having died, we should turn into a healing
ointment "
This almost four-worded line of poetry too
Is found here upon the holy pitcher !
It may convey only the sense that '*Bhī*'
How hardest had been
Our stone-like life !
We got stumbled upon it,
We were taken aback, we fell down !
Having forsaken the right path
How many of us turned back !
Then,
How many feet got blood-stained,
How deeply wounded they were found !
When were they provided with proper treatment,
How it was possible by the sinful stone...!
Merely an idea of treatment

Took rise in it today !
It also is an indication of good luck
It is not possible to take some step ahead of it.
O Lord ! the depraved sinner prays simply,
That
If not within this life-span
At least in the next course of birth...indeed
After death, we should become a '*salve*'...![50]

One more verse of four syllables–
"I'm double-throated"
The first sense which it conveys is that
I am bi-linguist
I speak internally something different
Some thing else externally...
I mingle poison with the milk.
Now its second sense seems to appear :
I'm a bastard
I'm deceitful, cunning and fraudulent
Due to ignorance and arrogance indeed
I have been concealing this perfidy
Thus you too all the well-wishers
Acknowledge this bitter truth,
Where does your well-being lie ?
And
What is the third sense which it
carries –
Is there a need to ask about it ?
Let the root of all the ill-wills and
passions
'I', that is, egotism
Be melted –, be eradicated

I'm...a wretch...! I...a betrayer !!
I, the one to be freed from self-conceit !!!

□

Some watery portion is still left into the pitcher
It has to be fully absorbed
And
The Artisan places the pitcher
Upon the basked open ground.

Without penance, the wateriness–the ignorance,
Can't be annulled
And
Without heat the rise of wateriness–of rains,
Is never possible.
In absence of austerities
This inner heart has been feeling uneasy
Since time immemorial with so many resolves
and options.
Only failure has been achieved,
Only restlessness has accompanied all along,
How to tell, how to bear
And, how to live ?...
Only, indeed,
The tidings of success have been achieved,
In this life, till today…!

To be lost into the Fragrance of the Infinite
Is constantly persisting,
To go beyond the limits of the extremity
Is leaping forward,

The restless heart of a saint, enquires thus :
'O Thou Vernal-hearted !
Mother-Earth ! where hast Thou vanished...
O the Majesty of Spring Season ! where has
thou gone ?'

At this,
Some words reach the ears of the Saint,
That
" The spring season has come to an end
The finite has lost itself into the infinite,
And the last funeral ceremony of its body has
to be performed.
The summer season was called for, hence its arrival,
There is violent countenance of the Sun
The sun-shine is sparkling,
The heat of the glowing flames is spreading
Inside and outside, rightwards and leftwards,
To and fro, Upwards and downwards,

Lo ! falling down all-around is only
Heat…heat...heat...![51]

The condition of all
The ten directions has changed,
The broader heart of the Earth
And
These thighs and stomach
Have become full of heavy fissures –
Wherein enter
These extremely hot winds,
As if extending their acquaintance
With the boiling lava of the regions below
the earth.

Here, there is burning only
Heat...heat...heat...!

These lakes of blue waters –
These drains-rivers
Full of even endless water,
Flowing as undercurrents
Have become waterless;
They have been transmuted reversely
That is,
Na...dī...dī...na.[52a]
On being waterless
The river suffers from inferiority,
And
Nā…lī…lī…nā…[52b]
It is being immersed into the earth
Due to bashfulness,

Here is going on only
Heat...heat…heat…!

Despite having ascended the 'Mount of Sunrise'
even instantly,
But approaching the 'Mount of Sunset' with delay
The Sun
Is taking more time
In accomplishing His journey.
It seems,
Some slackness has entered into the movement
of the Sun,
Otherwise,
Why this enhancement in the day-time these days ?

Here the force behind it is only
Heat...heat...heat...!

Whatfrom that 'greenness' is green ?
Of what avail remained
The Lord's jubilee, then ?
The delicacy of a flexible creeper
The relish of the ripened fruits
Where have all these vanished ?
The blowing of that slow fragrant wind,
That light gust
Where is that swinging of the bunches of fruits ?
The smile of flowers,
The clappings by the leaves every second
Where is that melodious audible humming
Of the row of the honey-charmed large black bees ?
Of the yellow vine the grey-haired splendour too,
Which, hidden from the touch of the creeper of coldness,
Did not stay even for a moment ;
Was inflamed, vanished, without leaving a trace behind,

Here is being nourished only
Heat...heat...heat...!

Where is that charm, where that pollen,
Where is that awakening of the soul ?
Neither that odour is there, nor that warbling,
Neither that receptiveness, nor that cheerfulness,
Where is that bird, where that poet,

Where is that Sun radiant with lovely rays ?
Where is that system, where that eminence
Where is that sneer of the Cupid ?
Neither, that gesture is there, nor that feeling,
Nor the graceful shadow of the consciousness,

Here, there is going on only
Heat... heat...heat...!

The objects of worldly pleasures have stayed behind
The pleasure-seeker has passed away,
The yogic observances have remained behind
The ascetic has left the world,
What stands stable, and for whom –
The wealth for the sake of life
Or the life for the sake of wealth ?
What upholds the value –
The corporeal or the incorporeal,
The material or the spiritual ?
The decorations and the ornaments have been put off
From the body of the Spring,
Under the cover of which, the sensuousness gets concealed
That cloth too has been taken off.
The abode of sensuousness
Is neither there within the body, nor there in the dress
But
It is there within the conscience affected by fraudulence.

Being utterly inert and unscreened
The physical body of the Spring is lying,
Like a dry flower without fragrance.
Its mouth is gaping a bit,
The tongue is protruding out of the mouth
Somewhat turned and twisted,
It seems as if she is almost uttering –
– There is no real joy in the corporeal life indeed !

And
Ra...sa...nā, nā...sa...ra...[53]
That is, the Spring is without head
It is without wisdom to examine the beneficial and
the harmful,
That is the reason why
The preachings of the saints
Fall flat upon the vernant lives.
The moment of burning ceremony has arrived at last
The atmosphere of non-attachment seems to be prevailing
From the body of the Spring,
When is withdrawn it –
The shroud...shroud...shroud…!

Here, there is melting merely
Heat...heat...heat...!

Before the very eyes, exactly…
The sight fails,
The deadbody of the Spring also
Disappears into the lap of the past,
Only remains the existence of the bones.
And,
While uttering these words
The bones are smiling
Upon the folly of the world, that –

The one, who has embraced death,
Must re-gain birth
And
The one, who has embraced birth
Must obtain death,
It is a lasting law, without exception !

The counting is not possible,
The earth got dug out on countless times
On countless occasions, these bones got buried
Deeper and deeper, into those very places !
At least now, don't arrange our
Burial...burial...burial...
This very burial of ours,
For the future reception of Spring is
The sowing...sowing...sowing...

Here, there is going on only
Heat...heat...heat...!

Often the dreadful black Rahu
Is seen swallowing fully
Even the radiant sun,
At times, that sun also
Is noticed emitting out flames.
The emission is such in which
The trees, the plants, the mountain-cliffs
The whole of the universe upto the lowest region of
the underworld
Appears to be melting and fusing
Some times the flames turn into winds
Sometimes the wind changes into water
And
The water is soon transformed into soil,
Effecting exchange while rolling into each other
Some times, is shaped, into an admixed marsh.
The night full of nectar is seen
Some times, the smiles of the moon are visible –

At times, rejoicings and laughter,
At times is seen the deep dark night,
Often fragrance, often bad-smell
Often alliance, often a secret plot
Sometimes eyes, sometimes blindness,
–Free from fetters, again confined

Occasionally, even the sweet one
Was found devoid of sweetness,
Ever and anon the crooked one
Was seen distressed with crookedness,
Now a kinsfolk, some time without kinship
Who plays a trick of sentimentality,
A young one who sometimes steps forward,
The perplexities grow, and go on growing,
Becomes protector, assumes guidance,
In due course, his hair turn grey,
At times, suppression, then pacification
Occasionally, the garden of delights
Now, the emittance from the mouth, then the show of salutations
Now and then some fulfilment..!

Even now, without coming to a halt,
Feeling no fatigue while relating,
The bones add something more,
That
Keeping in view such situations and conditions
Don't ever hold such opinion that
Whether they possess some significance or not!
All these are merely night-nourished
Dreams ...dreams...dreams..!

Here, there is going on only,
Heat... heat...heat...!

What is that which causes
This ephemeralness into a thing
And
From what corner does appear
This dignity into a thing,
Innate naturality, fixedness
Seems to be some-what concealed here
Who is He ?
Why is He silent ?
When shall His image and identity be manifested ?
When shall that brimful juicy well be attained ?
And
This dewy grace of joining and separating
This innocent grace of momentary throbbing –
Why it doesn't come within the grasp?
The smile of the skeleton
Is the answer to all these doubts !

The sages have expounded this aphorism –
" *Utpāda-vyaya-dhrauvya-yuktaṁ sat*. "
–"The entire Entity is imbibed with birth-decay-fixity" [54]
The present reality (Existence) of the infinite
Has almost been condensed herein.
This is that mirror,
In which
The past, the present and the future –
All is being reflected,
...Is appearing afloat,
Is visible on seeing through the 'Eye of Faith' !

The interpretation of the aphorism
Is presented thus in the colloquial wordings :
'In-coming'and 'out-going' is in force
In-coming, that is, birth - is 'production'
Out-going, that is, death - is 'destruction'
In force, that is, fixedness - is 'continuation'
And
'Entity,'that is, the eternal 'Being', is there
This is the 'Truth' indeed, this very the 'Reality'...!

The further resultant of this is, that,
All these substances have mixed up,
While bestowing shelter to each other
Have dissolved like milk and sugar
–Looked splendid, with their own qualities
But did not shed off the inherent nature
Since ages by gone !
Then who can catch up with
Whom, and at what moment ?
Then who can steal away
Whom, and when...?

Thou art the Lord of thy own self
Thou art the Wisher of thy own self,
Then, who can nourish whom
And at what moment...?

Even then, alas !
The feeling of seizure and collection exists –
So...it is a sin, which remains with the next births.
Enough of more narration,
When has this mystery been revealed till today?
The entire 'Entity' that exists –

Is reformed naturally through thy
Own-self...own-self...own-self...
Even now, be alert, be thoughtful
Behold thy own self,
– All of us...all of us...all of us...!

Here there is going on only
Heat...heat...heat...!

□

The vernal season departed
Its body was put to flames,
Even then
It has left behind its impact
Upon forests, parks, on every particle
Upon each and every form of life here;
That flavour, having taken the form of blood,
Has penetrated into each and every vein.

As a result of coming in touch with it
A deeper paint has affected strongly
All the folds of beauty, smell and taste.
All that was natural has been covered up
That subject has assumed a deeper secrecy
Therefore,
Even after the funeral ceremony,
The entire campus
Has to be necessarily bathed and washed.

But, how strange it is !
Despite being a guest, why this excess ?
No matter if income is meagre –

No worry over the expenditure too
But
Extravagance is highly detrimental.
The future doesn't appear to be good now
The forehead of the Fate is gloomy !
As is hanging over the empty space
The thickness of the band of clouds,
Why this untimely appearance of death and
destruction ?
Thus, probably...turning the entire world
Into only one single morsel,
Wishes to gulp in its entirety
Without chewing…,
Indeed, at one stretch.
Pushing the universe into the fierce jaws of
annihilation !

□

CANTO : THIRD

The Preservation Of Virtuousness
The Purification Of Sinfulness

Whenever the universal destruction descends upon
the earth

The concern goes only to water

By extending the allurement of coolness to earth,
It has been plundered,
That very is, indeed, the reason
Why this earth has remained bare ground to-day
Neither could it become rich nor wealth –
sustaining earth !
And
That water has become an ocean –a mine of
jewels –
It has carried away with its rolling waves
The splendour of the earth.

The turning of one's eye towards the other's wealth
Is an indication of ignorance,
And
The amassing of fortune through the seizure of
other's wealth
Is the excess of illusion and infatuation.
It is a deed of very low quality,
It is to torture one's own self as well as that of the others,
It is to lead a life down into the hellish regions.

By doing this derogatory deed
The ocean has acquainted us with its
Senseless mind and irrational intellect,
It has proved the significance of its own name.

The Earth has taken a vow
Not to retaliate
On being even ill-treated,
That is…why…the Earth
Has been called all-enduring
And not all-destroying...

And
To be all-enduring, indeed,
Is to attain the whole substance in life –
The path of the saints sings really thus.

Being the way-farer of the path of justice
The Sun-god can not see,
Can not bear this injustice
And
Can not give out, indeed,
His tongue to none else !
Even then, he does not become inactive
The endeavour of the Sun goes on continually,
For the dismissal of the side of injustice,
For the victory to the side of justice.

Lo! through his hot and hotter rays
The water of the ocean
Is heated on to get dried up,
The endless wealth and splendour
Which is stealthily hidden inside
Comes in view of the gods, the celestial chiefs !
Despite this all, behold... the real nature,
The burnt up water turns into vapour

Being moulded into the clouds, keeps on raining
And
Goes on concealing its faults and frauds
By filling up the ocean once and again...!

An effort is made on many occasions
To bribe the Sun
But, from the path of justice, does not flinch
...He
But,
On the other side, the Moon gets distracted
And
Having taken the side of the watery substance,
She, deviating from her aim,
Takes the bribe to her heart's fill.
That is...why
The owner even of a little of wealth, the Moon
Becomes the 'mine of nectar' to-day !

All the nectar of the Earth
Flows into the ocean and gets deposited there,
Then, it is remitted...upwards...
And
It is utilized
By the moon, and not by the ocean,
Only salty element is fated for the ocean.
'It has not been a deed according to
the dignity–
It is improper for me by all means' –
Thinking thus, the Moon feels ashamed
Her brighter fore-head gets stained –

Otherwise,
Why does she set out from home at night,
Why not at the day-time ?
And that too, suspicious like a thief
Hiding her tiny face...!
And
Why does she dwell at a very long distance
from the earth?
While the Sun
Performs his sojourn at close quarters with
the earth !

It's a matter of regret !
The stars too
Follow the footsteps of the Moon.
Hither, the position of the ocean too is the same,
On beholding the Moon, it rises and rolls with joy
And
On seeing the Sun, It boils.

'It is a bitter truth that
The eyes of wealth and money
Are unable to see the transcendental reality,
The greedy desires for wealth
Have made shameless even the high-ups.'

□

It's a peculiar point, that
The ocean too is the treasure of genuine pearls,
The reason is that
The material cause behind a pearl is water,
That is, the water really transforms into a pearl –

Nevertheless
It we ponder over it
It is found that
This achievement is obtained mainly due to
the earth-factor.
In transforming water into the shape of a pearl
The pearl-oyster is an eminent cause,
And
The pearl-oyster in itself is a part of the earth.
Having trained the pearl-oyster, the Earth itself
Has sent it into the ocean.
Having relieved the water of its stupor
And to mould it into a pearl form,
Having taken it out of the pit of decline
And to place it on an elevated position,
Is the objective of the patience-retaining Earth.

This is the real nature of compassion
This is the *kārmic* action of the Sentient Being.

– Even then !
How is it possible
That every body's nature is honest and upright ?
The reverse move of water can never be uprooted
The nature of water is not that of gurgling with a leap
The leaping forward is only an excuse
Its nature is really…that of hoodwinking.

Being open-mouthed, supine-faced,
Countless pearl-oysters keep floating
Upon the broad chest of the ocean,
Waiting for the drops of water.

As and when one or two drops enter the lips
The ocean, having mouthed them,
Instantly makes them sink,
Due to the fear of being snatched away by someone.
And, conceals them
Into its bottomless unfathomable depths.
The diver who endeavours to reach there
To bring up the wealth again on the earth
Is himself really sacked.
It is difficult for him to come back empty-handed even...

The army there remains at alert day in and day out
The dreadful venomous dragons, crocodiles
Move around the wealth fancifully,
They, at once in entirety, swallow up any one
Whosoever appears them to be a new-comer !
If he escapes their grip
Then...then…what ?
The atmosphere is made poisonous
At once by diffusing the poison.
That is why there is found
A huge storage of poison into the ocean.

□

Despite being fully acquainted with water
The earth did not budge
From its self-obligation.
Far from creating an obstacle
For the one who is thankless,

It did not even brood
In its mind over creating some hindrance.
For leading an unhampered life
What broad-heartedness of the Earth is this !
It keeps on thinking, indeed,
Constantly about the means of deliverance for all.

Look here, please !
The bamboo too is a part of the earth
The earth has told the bamboo (*bānsa*)
That
The posterity/bamboo/ that is, '*vanśa*'[55] is aggrandized
only when
It shall go on converting water into pearls
For ages to come...
Even in the days of struggles
While taking a heavy sigh too
In the moments of joy also.
Then, how wonderful !
On being ordered by the Mother Earth –
Inside the huge dense forests
Above the sky-kissing mountain-chains
After coming in company with the bamboo,
The water fallen from the clouds
Starts transforming into bamboo-pearls...
That is…why…
Even Lord Krishna too.
Bestows his full-throated praise upon the flute
While wearing the pearls around the neck,
And
Caresses the flute
With his lovely ruby lips.

Then, in return
Hears melodious musical notes with his ears
Being enchanted, forgetting himself
And his day-to-day nightly dreams !

In this very way,
In obedience of the order of Mother-Earth are occupied
The serpents, boars, milters, elephants, clouds etc.
After whose names the pearls are prevalent–
The bamboo pearls, the oyster-pearls
The snake-pearls, the boar-pearls
The fish-pearls, the elephant-pearls
And the cloud-pearls !
In the formation of the cloud-pearls too the earth plays its role
So...it shall be explained here under...

Due to all these characteristics
The pre-eminent fame of earth augments,
The fever of the Moon-beam
Goes up excessively high.

The sense of disregard towards the earth
Increases more and more,
In order to
Insult and defame the earth
That watery element, very swiftly,
Starts its chess-like moves
Under the directions of the moon,
By making some sporadic rains to fall occasionally
Begins to create morass over the earth.
In order to damage –

The unity and integrity of the earth
Starts setting in the lagoon !

The factional multiplicity is indeed the killer of peace !
As many heads, as many tongues
As many moves and manners,
The wateriness flushed with wine
Is the mother of weariness, indeed !

That is the reason
Why the heavy outpour of rains, want of rains
And
The untimely rains are being hereat justified !

For the petty selfish ends
For some futile fame
All offences can take place !

Where is there that prayer for the Lord
Where is there that adoration to the Lord
Which is meant for the wealth of the most
Sublime Truth ?

Meanwhile, standing with its
Large eyes widespread
The writing pen speaks out thus –
" Fie once and again
To this evil-mindedness
Which forges downfall, universal killings !
Curse once and again
To this tyrannous, oppressive
Huge vulture-like
Greediness for wealth ! "

□

Three or four days elapse,
Due to some reason
The Artisan
Has to set out under compulsion.
But, on sojourn
Travels only his body,
The inner mind once and again
Turns back there at the residence !

The body, has been described as sense-organs
The inner mind has been told as an unembodied
conscience
It is the birth-place of the Cupid
The generator of all types of attachments
The spring-board of all the colours of emotions…!

It is easy to control the body
And
It is not impossible to control the inner mind,
Yet
It is certainly an intricacy
A bitter-drink poison is it.... .

The absence of the Artisan
The presence of dryness into the holy pitcher (*kumbha*)
Is a golden chance for me –
Thus ponders the ocean.
And
On the pretext of the splashing waves,
With its…diplomatic…move
Intimates the clouds
Which are really trained beforehand.

The ocean is imbibed with 'Dullness' of intellect'
It doesn't mean that it is devoid of intellect
But,
Dullness implies 'materialistic', that is, 'senseless'–
It means not to make proper usage of '*dhī*'
i.e. intellect,
With the life-less objects like pot and cloth etc.,
And
Not to adore and receive supreme spirit.

The benevolent wisdom lacks with the ocean,
It is its inborn nature.

The wisdom is really that
Which is the executor of well-being and fulfilment
And
Destroys the disaster of ourselves and that of the
others too…!

Like wandering women with an elephant-like gait
Like, frail females in the lane of sky
With a lean and thin waist,
Which have become respectfully alert
Which have pooled a huge store of water
By filling up their pitchers from the sea –
–The three cloudlets have set themselves out
On receiving the signals from the ocean.
Wrapped into a white curd-like s*āḍī*[56]
That first one cloudlet
In its appearance…
Looks like a devoted nun.

The one, whose heart is opposed to cupidity
The one, who acts according to her husband's mind –

Which follows the first one, the middle cloudlet,
Like the laughter of a *Palāśa tree*[57] wore a *sāḍī*
Which diminishes the splendour of a rose,
Which makes blush the loveliness of a lily
Having ruddy feet-soles stained with myrtle;
The splendour of the *Sāḍī* of this cloudlet
Where-ever moves on, sliding and gliding,
The brilliance of that spot too gets changed.
And,
Not a false, but genuine
Gold-coloured *sāḍī* is wrapped
By the rearmost cloudlet.

Their first and foremost attempt is
To thwart the radiance of the Sun !
Having taken the Sun amid themselves
They start circumambulating it !
Within a few seconds
The radiance gets affected indeed,
But,
The valour of the sun
Isn't thwarted or defeated,
No decline is observed in its movements.

On seeing its better-half under the sway
The preachings of the Sun start up.
The discourse, though relevant, is really wrathful !

"In the limitless time-stream of the past
It has neither been heard nor observed –

That the universal destruction on the earth
Is wrought by the woman-community.
Do these cloudlets arriving for annihilation
Wish to change their culture
Into a distorted beauty ?

Whether her own or those of the others,
On seeing the children hungry or thirsty
The milk can't tarry within the breasts of a mother
It flows out with a gush
That milk
Remains in wait for this very occasion.

Has even the kind-hearted
Become thirsty of universal destruction ?
Is the religiousness being sold
For patronizing the body ?
Is the self-respect being bartered away
For the hoarding of wealth ?

There are so many virtues of the fair sex
Which hold forth an ideal before the manhood.

In spite of being subjugated every moment
The pan of the sins doesn't get heavier
...Even for a moment !
Sin-awareness remains latent within them
Otherwise,
Why is the adjective 'timid' assigned to them ?

Generally, on being compelled by the man-tribe
The women have to take to a wrong path
But,

The fair sex has upheld her dignity
In examining the fair or the foul ways.

Their eyes are an aphorism of compassion
Hostility can't even touch them
Courteous friendliness
Is a free gift from them.
That is the reason why
Their meaningful name is '*Nārī*'
Which means–
'Not-a- foe' '*na*' '*ari*' *Nārī*...[58a]
Or
They aren't like a handsaw
...Hence... *Nārī*...!

The one, who
Brings a great festivity in life,
'*Maha*,' that is, an 'auspicious' atmosphere – '*Mahotsava*'–
Is called a '*Mahilā*'– a lady ! [58b]

The one who is groundless and helpless,
Hungry for support
Dejected and disheartened towards life
In that man...
Unprecedented faith is awakened
For the '*Mahī*', that is, the earth–
For the Mother-Earth possessing fortitude.

And, who indicates to man the path
Towards the genuine destination –
Is called a '*Mahilā*'– a lady !

Not only so much, listen more !
The one who has suffered from the malady of
chronic diarrhoea

Whose digestive power of temperance has diminished
Who is sick of possession and accumulation
– To that man, she makes drink '*Mahī*' –
That is, a dish of sour butter-milk,
Hence she is called '*Mahilā*'...[59a]– 'a lady' !

The one who brings '*Ava*', that is,
'*Avagama*' - i.e., 'the flame of knowledge',
Having effaced the darkness-ignorance
Brings awakening to life –
She is called '*Abalā*' [59b]-'the fragile woman' !

Or, the one, who
Having fully removed
The inclinations of man's heart
From the conditions of the past
And
The expectations of the future
Holds him over to the '*aba*', that is 'now',
The living present
Is called '*Abalā*' – 'the fragile woman'...!
'*Balā*', that is, 'problem', 'hazard' –
Not '*balā*'... therefore, '*Abalā*' –
– A solution without any problem !
In absence of an '*Abalā*', i.e., a 'so-called fragile woman'
Even a strong man becomes weak,
All the wide world then,
Proves to be a multitude of problems,
Hence, consigned to ladies,
This name '*Abalā*' carries sense !

'*Ku*'[60], that is, 'earth'
'*Mā*', that is, '*Lakṣamī*'
And
'*Rī*' means 'giver' or bestower...
It all carries the sense that
This earth shall remain well off with prosperity
So long as
There remains a virgin, that is, *Kumārī*, here.
That is why
The saints have acknowledged them
As the prime benediction…!
Among all the conventional benedictions !

The house holder's-life is glorified
Through the supreme objects of life-i.e., *Dharma, Artha , Kāma* –
– The attainment of religiousness, prosperity and fulfilment of desire.
In pursuit of these supermanly acts
Generally the man, indeed,
Owns the eligibility for sinning,
That sin be converted into the goodness–
The ladies always take pains
With this object in view.
The passional desires of man should be controlled,
And
The adoration of man should be consistent,
That is, the exertions for the fulfilment of desire should be faultless,
– Only with this very purpose in view
She bears pregnancy.
She always protects the mankind
From the habit of hoarding and the disease of dissipation,
Through the proper distribution of the earned 'money'.

With her co-operation, getting the holy deeds
Of donation, worship, service etc. performed
By the man, along with all the family-rites,
She safeguards the religious traditions.

Thus, the word '*Strī*' is itself sounding the sense, that–
'*S*', that is, equanimity, good conduct and self-discipline
'*trī*', that is, carries three senses –
The one, who imparts wisdom and discipline to a man
For the attainment of *Dharma, Artha, Kāma* -that is–
Religiousness, prosperity and fulfilment of desire –
The super objectives of life,
Is called hence a '*Strī*'...[61], that is a 'lady'.

O, thou seekers of happiness ! listen,
The word '*Sutā*'[61] is itself telling
'*Su*', that is, heart-winning goodnesses
And, that suffix '*tā*'–
Is used in the sense of 'essence' or 'substance'
That is,
The one, who is a fountain of joys and comforts,
Is, therefore..., called '*Sutā*', 'the daughter' –
Thus preach us the sacred maxims !

The one, who is infixed with the twin-well-beings
Is called *Duhitā*–[61] i.e., 'the daughter'
She is able to perform her own well-being herself,
Even the life of a most wretched husband
Is beneficially set aright,
Hence, she is called '*Duhitā*', 'the married daughter'.

The one, who is the bestower of bliss for both the families,
The one, who is the creator of happiness for both the worlds
The one, who, accomplishes the well-being of her own and that of the others
The one, who, staying anywhere, somehow
Continues the milking of the welfare –
She, therefore, is called…'*Duhitā*'- the married daughter.

We should understand
The significance of the word '*Mātṛ*' too.
Valid 'Testimony' [62a] – *Pramāṇa* – implies 'Right Knowledge'
A demonstrated conclusion '–*Prameya*'- implies 'the object fit to be known'
And
The '*Pramātṛ*' is described as 'the perfect Knower' by sages.
That 'Power of Right Knowing'
Is nowhere available, indeed,
Except with the '*Mātṛ-tattva*', i.e., the 'Mother-element' –
That is the reason why, here,
There is none as Father-Grandfather, Man
Who is the foundation-stone of all,
Only the 'Mother-element'
Is the actual procreator.

In the unavailability of the 'Mother-element'
The '*Knowable* [62b]- Knower' relation ceases to exist !
Under such a situation, you please tell yourself,
Who can attain that
Happiness, peace, deliverance
Why and how can it be attained...?
Hence, during this life-span
That very mother should be honoured and respected,
Only her songs of triumph should resound always,
How blissful...!

She has been preaching the mankind
For many centuries bygone –
O those, who get fired with the attachment
to Cupid,
Hark ! listen to me, indeed a bit...!
I admit…that
I am a woman
But,
I am not a bodily organ only...
I am something much more...!
Try to peep a bit,
Through the corporeal existence,
Try to ask something
Even beyond the limbs,
Do you have the heart to accept
What I wish to give !
'That thing' is eternal and immortal
'That gift' is faultless and luminous –
You should feel obliged for that
weightless radiance !"

□

This discourse of the Sun
Went to the heart and touched it
The contrariness of the sentiments
vanished
The point of debate was forgotten,
. After, some moments, indeed,
The point of dialogue too was lulled
In accordance with the external relevance
The internal change was also affected
By all those *three cloudlets.*[63]

The favour of their own lord – the ocean
Seemed to be contrary to them
The side of the lord of universe – the Sun
Appeared to be agreeable to them.
On hearing about their bright heritage
The sense of repugnance was reflected
For the offence that was chanced
And for themselves, as well,
Hence...they instantly added :
" The error should be pardoned, O Lord !
The female devotees wish to offer their services,
When that manifested beauty
Be visible to these eyes ?
The dust should be pacified, O Lord !

That which had been an unacquainted nourishment,
That which had been an enormous base –
The source of the element of joy
Should, fundamentally, be understood, O lord ! "

What ought to be done, what ought not to be done, ?
The discretion to recognize milk-and-water was aroused,
We became the lady-attendants of the divine one...

The observers with the eyes of equanimity,
Whose playful performance was imbibed with
The mildness and delight of the body and the mind,
And the manner of speech, as well...

Who were absorbed in the acts of charity
Who were skilled in the virtue of mercifulness
Who looked like an humble Indian lute...!
Who renounced passions and pleasures,
Who were devoted to non-attachment
Who looked like an innocent lovely she-goose...!

In whom
Forbearance made a resolve
The killingness was beaten out,
In whom...
Modesty and a sense of salutation
For the saints and sages awakened
The sense of holy offerings for the ascetics
was aroused
Being devoid of partiality
The verses of righteous thinking became
opportune...!

As if cursing
The longings for future worldly pleasures
The white, red, yellow 'fairies' of coloured emotions,
Filled with a sense of humility and courtesy
Having moisted feelings and damp eyes
Were circumambulating the Sun
For converting the ripeness of sins into moral merits.

The eyes of the Earth beheld
The occurrence of this event,
The external corporeal existence glimmered
And paid a visit to the internal affection.

These countless hands of the earth
In the guise of innumerable atoms,
Would raise themselves up into the sky soon !
And,
Would reach the spot of occurrence
To rub gently the trickling water-drops
Rolling down from the eyes of the cloudlet
And resting on the cheeks for a while, –
– The symbols of bright pious life,
White, graceful and refined.

As soon as...
The distance of the zone shrinks
The dense atoms
Mingled up with the liquefying atoms
Which embrace each other closely !

In the form of the remaining purificatory rites
The inner core of deception is worn away,
Everything appears to be guileless
And
The watery portion is emancipated.

Lo ! thus
The procreation of the cloud-pearl like the cloud !

Whose capacity is this –
What is that eminent cause ?
Whose co-operation is this
What is that meritorious work ?
Whose agony is hereat
What are those vital breaths ?
Whose inspiration is herewith
What are those means of protection ?
All these doubts
Feel themselves doubtless,
Now all the mystery
Is fully unravelled,
The pearls rain down
Upon the unripened jars
Within the courtyard of the Potter–artisan…!

The advent of the adorer !
Stoopings upon the revered feet.

□

The showers of pearls over the courtyard...
In absence of the Potter–artisan
The whole of the atmosphere is drowned into an
amazement,
The sense of greed peeping through
The eyes of the neighbourhood around !

Hastily catching the winds, the rumour
Reaches the ears of the King.

Then, o thou animate being!
Why the King's mouth...
Shouldn't begin to water !!
The King approaches with his retinue-
The band of attendants enamoured with allurement,
Enchanted with temptations
Having observed the spectacle previously unseen
Feels as if deployed in vain…!

The party gets a hint
Of filling the heap of pearls
Into the bags.
Having taken the King's hint
As a royal command,
The party as soon as...stoops
For picking up and packing the heaps,
At once, comes from the blue…
A heavily grave thundering :

"A great misfortune...an offence...a smash !
A sin...a crime...an evil...!
What are you undertaking...?
Work hard
Sweat your souls out,

You have got the strength of arms
Engage yourself in right endeavours
Recognize the genuine person,
You may well swallow a ball of butter,
Without hard work,
It shall never be digested
On the contrary, the life is imperilled !

> The other's better-half, be regarded as mother,
> The other's riches, even a piece of gold,
> Be merely a clod in the eyes of a virtuous man !
> Alas !
> In the whole of the world of creation
> Where is to be found that decorum ?
> Only the wickedness has prevailed !"

Thus, in spite of even hearing
The discordant, offensive, sarcastic utterings
The company stretches out its hands,
And
As soon as the pearls are touched off,
The agony of the sting of a scorpion,
Like the thin crisp cakes of pulses being roasted
The bodies of all of them start tossing and
tumbling about
And begin to change sides...
It seems as if all of them
Feeling agonizing pains in every limb
Are poisoned from head to heel
The enchanted party faints
The slender bodies of all of them grow bluish !
A long with that of the infatuated counsellor...!

On seeing all these happenings
The mind of the king too felt afraid,
His lips did not move apart
As if the mouth was somewhere locked-up,
The throbbing in the hand-pulse was loosened,
The king feels, that
He has been nailed down
By the influence of some incantations
The hands have become motionless, ...Have stiffened
The feet can't move on
...Have become co-agulated.
The sight has become dim and foggy,
The ears have lost audibility,
... Have become distracted.
The idea of retaliation lurks in the mind
But, the revenge can't be taken,
The king found himself into a fix
And
The aim and objective of the surroundings became obscure !

The crowds of the world thronged around
On this very occasion !
The Potter–artisan too arrived,
At the very sight of this scene
The three lineations of wonder-sorrow-desirelessness
Spring up together
Into the eyes of the Artisan !

That vast assemblage
Was the cause of wonder;

The fainting of the royal retinue,
The nailing down and stunning of the king
Remained the reason behind the sorrow;
And
Those who were caught into the snare of
woman and wealth
Never got rid of the unbearable agonies –
This point clearly seen
Was the cause of indifference to worldly pursuits.

The Potter–artisan felt like weeping
A component of this tragedy was the courtyard,
That which was the cause of heaven and 'liberation'
Provides the cause of calamity by evil spirits, today,
Why such a noisy quarrel, O Lord,
Inside the auspicious courtyard ?

It seems,
The ripeness of our own virtuous conduct
Has acted as an efficient cause, in this happening
Thus
For experiencing the 'Self' and the 'Non-Self'
Makes an entreaty before the Lord, that

The life shouldn't be robbed
Happiness and Peace be adorned,
The internal as well as the external delirium
Of these persons should be wiped off,
They should be filled with vitality.

For some moments
A motionlessness prevails inside the surroundings.
That uttering immerses into adoration –

Then, that
Reticence gives way,
With the loud pronunciation of *Omkāra !* [64]
Having placed cool water on the folded palms.
Consecrates with the internal utterings,
The welfare and the well-being
Is invited with the internal competence,
After sprinkling the water consecrated by 'Mantras'
Upon the faces of the fainted council of
Ministers.
Then, how excellent !

Within seconds, the eyelids fluttered a bit
The closed eyes were unfolded,
In the same manner
As a water-lily blossoms into a pond
With a tender smile on its lips,
On being touched by the sun-beams.

The swoon being faded away
The retinue stayed off at a distance from the pearls,
The King too was taken somewhere else
Due to the fear...
Lest the recurrence should take place...!
Then,
No eagerness is there in the heart
The throat seems somewhat choked
Into the suppressed trembling speech.
With wet eyes
With folded hands,
In all humility, the Potter–artisan says :
" The offence be pardoned, O Lord !

You are a sovereign, O thou the Treasure of Mercy !
We are the people, an object of compassion,
You are the protector, we the youngsters,
This is really your own treasure
We belong to your Holy Presence
A Shelter !

You elders faced troubles
Due to my absence,
Now, no more of such repetitions, my Lord !
You kindly rest assured."
While making such utterings,
Fills the heaps of pearls
With his own hands, into the bags
Without any sense of terror.
On beholding this scene,
A voice at once spreads out
From the lips of the King, along with his retinue,–
" Victory to the true religion !
The true religion be triumphant !! "
□

In this very context
The immature pitcher too
Relates a relevant point
By dropping a hint to the Sovereign :
" You made a narrow escape, O King !
Take it as the dawning of a favourable fate !
Otherwise,
You, having burnt yourself,
Would have evaporated –

Into the vacuum…since long time.
And
What wisdom does it indicate –

Where was the need to touch
A burning incense-stick ?
If
The incense-stick would have
Drunk its own fragrance itself,
Then...there was something remarkable,
But,
It was remitting, indeed,
The mild fragrance upto your very nose !

The other point too is that
" The violation of *Lakṣmaṇa Rekhā*, that is, the lawful limit,
Would surely deserve punishment for the one
– Whether he is Rāvaṇa or Sītā
Or, whether it comes even to Lord Rām Himself ! "

The one, who has scorched himself
In pursuit of his burning anxiety for unlimited wealthiness
For whom only wealth is life, only wealth is deliverance,
And after knowing and believing so
Who has been infatuated with power and pelf,
– He isn't a man of keen wisdom
So far as such money-policy is concerned.

Under the sensuous shadow of the '*kali-yuga*'–Iron Age,
This world has often learnt
In the atmosphere of trade-mentality –
To tender its due services for the lustful malpractices...!"

□

Due to the sarcastic remarks of the pitcher
The broad forehead of the King
Was reflected
With three feelings simultaneously –
The flush of bashfulness !
The expanding and shrinking of anger !!
And
The thinking mixed up with anxiety
About the reality of the occurrence !!!

On discerning some change into the facial halo
The King's mind was held under reference,
Then
The Potter–artisan cast his curved eyesight
Towards the pitcher.

...Some how should be ceased
The utterings of the pitcher,
Which were heart-rending !
Though self-explanatory,
Which were future-sweet, but, bitter today.

And
...With this very intention that
Our goodwill for the King should be expressed.
Lo, the pitcher is acquainted with –
The mild nobility of descent
Inherited through parentage !

To preach, even by mistake the eminent elders
Despite being youngers,
Is a prominent folly which is vainly troublesome,
But,
To acquire virtues from the Spiritual Guides i.e., *Gurus.*

That is to say,
To take a vow before them in the manner that
We shall tread upon the path of spiritual wellbeing,
Is a great boon for the nectar of happiness,
And,
Being a Spiritual Guide i. e., a *Guru*,
To bestow a promise even in a dream to the young learners,

That is
To follow their ways
Is to demolish the way to happiness.

But, yes !
If they ask something about their well-being
With an earnest request and humility,
– Without any partiality
– Without winking a trickful eye,
To instruct them
With worthy, and suitable and sweet preachings
Is to efface the agony of sufferings.

Little by little
Like risen mercury fluctuating down
Inside the clinical thermometer !
Or
Like the milk boiling-bubbling
And, having risen up, refracting
To jump out of the vessel,
Getting calmed down and pacified
On some water-drops being mingled with it !
Through the utterings of the Potter–artisan instructing the pitcher

The boiling up of the King's intellect–

The excitement seemed to be decreasing,
The position which seemed to be confused
On being found now…
To be entirely sound and quiet,
Again an entreaty, a request with folded hands :
"O Thou Holder-of-the-sword, O Thou Merciful-at-heart !
Take pity upon thy object-of-mercy
Kindly do a good turn to this treasure
By accepting it !

Don't take it as a gift
It is the very necklace of yours, an embellishment,
Is your triumph indeed,
Its consumption and usage
Is our defeat, O Lord !"

□

Filled into the bags upto the brim, the heap of pearls
Peeping outside,
Hearing and understanding
The Potter–artisan's humble request,
Which is being made to the King;
And
Is grasping too
The ardent desire of the King's heart,
The bubbling up of the King's mentality
Which is inclined towards consent,
With an excuse of a faint smile upon the face :
– Is supposed to be whispering thus –
O King !
It becomes your high status, accept it –

But listen...!
That pearl, worth its name,
Neither indulges into affection
Nor fills itself with malice !
Nor vanity, self-conceit, jealousy –
No other passions can touch it !

At first, it gets rained upon the courtyard
From the blue sphere,
Then, it is scattered around in portions
And is packed into the bags.
Now it is being carried, with due regard,
Towards the royal palace...
It is being admired, without any reserve,
But
When does it listen to it being enchanted ?
It is enshaped into the safe-guarding necklaces
of the ladies with buoyant faces !
It extends blissful touch of its palm
Upon the heads of visitors and guests at the door,
It is utilized as the liberating gate-festoon,
Despite this all
That unchained one remains a liberated-'pearl'
Unstained with arrogance...unfettered…!

The king, pondering over
The submission of the Potter–artisan
The admiration and backing
Of the pearls and the surroundings,
Extends his welcome to the offer of acceptance,
Delightfully !

And
Having received the rare treasure of pearls,
Enriches the state-treasury further more.

□

In the same manner !
That bright glory of the Earth,
As if putting the moon-light to shyness,
Piercing through all the ten directions
Is constantly growing
High around the limitless firmament.

That of the sun-like heroes and the braves
That of the wealthy and the wise
That of the firm-minded and their paintings
That of the children and the animals
That of the fortunate adolescents
That of the lads and lasses and the group of saints
That of the feudal lords and the ascetics
That of the chaste women adorned with character
That of the toilsome hermit-like farmers
That of the workers with sword and pen in hand
That of the accomplished sages and
the inspired seers
That of the divine personages and
the virtuous elders
That of the grand trees and the great Spiritual Guides
That of the fragrant buds and tender leaves
That of the dense cluster of shrubs
That of the soft flowers and the bunches of fruits
That of the new-born leaves like smooth sprouts
That of the mountains and the observance of
festivals, –

That of the ever-gliding rivers
That of the pool with the loveliness of lotus
Etc. ...etc. ...thus
That of the diverse splendours –
Natural that love with the Earth
Is prospering more and more
Is growing ever and ever...!

□

Oh, what is this reverse-like tendency !
The practice of the ocean is venomous...
It is getting more and more irritated
On seeing the growing glory of the Earth !
O dear friend !
It is a malicious feeling
…Undoubtedly...!

Having destroyed the pitcher
Having dissolved and mixed it into the dust,
– Which are trained and directed messengers
To make the soil flow as waste –
– Which, having adored the opposite side,
Cause the pearls to fall out, –
On beholding those shy cloudlets turning back
After enriching the glory of the Earth,
The anguish of the ocean
Reaches its climax within moments .
Its eyes turn reddish
The eyebrows get knitted together
The gravity changes into fright –

The forehead of the future doesn't appear favourable
to him
And
Thinking thus, the ocean,
With a mind marred by foul emotions
Expresses some of its feelings
Quotes some lines - that :
" Whether our own better-half or that of the others,
It is the nature of the woman-folk
That
She doesn't keep herself stuck to any side.
Otherwise,
Is it a trivial job to give up
The mother-land, the mother-side
And that too...
Without anguish, without special trouble !
This
Is not only a very tortuous job,
But an impossible act in all the three spans of time
For the man-folk !
Hence, even by mistake,
The woman shouldn't be entrusted with
The highest office of the hereditary tradition and culture.
And
The background of the deliberations
Relating to the confidential plans
Shouldn't be disclosed to her... ."
A sense of enmity and ill-will for the Earth
A proud attitude towards the venerable elders
An uncontrollable ambition
For keeping the all under subjugation.

And all-devouring tendency....
On seeing this position of the ocean
The luminous Sun
Couldn't tolerate this all !
Therefore it
Informed the lustrous element
Residing at the sea-floor
With mysterious hints aroused it
Which was governed by the Sun itself,
– Where there was found communal
similarity too;
The result was that at once
The submarine fire fiercely boiled up,
And
'O thou sea, an endless deposit of salty matter !
Even a single second is enough to me
For drinking thee off upto the last drop'
– Thus grumbled it out.

On some inevitable occasion
Even the gentle and saintly persons
Have to fulfil their responsibility
By taking recourse to flurry and fury.
Otherwise,
The goodness gets defiled
The villainy gets extolled
Has it ever been desirable in the eyes of the well-bred...?

There is a veritable difference between the
word and the deed,
The one who says doesn't act –

And
The one who acts doesn't say,
Thus, bursting into laughter
The ocean again passes a sarcastic remark,
" The sun is burning from above the sky
You are boiling from under the ground !
And
In spite of dwelling in-between
...When has this ocean got burnt or boiled ?
When has its cool character...
...Got itself altered...?
Ah me !
Where have you become cool
Despite being one with coolness ?
When have you spitted out haughtiness ?

The second point as well is, that,
Your bilious humuor always remains fretful
Because of your nature being hot
And your mood is found always under excitement,

Otherwise,
Like a frenzied one
Why should have you indulged into absurd talks ?
For subsiding your bilious humuor,
Having made an entreaty with me,
You should make good use of the moon-like nectar,
And
Shouldn't take sides with the Sun !"

□

Within the ocean, the diplomacy
Has been filled in a compact form.
The special endeavour gains momentum again.
The main objective, indeed, is
To bring total annihilation upon the Earth !

That is the reason why, this time,
A man has been trained
By bestowing ample and mature opportunity
to him.

And those personages are–
'*The three dense clouds*' [65a]
And not the cloudlets, often changing
the groupings
On being melted soon out of mercy.

Their first and the foremost job has been
To obstruct the auspicious ceremonies.
Their feelings are detestable
– Performance abominable, indeed !
And
Their name is '*ghana*', [65b] that is, '*the cloud*' !

Having risen from inside the ocean
Filled up with alkaline waters,
They fly high up into the sky
Like the lined-up aeroplanes
With their different rings.
The very first cloud is so dark
That, at the very sight of which
The band of bewildered and deviated big
black bees,
Separated from its fellow-partners
Mixes with it once and again,
As if doubting it to be its own companion

And
Turns back, on being disappointed
That is to say
The first band of clouds...
Is even more dark than the big black-bee.

The second one...right from a distance,
Is like a dark blue serpent, spitting out poison
The blue-necked one with sportive performances –
By the pomp of which
Even the ripened yellowish farm of paddy
Assumes a greenish splendour !
And
The last band of clouds
Reflects the colour of a dove.
Thus, all the three of them,
According to their bodies, are corrupt too in their minds.

Their mental analysis is being depicted :
They possess a violent character like that of a
merciless wretch
They have turned into a solid mass of pride.
Their hearts have fashioned into an abode of cruelty,
They go on indulging into strife
By fits and starts,
Without a quarrel, they are unable to get their
diet digested!
On beholding them from a distance
The ghosts take to their heels out of fear,
Even the frightened last night of a dark fortnight,
Keeps Itself hidden away... from them
somewhere at a distance;
That is why
Only once in a month –
It sets out abandoning its dwellings.

The night is related to them as their sister,
The moon sought its friendship with the ocean
The moon became an object of disgrace and blemish
Due to its failure in getting itself related
With some lovely lass,
The moon was married to night,
Hence...this credit goes to the ocean !

Being infatuated with the ghost of delusion
They are never subdued by anyone in any way,
They are ill-intentioned and have been the
wicked ones,
They have been strong in their malpractices,
They feel satisfied and satiated
Through inflicting sufferings on others;
At the very sight of others
They feel displeased and agitated
Their tendency to take revenge
Is spontaneous and inborn
Their complex for hostility and discord
Doesn't relax itself easily.
They slander the innocents
They awaken anger among the contentments
They scandalize even the venerable elders
The auspicious acts are blinded by them;

They don't like to smell, even by mistake,
The charming fragrance of the good deeds,
They have resigned themselves to the tastes of senses
They have become the farmers of the harvest of foul passions
Their denomination – '*Jala-dhara*'[66] i.e. 'jealousy-
holders' is meaningful.

Those who have become dull-minded and intoxicated
By retaining senselessness with them.

Though they bear another name *'Payodhara'* [67] too,
Even then
They shower poison in the rainy season.
Otherwise,
Why are they as dark-black as the large black bees?
It is something remarkable that
The 'poison' transforms into nectar
As soon as it comes in close contact with the Earth
And, one more doubt lurks, that
Why do they look as bright as diamond.
After the rainy season, in the autumn...?

□

Only the presence of some endeavour
Isn't enough,
For the attainment of the 'beneficial'
The absence of the 'injurious' is also inevitable.
And that too
Is accomplished by special effort, and not all of a sudden.

Keeping in mind, indeed,
This discipline of the cause and effect,
At first, those bands of clouds
At once, within the twinkling of the eye,
Get together against the Sun
Which poses a hindrance in their way.
And
They, melted with high pride,

Resounding with heavy roar say that,
"Why do you take sides with the Earth?
Why do you get irritated with the ocean?

O thou sharp-edged Sun, listen !
well good ! thou art recognized as the jewel
of the sky,
The deity-planet of the solar system –
The presiding planet of the galaxy of planets,
There appears the apex of uneasiness in thee
O the most fiercely hot jewel of the crown !
Thy incarnation into a body...that is, –
Thy embodiment is of no avail.
The reason,
Where is the rest-house with thee ?
That is...why
Thou hast to wander, the day in and the day out,
Door to door, like the poor and helpless one !
Even then,
With what notion does thou venture
For an encounter against the ocean ?

Hark, ...even...now
Take the sides with the ocean,
Have some pity upon thyself
And
Treasure happiness, peace and fame for thyself !
It is an occasion,
Take advantage of it
Now, make good use of thy brain !
Even…now...get rid of the perverted craze
Otherwise,

The arrangement for the 'eclipse' shall be made
without delay.
The reason behind ignominy is evil practices
The person with evil conduct has always
Met with that imprisonment !

□

On facing the strokes
Of the hard, harsh and bitter wordings
All the ten directions went deaf,
The heavenly sphere lost brilliance, indeed,
It got drowned into the scattered band of clouds
The space provider for plunging seemed itself
to be plunged into !

And,
The halo of light of the Sun too
Losing a little of its lustre says,
That
O thou the swindlers, having cheated others,
O thou the enjoyers of the peals of laughter,
O thou the seekers of a fragmented life,
O thou the high-soarers with the wings of hypocrisy !
You will take time
In grasping this point of mystery !

Not a filthy one
But a devotee is afraid of
The odd and the worthless world –
And,
Not the blind,
But the one having eyes indeed, is frightened
By the immensely dense darkness.

To nullify the violence
Is to adore, to appreciate...non-violence,
And
To kill or worship a destroyer or killer
As a rule
Is to murder non-violence...is brutality.
That very natural tendency of thoughtfulness
Is the steadfastness of the Earth
And
That very natural tendency of being absorbed into body
Is the cowardice of the ocean.

Thus,
Rewarding according to the due dignity –
The supremacy of the Earth
With the tender flowers of adoration
And
The lowliness of the ocean
With the harsh thorns of reproval,
The Sun, then
Was filled with a sense of self-respect,
His that sharp heat
Sprang up to the full extent
Which was there within him.
The eyebrows, supine under tension
As if bathed into blood, arousing fear,
Took the form of a brandishing tongue –
Seemed to be dripping the drops of fire,
Densely...somewhere...
'No, no, none shall be excused.'

Roaring thus
Appeared as a small forest blazing up like
wild-fire...!
It is beyond exact comprehension.

In both the eyes fully opened
Does there flash a call of *lāvā ?*[68a]
...It is a deception!
The volcano is staring outside
The original source of the element of lustre
The electrical centre of the universe.

The element of lustre is exported from here
Into the every nook and comer of the world,
In absence of which all the traffic
Of the animate and the inanimate stands still...!
All around there prevails utter darkness... .

□

Which were indulged in viewing with an eye of calumny
Which descended down nearer
Which pursued a lowly and strange policy –
To burn off such bands of clouds,
The ocean remembered (*the dragon-headed planet) Rāhu* [68b],
After seeing the endeavours of the Sun,
And said :

" Till what period, the arrogance of the Sun
shall continue,
(Under the sway of the Earth, the Sun)
Is going on devouring
The decorum of the solar system !
Devoted to the service of the Earth
Influenced by the Earth

Isn't the Sun familiar with you ?
While standing before a lion...
Does even a deer act according to its own
sweet will ?

Can even a frog being arrogant,
Play sportively
After finding itself upon a snake's hood ?
Probably is it not so, that
Under the pretext of serving the Earth
He (Sun) should have been mocking at you !

Come what may, take what-ever you should,
The desired, the requisitioned thing !
The demand shall be met with due regard,
This unlimited heap of wealth is awaiting you.

The civilized ones should be produced and protected
The wicked ones should be uprooted and squeezed,
The success of prosperity
Lies there in its due utility, indeed ! "

On seeing the availability of wealth in the way
The-*Rāhu*-goes astray,
Alas ! it is a matter of sorrow,
The very path of the '*Rāhu*' is altered, indeed,
And
All these sinful acts are committed
Stealthily, in the broad daylight –
The export from the ocean in toto
Towards the solar system...!

Having loaded into an aerial car
The treasure of countless
Dazzling and glimmering gems

Giving out such bright smiles –
The charming diamonds, the original jewels,
The pearls and corals the splendours of rubies
The saffron slabs of topaz
The silvery wands set with jewels of sapphire –
Which evoke fascination among the kings.

The side of the ocean gets vindicated
The *Rāhu* agrees, a heap is granted
Hence..., the weakness ceases to exist,
The side of the ocean becomes stronger
When
The *Rāhu's* house is filled
With the unlimited hoardings got without efforts
Then
The *Rāhu's* head is filled
With the poisonously wicked sinful heaps of money.
That is
Due to the touch of the untouchable hoardings
The *Rāhu* turns so dark black, that
He, the store of sinfulness, goes out of sight,
The one whose good fortune turns most feeble,
Who can not make his appearance before spectators
Who does not remain touchable for contactors !

Lo, a sense of similarity is melted into the thoughts
Two forces inter-act upon each other.
A bitter creeper is, indeed, pungent
And if it mounts over a margosa tree,
How excellent then !

The good and the bad lies in the lap of future
At present, it is turning sides, while lying !
In spite of this,
Aren't the hearts of the both of them restless –?
The uneasiness has multiplied several times.

Day in and day out
Under daylight, under the cover of darkness
Even after closing their eyelids
Both of them see only the universal destruction,
The annihilation has been their foodstuff
The annihilation, indeed, their purpose...!

□

How shall an abode be found
In the universal dissolution of the Earth ?
And whereat those means of life...?
In the triumph of Earth
Who shall not obtain an assurance of fearlessness ?
And hereat, a treasure like the very 'Life' itself !

For us, for you and for them
Whosoever seeks these here,
Alas, but !
– Where do they get
The evolution of this thought ?
That who possesses a crooked serpentine motion
That who possesses terrifying jaws of death –
– Became devoid of the saintly strength,
And gained the physical force.

The wayfarer of the boar-way, *Rāhu* –
Who lacks discrimination between the beneficial and
the injurious,
Who is cruel by nature, feels enraged,
On being filled with fury, becomes sulky, –
Without raising any hue and cry
Without making one or two mouthfuls,
Swallows up the Sun, the heap of radiance,
From heels to head, entirely.

The Sun is settled into the jaws of *Rāhu*
like a drop Into an ocean
Like an infant into the intense lap of a mother.
The Sun disappears...therefore...
It seems to be the close of the day,
The feeble and the forlorn day looks
Like a poor householder, surrounded by miserable days.

Is it the twilight-hour
Or the untimely advent of the end !
Like the fore-head of a lady
Without an ornamental mark on it,
The courtyard, of a celestial nymph
Has where remained fascinating?

The state of directions has changed
Like the body afflicted by chronic fever.

The lotus-friend, the Sun, doesn't appear...
So, the assemblage of lotuses remains blinking
A decline out of order...is discerned in their
loveliness !
That life of the forests, gardens
Seems to be deserted,
And

The restorative drink of air to life
Seems to be plundered.
The fire is really a friend to air !
The Sun, indeed, is the source of the element
of lustre !

Despite being an undaunted and untired traveller
The steps of the wind have got jammed today
On seeing the livelihood of its friend being robbed.

– Which is innocent, an image of affection
Roaming about at its sweet will, free-minded,
Living upon music, with a mechanism of self-control
Liberated from all bonds of attachment...non-attached
Whose very limbs are its friendly companions,
A servant of its union and society
With an affectionate chest !
–Which dispels the demerits of ignorance and avarice
possessing the quality of goodness and richness
of labour
Which is opposed to enmity, having knowledge
and understanding
Afraid of the hazards of evening
Distressed due to the unexpected fears –
Whose feathers have got tired –
– That fatigued ring of birds,
Having left its bird's eye view of sight-seeing
Makes its bodies descend silently
Upon its respective nests,
And
Whose heart dives down
Into the far-fetched...depth of anxiety !

All the moments are thrilled with sympathy
Hence...a shiver runs through their bodies,

The moisted internal particles
Are lamenting
Due to distress, while flowing out !

These are the ears only of yesterday
But, alas ! where is that singing of the birds?
The humming of the days gone-by !
Even the throat of the cuckoo goes blunt,
In the forests, parks and gardens
Has prevailed only
A pitiful weeping and bewailing !

Among the crows, the cuckoos, the pigeons
Within the heart of the kites, the birds and the *Chātakas*[69]
Among the tigers, the sheep, the hawks and the ducks
Into the organs of a peacock, a spotted deer and a lion
Among the winged creatures, the rabbits, the asses and the wicked ones
Among the lovely, tender and bashful creepers
Among the sky-high mountain-tops
Among the grown-up trees and the plants
Among the off-shoots, the leaves, the fruits and flowers
The awakening of the pains of separation
Can't be endured to see even for a moment
Therefore...
The ring of the birds takes a resolve, that –
Unless this calamity of solar eclipse
Is warded off
Uptil then, the renouncing of the meals and drinks !
The abandoning of celebrations and recreations!
No wonder that,
The giving up of even the gestures of the night !

□

On hearing the loud bewailings
Of the beings moving on the earth and in the sky
On beholding the Sun
Tossing and tumbling about into the jaws of
the *Rāhu*
The heart of the cloud is invigorated,
Thence
His blood is enriched manifoldly !

It happens so, indeed
In the defeat of the opposite side,
But, it shouldn't happen so;
And
In the subjection of our own side
There runs a wave of heart-attack–
All this is the folly of the world.

Who can now obstruct
The showering of the clouds ?
Who can now-repress
The gladdening of the clouds ?
The background of the annihilating rains
Has gained momentum at a proper place –
On seeing the atmosphere telling thus,

When the air goes ineffective
Then, the medicine works,
And
When the medicine becomes inert
Then, the blessings bear fruit,
But,
When even the benedictions are incapable
Then, what else remains to supplement ?

What support ?...So...listen!
The firm, the constant, embraced with
self-discipline
This consciousness,
Acts self-existently –
To the Earth, thinking in this way,
Tell with a sense of decorum and courtesy,
All these particles :

" The honour of the mother should be held respectfully
They are the part and parcel of *the race of Rāghavas*,[70]
The admirers too of the skilful dynasties
But,
They are, Mother, the destroyers of the arrogant dynasties,
– Which were trained in the egotistic mental mould.

The lineage in 'which great saints and Supreme Souls
Were born, are taking birth and shall be incarnated–
The memory of that lineage shouldn't fade
away, Mother !
Let us attend to our own traditional lineage,
...Which remained simply a sharer of hard work !
Only a discussion–
– Let it be stopped for a time.

Today, indeed, a dry diet
Is appearing to this consciousness
More tasteful and health-giving
Than a sweet speech."

They would offer salutation, bowing their heads,
At the auspicious lotus-feet
Of the universally benevolent Mother

And
Would hear thus the blessed benedictions
Through the utterings from the Mother :

" Hit hard at the sin and hypocrisy
Earn excellence in performing virtuous actions ! "

□

Like the firm-minded competent ascetics
On being intent upon accomplishing
their objectives
Filled up with immense enthusiasm !
These countless particles soar high
Into the fathomless empty space...!
Like those self-respectful lovers of freedom,
With warrior-like reddish eyes,
Who jump into the battle-field
On hearing the trumpet of battle
Or
The fiery mass of iron, being hammered hard,
Diffused with a crackling sound
Like its showers of sparks,
These scarlet particles of earth,
Despite being separated as single entities
each moment,
Are only constantly absorbing,
Are going on soaking up...
So many drops of water;
In spite of applying their full force
The water-particles
Having pierced through the mass of earthly particles,
Shouldn't come across the side of the earth.

With the countless water-particles
Falling down from the upper stratus !
There is a forceful encounter
Of the countless earthly particles–
Soaring high from the low levels
The result is, that
Each and every water-particle
Gets itself divided into many pieces –
There is a very strong dispersion!
All around...stress...noise...
And
Into the endless solar system
A smoky encirclement...!

While sparsely overspread the disturbance
upon the clouds,
The earthly particles, despite being dense,
Remain guileless, beyond the guilt ;
Where are the particles of the clouds sinless?
They are fleeing away out of fear
Due to the hundredfold burden of sins,
And
These hungry-looking particles of Earth
Assuming the form of a calamity,
Are running after the particles of water
In a horrible shape.

On this occasion, Indra too,
The Lord of gods, lands down in human form.
– But

His incarnation remains a secret
He can't be sighted,

Only his bow, comes to view –
The active rainbow of Lord Indra !
The great personages don't come to light
They don't wish to,
They take delight
In giving away the light.
This point is peculiar in itself, that
The light shall indeed enlighten all
Whether it is self or non-self, only that
Which is required to be illuminated...!
Moreover, where is there a non-existent thing also?
Then, how is it possible,
That
There be the existence, and it should remain
non-manifested ?
He also wishes, like Lord Indra, this very thing.

I wish *to achieve supreme reality or to be a True Self*[71a]
And not a mere relater of pains or troubles.
And
I wish *to be a perfect ascetic or an enlightened one*
(Tathākāra)[71b]
And not a story-teller or a mere preacher.
This is the genuine feeling behind this penmanship –
The true performance should stay, the true culture
should stay,
Through the endless future
Wakeful...alive...invincible!
Where-in is moulded
Into a truly beautiful and heart- touching shape
That decoration and glory
Of the inherent nature.

Never before the world
He should remain the doer–

Wherein wakes up
The alkaline world
Of the odd distortion
With its loud cry of self-conceit
And
The true well-being of our own 'self' and that of the others
Is definitely destroyed !

□

Today, the valorous acts of Lord Indra,
Are touching their farthest limits,
Having fully stretched the bow-string
With the right hand upto the right ear,
All the bodies of the bands of clouds
Are being pierced and dispersed
Deformed and rent asunder
Through the sharp needle-headed arrows
Being continuously set in motion.

Their condition of wild rustling refracted into
A piteous state, which makes one weep !

Where-ever we see
The particles of Earth only are found spreading out
The particles of water remain in small numbers.
This is the very reason
Why the ocean remitted again
The bands of clouds filled upto the brim with water,
And, abreast of it,
Has also instructed
As to what step should be taken in future.

In accordance with the informed idea, at once
The clouds produce electrical power,
The fretful lightning dazzles and thunders,
The eyes of all are closed in such a manner
As if they are stuck with gum !
The wit of everyone seems to be depressed
Not to mention others,
Naturally, even Lord Indra, who looks
unwinkingly
Becomes a blinker within moments,
That is to say
Even the eyes of Lord Indra
Start twinkling once and again.
At that very moment impulsively Lord Indra
Having taken out his infallible weapon–the
thunderbolt
Launches it towards the clouds... .

Being wounded with the stroke of the thunderbolt
A deep sigh of pain burst out of the throat of clouds,
On hearing which
The solar system goes deaf.
Like an outcry by Rāvaṇa
That shedding of tears of the clouds
Proves to be an unlucky omen for the ocean,
And
Entering into
The eyes of the lightning vomiting fire,
The particles of dust in heaps
Create unbearable troubles.
On seeing such an odd situation,
Even the lightning starts trembling
Perhaps, due to this very reason...

The lightning would have acquired
A transitory, passing and momentary life-
breath...!

On beholding this mishap,
...At once,
A message is again communicated by the ocean
To the frightened clouds, that
Lord Indra launches an unfailing weapon
Hence... You
Make good use of the unfailing arrow of
Lord Rām !

Keep yourself aloof from retreating,
Pelt a stone for a brick !
Instantly, without any delay,
Start a hail-storm...a shower of hail-stones !

Lo, some agility appears again among the clouds
A sense of self-respect awakens
The production of hail-stones gains a fillip !
Hence...it seems
Not the production, an opening-unveiling has taken place
Of the unlimited storage somewhere !

Light and heavy, tiny and huge
Those having three or four angles
And those having five sides,
Those having different forms
Those having various weights,
The rounded and well-shaped hail-stones
How to tell, what to tell, did they say,
The hail and hail seen everywhere
The solar space is filled with them !

Hence...this penmanship tries to compare
The solar sphere with the zone of Earth :
High above, the force of atom is at work
Then, hither...downwards
The power of Manu exists !
Over and above, the machine is thundering
Beneath it, the holy incantation is being sung
The one is a killer
The other a saviour;
The one is Science
Whose subsistence is 'argument',
The other is Faith
Which doesn't worry, for a calling,
The one is hanging into the empty space,
It has no support for footing,
The other has got shelter upon the Earth
That is why the high-ups
Only possess a brain and no feet...
May be, white ants have eaten up
Their feet of conduct ...!
The down-taker moves also on foot –
On some occasion who can move
upwards too;
Aye !
The uptaker's mind may get heated up
When he
Can learn a lesson
Only of destruction or degeneration.

It is also known to one and all that
The mark of interrogation –

Is always found hanging above,
While
The full-stop stays downwards.
The answer of a question is indeed found underneath
Never upwards...
In answer, there is repose, lasting peace.
The interrogation remains ever-agitated
After the answer, the question doesn't arise at all,
The life-end of a question –
Like a drop of water vanishing into an ocean...!

□

By this comparison through the penmanship
The masses of hail break down cruelly
Upon the particles of the Earth
As if taking it to be their devaluation.
As a measure of counter move,
Acquainting with their strength,
The particles of the Earth too, turning upon
their heads,
And having protected a clash with the hail-stones
Toss them about into the sky
At a farthest distance...out of the orbit of Earth,
just as a missile
Hurls the satellites
Like '*Āryabhaṭṭa*', '*Rohiṇī*', and so forth !

Due to this collision, a part of hail-balls
Scatter into many sub-divisions
After being broken into Pieces within seconds,
And that scene –

Is appearing as if,
The flower-petals of the fragrant coral-tree
Are being showered down from the heavens !
Are gradually descending underneath !
Scattering about their auspicious smile !
Like the welcome-greetings of Earth by gods.

The hail shouldn't feel pained
As if thinking thus, indeed,
The particles of Earth are flying
While keeping them over their heads !
Hence...it seems, that
Hanumān [72] is soaring high
With the Himālaya over his head !

This chain of happenings
Continue for hours incessantly,
In the face of it, the 'star-war'
Which has become a current topic these days,
Doesn't gather much significance.

The group of pitchers too, with its open eyes,
Is noticing this occurrence happening upwards.
But,
There is no trace of the uneven wave of awe
Upon the face of any pitcher
Every thing is experienced, only
With a natural sense of testification –
The simple and the poisonous, the part and the whole-all !

In spite of this
The point of wonder, really is
That,

Even a single piece of hail-stone coming down
Can't leave a pitcher broken !
So far as the victory or defeat is concerned –
The particles of Earth have come out triumphant
And
Around the neck of the clouds and the hailstorm
The necklace of subjection is hanging –
Devoid of sweet smell and fragrance,
Almost dead and faded.

Even then,
The advent of fresh and new clouds
The creation of additional hail-stones
The intermittent flashes of lightning
The uprise and intensity of friction
A conflict, a tug-of-war, a cunningness
The odd gestures from the ocean, cruelty
Etcetera, etcetera,-this all
Is the distressing result growing after the defeat,
The overthrow of anger is not an easy thing !

□

Even under this reverse state,
The courage of the hungry particles of Earth is
astonishing,
The sense of renunciation and penance remarkable !
The dignity of the Motherland
The honour of the Mother-Earth
Can't be upheld intact
Without firm faith,
It can't be kept up here,

It would have been sacked...then and there –
Recollecting this idea into his memory
That Artisan being engrossed into the worship of his deity...
He doesn't ask for anything till today !

It doesn't mean that
There is no trouble at all here,
The perception of want may not be present indeed;
Aye,
The want of money is no deficiency
And
Even to ask for money from the Lord Himself
...Carries really no sense !

Why ask for a thing
Which is not there with you, indeed,
Which you don't wish even to retain?
But,
The absence of the *summum bonum*, that is
the highest good
Has become intolerable at this point, O Lord !
When would this deficiency go ?

The smell of the pent-up agony is sensed,
And that too by the nose of the mother,
Into the subtlest sobbings of an adolescent
Who has slept in a corpse-like Yogic posture
– Having become wearied and tired after
getting distressed
Due to some typical reason.
The motion of his respiratory system,
The listening of its rise and fall
Can only be done by the hearing of the mother.

He isn't tearing off the dress worn by him
Isn't beating down hands and legs over the earth,
And
Isn't lamenting furiously
While making his facial expressions distorted,
Due to this very reason,
To take the decision of the lack of grief in him
Can't be regarded as a true judgment.

The expression of pain only –
Is not found here
But,
The internal horizon
Is covered with the cloudiness of sorrows!
If even the Almighty shall not be capable
Of visualizing it,

What...then...
Whose gifted eyes are those
Which can see him
And at once
Being tearful, may console him ?
The dignity of Mother Earth, Should remain
safe, O Lord !
The prestige of water should get consumed,
O Lord !
There is a limit of putting someone to test,
Excessive testing too, generally,
Deviates a person from his chosen way,
The affection also for the provisions of
a journey decreases.
Due to the deep-drawn breathing once and again,
The embankment of endurance and courage is shaken
And there is every possibility of a crack.

Ah me !
Will the life have to be
Relinquished untimely ?

Day after day passed away
...So many days !
When the reason of the Artisan's absence is known
An affectionate soft smile
Something of fondling and loving.
That tickling of the tender leaf-like palms
Rubbing gently its hand upon the body,
The endearing sprinkling of the cool water...
Conferring assimilation with the music...
All this pre-eminence bestowed by the past,
On becoming a recollection of memory
Reflects before the sapplings of roses.

And
The row of plants at once cast its glance !
Towards the Artisan seated in the distant...courtyard,
Who
Has been fed up with the worldly pleasures and luxuries,
Has been absorbed into asceticism and devotion,
His such understanding
Has become a devotee at the feet of the Lord,
But
There dwells into his facial expressions
A thin and dim sense of dejection !...So...

On seeing his Lord caught into scruples
The rose-plant speaks out :
"The end to this trouble should come within
the reach,

From difficult to most formidable dangers too
Are warded off within seconds;
Then...indeed...O Lord !
Instantly, while remembering You,
By taking a closer and the closest view;
How is it that delay is taking place
In the performance of the high Personage (*Ārya*) –
Despite you making a dwelling within the heart...? ”

□

On this very occasion, that is,
About the advent indeed of the approaching peril
The thorns of roses also grind their teeth !
Utter something bitter, in this way :
“O Thou, the Calamity !
Thou heartless unknown swindler !
In the form of thorns, don’t get thyself scattered
Upon the path of the disinterested
Innocent, simple-hearted and passionless
wayfarers !

Give up thy obstinacy
Even now stand off
Out of the way...go somewhere...else,
Otherwise,
A thorn is ousted with the help of a thorn –
Don’t thou knowest this saying?
Beware thyself,
Within seconds, thou shalt leave even no trace behind !”

...And
Meanwhile, in this context,
The flower hanging upon the bough –

Becomes specially active
Neither it interrupts against the thorn
Nor does it rebuke the thorn,
But
Makes timely utterances
For the pacification of
The excitement and heat of the thorn.

Where a needle may work
Why should a sword be blown ?
When a flower can serve the purpose
Why should a thorn be made use of ?
When, basically, while living, indeed, upon the earth
The fruit is being acquired,
Then, to climb upon the pivot
Is not only a wastage of energy and time,
It also proves the lack of true evaluation.
Thus, a treasure of fragrance, the rose,
Explaining the method of right policy and good conduct,
Showing the wealth of affectionate performances,
Introduces the fragrance
With its intimate and unique friend
– Each and every atom, each and every particle,
Remembers the odour-carrier winds
By spreading it upto heavens and horizons.

A few moments are gone, when
Arrive the winds,
Which are rapt with humility, trust and
thoughtfulness
Having a nature like that of the Nature herself
Which are habitual of wandering into forests
and gardens –

Possessing the attributes of Spring, Summer,
Rains and Frosty Winter
And moving uniformly through all the seasons,
At every moment of life
Which tastes the sense of friendliness
At every moment of life
Which salutes the sense of ancestral care.

With reference, indeed, to such personality
These sayings of the saints are meant, that
'Whose dutifulness
Is found touching the height of eminence,
His universally acknowledged honour, indeed...
Surpasses even the highest limit itself.'

□

Lo, a meeting with the friend
By having only a remembrance of him, is availed
Hence...the rose feels overjoyed,
With a jubilant face
It starts swinging into the cradle of delight,
The result is –
The reception of the visiting friend occurs by itself.

The flower bathes
The wind with affection,
And
In return of it
The wind moves
The flower with a caressing touch !

Silence for some moments !
Then, the wind utters meekly, that
"You remember me...therefore,
I wish to know the reason thereof,
...So that
I may perform the relevant duties
May fill up myself with virtuous deeds,
And
Only sanctify myself,
No other purpose is there...
Yes !

I should do something for the others also
May become co-operative, helpful,
This sentiment is a pretext,

To advance towards the 'middle', that is,
equanimity,
By making good use of others as medium...
Only, it is the easiest way,
It acts as a purge for aversion and hatred
With which we are filled for the others !"
Upon this intention of the wind
The flower doesn't say even a word,
As a reply to it !,
It keeps on staring at the ground
With a grave face only.
Then,
Being melted by mercy
It turns its eye full of pathos
Towards the Artisan, sitting at a distance far
off...!

Who, what, to talk of others,
Doesn't look even at his own body.

Some seconds slip away, when
The face of the flower
Grows red with anger;
The petal-like lips of leaves
Flutter, with anguish;
With the reddish-yellow eyes –
It looks up at the clouds –
Which, being ungrateful,
Are drowned into the deeds of disputes;
Which are the visible-procreations of hindrances
Which display excitement and anxiety
Towards the life of good emotions,
And
Whose future, a horrible one,
Is only a wreckage of sublime sentiments !

Having seen the different characters
Along with the different modes of feelings
The vomitings, salutations, transmutations!
The turning and changing,
Of the flower, as such
Is sufficient really for the wind.
Yes ! Yes !!
Even the unsaid too is certainly known
To a diligent person
Then...indeed...
For the devotion with self-control
Shall the indistinctness of anything....

Make agitated ?
Everything shall unfold and blossom itself
Before it...without delay !

Thus, the relevant work being really known,
The wind girds up its loin at once
To get it accomplished joyfully.
Making others express their gratitude for the Earth –
While assuming the form of final destruction,
Tells with a sense of wrath –
" O thou wayward clouds !
Try to make good use of your strength,
You shouldn't take advantage of knavery !
No solution can be attained
Through the force of fraud.
You may do a thing or not,
The solution is only the end of grouping,
And that too
At close and closest quarters ! "

□

With the fastest motion like that of intellect
The wind reaches the higher sky sphere,
And takes the chief among the sinful clouds
Into its clutches, encircles them
And
Changes the direction of their facets
Towards the source of inanimate matter,
the ocean...!

Then, with its full force
Pushes them down –

Having raised both his hands a bit up
While planting one of his feet durably on the Earth.
Having pulled one of his legs backwards,
Having Kicked the ball like a boy,
By dint of his heel –
Who stands aloof wonder-struck
So, the wind remains an on – looker.

Now, it how wonderful !
Countless frozen drops of water, along with
the band of clouds
Moving fast headlong,
Fall together Into the ocean,
As the villainous hell-dwellers fall down, –
Leaping into the infernal regions
–On being subjugated by their sinful deeds
–On being entangled with horrible agonies.

□

Hither...
After so many days,
A glimpse of the unhindered cloudless blue sky.
Infused with jubilance into the wind
Filled with joy and zeal,
The Solar Sphere speaks out, that –
" The dignity of the Earth should endure, and
The faith of all of us
Should only flourish deeply into the Earth. "

Each and every atom, each and every particle
The forests, gardens and the winds –
All these have been purged with the lustre of the Sun.

Being unfolded, the buds get blossomed
With the laughters of the winds,
Their splendours mix-up together
In the lanes of the sky,
A new rapture, new colours
A new wave in each of the limbs
A new dawn, hence a new energy
The fresh celebrations, hence fresh adornments,
The new eyes with new reviews
A fresh sprinkling of water a fresh thinking
A fresh shelter hence a fresh selection
A new dieting with new decorations
The new steps, a fresh movement –
The new rituals, the new purifications
The new melody, the fresh pollen,
A new awakening, no escaping
The fresh gestures with fresh satisfaction
The new feelings with new grace
A fresh delight with fresh smiles
Thus, new and fresh this gloriousness.

The fresh welfare with the fresh Sun
A new forest with fresh soil–
A new time-limit with new understanding
A new consciousness with a new guidance
A new condition with a new direction
No falseness, then a new fame
A fresh hunger with a fresh thirst
A fresh nectar, then, fresh vegetarianism

It is new association, new experiment
These are new and newer usages of
the standpoints
The novel art has befitted with the greenery
The new prosperity is more superior
There is a new thrill into new eyelids
There is a new glimpse into a new longing
There are new touches, into the new mansions
Into the new touches, there are new throbbings.

□

Thus, this novel change occurs
Even then,
Where does it leave its impact –
Upon the silently seated Artisan,
That soft fragrant breeze
In spite of blowing constantly,
Remains ineffective.
Where do the rows of hair over the body
Of the Artisan feel thrilled ?
When can that touch
Influence the untouched...?

The fresh fragrance of the rose,
Despite reaching the nostrils of the Artisan,
Can't wake up his nasal sense
These things of worldly enjoyments and luxuries
...When
Can't satisfy
Even a pleasure-seeking enjoyer
Then...indeed...hither –

The ascetic is to be invited
He is to be enchanted for coming out !

Leaving behind their respective nests,
Beholding the bloom of forest while coming out,
Even the warbling of the flock of birds
While running in the series of waves
Couldn't touch the ears of the Artisan,
In absence of their eagerness,
And
It drowned into the empty Space.
That is,
Those ears of the Artisan
Did not become the receivers of the audible
warbling.

In such a special situation
In spite of being at a long distance
The dustless Sun itself, indeed,
Having extended his thousand-fold hands
Tickles the eyelids of the Artisan,
Like the closed petals of a lotus,
With his tender beam-fingers.

Through this tickling, the Artisan feels,
The sweet-loving touch of a mother's sense
of ownness.
The eyes are gaped wide wonder-struck
The glimpse of the abode of light, the Sun,
Becomes the home of unlimited capabilities.
In spite of viewing from a long distance
The tears of joy roll down from the eyes,
And hither...
For bathing and being pacified.
Into the bright drizzle of devotion

These particles of Earth feel desirously eager,
Thus, the whole of the surroundings drown
Into contacts, into visits,
Into rejoicings and keen eagerness !

□

On seeing the Artisan regaining
His healthy condition, the pitcher said,
That
The attainment of heaven and final 'Salvation'
Has never been nor shall be achieved
Without severe vexations and calamities
(*Parīṣaha* and *Upasarga*)
It is an eternal truth !

At the mature Faith of an immature pitcher
Which appears like the tacit devotion of
an ascetic devotee
The Artisan feels amazed,
And he says–
"I don't expect that
You shall be so successful
Within such a short period.
Before the hard and perfect devotion
Even the eminent devotees too
Have been found here
Breathing heavily, while kneeling down on
their knees !

Now I am fully confident,
That
The complete success would be achieved in future also,
Even then, your journey now onwards–

Is only crossing over the primitive valley,
The series of the valleys is still awaited !
And...listen !
You have to pass through even the river of fire,
And that too without a boat !
Yes ! O yes !!
Swimming off with your own strength of arms,
The coast can't be reached without swimming."

On hearing this, the pitcher adds, that
"Before the deep-insight of the devotee
No difference does remain
Between the water and the inflammable fire.
The journey towards perfect ascetic devotion
Proceeds, all along and ought to proceed,
indeed
From diversity to unity
From the perceptible to the imperceptible
Otherwise,
That journey is merely worth its name
The journey has not yet been commenced."
These few lines of the pitcher
Proved to be very vital
Very impressive.... .

□

CANTO : FOURTH

The Fiery Ordeal
The Silvery Ashes

Hither the heart of the Earth
Has shaken, has moved,
The lips of the Earth have trembled
That thing named 'fortitude'
Is found nowhere.

Whether it is that of an indulgent one, or
that of an ascetic,
Nobody's intellect can be of any avail.
The outward fertility of the Earth
The fruit-bearing power shall be swept away
Where shall it go, is not known...?
Generally it has been heard, that
Only scanty gifts are obtained
By the earthly beings from the heavenly
bodies,
They get plentiful of blows !
What can a worldly person bestow upon a
sage ?
What shall an ascetic get from an
impassioned one ?
And
It has not only been heard,
it has been found often
That
Before the holy rituals and self-discipline
Not only intemperance, but Yama, the Lord
of Death, too
Comes down upon his knees,
The heavenly bodies, the gods and devils
Have to concede their defeat !

Today, the potter's kiln is observed
With a cursory glance, now.
Without delay, within a certain period
The pitcher (*kumbha*) has to be entered into
the potter's kiln,
And
The potter's kiln is being made neat and clean.

Inside the downward portion of the kiln
The huge, knotty, zigzag
Logs of acacia tree
Having a blackish bark
Are placed carefully one upon the other,
And they
Are being supported
With the sticks of margosa
Having a reddish-yellow bark.
The sticks similar to those of the pine-tree
Which catch the spark instantly,
Are spread amid empty spots,
The smoothened timber pieces of
the tamarind tree too
Which get inflammed slowly
Have been erected around
At the brink of the circular pot-kiln
And
The batch of the pitchers has been arranged
Exactly in the middle of the Kiln.

On behalf of all the timber-pieces
The sticks of the acacia tree, with the choked throat,
Unfold their ultimate inner agony
Before the Artisan,
And

Its woe-begone posture
Ventures to say something, that
" Our nature is hard since the very birth
We have been the pieces of timber
Almost reaching the ground, we have been touching it,
The pan of our sins has become heavy.

At a very far-off distance...behind us,
The 'Compass' of moral merits has been
separated from us,
Not only the distance of the region
But also the distance of the time has occurred
Between the righteous conduct
And this degraded life...

Often we have been moulded into
The hard to the harder canes
For punishing the culprits.
Generally, the defaulters escaped punishment
While the innocents were put to beating,
And, while beating them every now and then,
We were broken into pieces.
How can we call it to be a democracy ?
This is simply an aristocracy,
Or
It is a despotic rule or autocracy !

The fruit-extract of this impropriety
We also have to relish,
And
This yearning, which has been started
To burn the innocent pitcher
By making us as its efficient cause–

One more link of a murder –
Is being interlinked with this life.
Now the bitter sip can't be swallowed up
The suffering has overbrimmed the throat,
Now, really, there is no empty space left inside,
Whether it is a draught of the poison
Or that of the nectar
For some time, the nectar too
Isn't going to leave its effect
Upon this life !
Which, while dwelling within the poisonous
surroundings,
Has itself become poison-like.

'Due to the delay beyond expectation
The injustice not as justice, but
The justice does appear to be injustice indeed'.
And this is what happens
To it, in this age."

The tongue of the staggering stick
Again speaks out while moving with a jerk –
" Not by harassing the weak,
But only by saving them through providing strength
and help –
The strength of the strong proves its worth."

On hearing this and without being agitated,
The Artisan utters
The sugarcandy-mixed sweet wordings
With his tender affectionate tongue, that
"While uptaking the down-trodden from
the ground
His hand may ache,
It is none of the fault of the uptaker, –

The lack of strength to rise up is the flaw, really
Yes, yes !
In that suffering, the uptaker is regarded as an
efficient cause
Only, in this context, it is exactly the point.
The life of the pitcher has to be uplifted,
And
For this work
You yourself have to be the efficient cause
And none else."

Thus, on hearing the words of the Artisan,
While taking a pretence of hesitation and shyness,
As if expressing its internal assent –
Almost like that of a woman before a man–
Moving a bit of its neck,
The wood-stick says that –

" The relevant point has been grasped and missed
partially,
Even then, keeping in view your liberality,
Where is the courage in it
To put aside what you say ?"...and
For that relevant auspicious performance,
Acceptance is extended from the side of
the timber-piece !

So...
Having pressed once and again upon the
mouth of the kiln
The crystallized ashes and soil
Are spread over in such a manner, that
Even the sound of the external wind
Can't enter the pot-kiln now...!
On the northern side of the kiln –

There is a tiny doorway in the lower part
Approaching that doorway, the Artisan,
Having remembered the eternal supreme soul,
Chants the holy incantation –
'*Navakāra Mantra*' [73] in nine rounds;
And
With a small burning stick,
The fire is awakened into the kiln,
But
Within a few seconds, the fire
gets extinguished.
Again, at once
It is kindled
Again it is extinguished instantly !

This activity of fire being kindled and being
extinguished
Went on repeatedly,...then
The Artisan again, in a friendly language,
Speaks out to the wood-stick :

" It seems,
The assent for co-operation couldn't be
obtained fully
At present, in this auspicious deed,
Otherwise
This obstruction won't have stood in the way !"
At this, the wood-stick again tells
With the gentle wordings of welcome, that
'No, no...this hindrance
Hasn't been projected from my side !
Assent does mean...assent…
Dedication does imply...dedication…

Do what you say, say what you think,
By deed, word and thought
The uniform conduct, the one and the same only–
It's here that the current of conscious
attentiveness flows !

And listen,
Here the obstructive cause is indeed different,
It is the fire itself.
I do myself want to be burnt off
But,
The fire doesn't wish to set me on fire
The reason thereof is known to it only."

□

In what words should I entreat the fire,
Shall it give me a hearing ?
Shall the enlightening effect of this heart
Touch and impress it ?
Shall the burning turn itself into water,
Shall its thirst get itself quenched ?
What, if it does frown upon me...?
Pondering thus, the suspicious Artisan
Kindles the fire once again.

Lo, the burning fire adds thus :
" I acknowledge the fact that
None has attained liberation till to-day
Without the ordeal of passing through the fire,
Nor shall it indeed be achieved in future too.
When, in this connection, thus goes the law
Then, what !

Shall the ordeal of fire itself not take place ?
Who shall put me to test– the fire or the water ?

To examine ourself on our own touchstone
Is so easy...but
It is very difficult to take the right decision,
Because,
'The ruddiness of our own eyes
Isn't visible to us'.
One added point too is there, that
The life, which has become
A touchstone for others
Should act as a touchstone also for itself,
It isn't an inevitable rule.
In such a situation, generally,
Having taken a false decision indeed,
One has to affirm himself
In the rank of a testimony...therefore,
It's not possible in the life of the fire.

'The life moulded into
The cast of magnanimity and virtuous conduct
Is regarded by me the true touchstone of myself.'
Then, far from really burning the pitcher,
Even to think of burning it
Is taken by me as a curse, a sin, dear Artisan !
...Well, then !"

On hearing the words spoken out above,
The pitcher tells the fire from within the kiln
With a sense of humility and conciliation, that
" To do a favour unto the mannerly persons–

Is to make good use of
Naturally obtained strength, is religiousness.
And,
Not to chastise the wicked ones
Is to misuse the power, is irreligious !
I'm not a faultless one
I'm a treasure-house of sins
I'm filled up with those faults.

Until they are burnt off
I can't be faultless.
You have been entrusted with the power to burn
Where am I asking you
To make me inflammed ?
Let my faults be burnt off !

To turn my evils into ashes
Is to make me live indeed
To burn away the faults of our own 'self'
And those of the others
Has been acknowledged by the saints
–As a supreme religious performance.
The faults are inanimate elements,
Are the by-products of some accidental cause,
Arrive somehow from outside;
The virtuous merits belong to Soul,
Such merits deserve reception.
You shall attain the most sublime Truth through this deed,
This life shall be infused with a true purpose by you,
I possess the capability of retaining water
Which is awaiting you,
Your co-operation is inevitable
For its perfect expression." □

The fire comes to know the purpose of the pitcher
Lo, the face of the Potter-artisan looks delighted !
Having manifested itself fully
And being transformed completely
Into the sense of hope and faith,
The mark of despair on the face of the Artisan
Brightens as active, and not indolent.

Lo, within the winking of the eye,
The fire goes ablaze with a crackling sound
While encircling the whole of the Kiln
within its stretch
And gathering up all the tiny and big logs
Inside its belly !

The kiln spits out entirely
The bullets of lamp-black smoke,
like the dense, thundering, frightful –
Cloudiness in the month of *Āṣāḍha.*[74]
Around the kiln
A circular space of about thirty or forty yards
Became devoid of light...so
It appeared, as if
The darkish huge hellish stratus
Is somewhere spreading out
The stark darkness over and above itself !
The Artisan peeps out through
The smoky insurgent zone,
The very kiln is sighted nowhere –
So horrible is the prevailing external
situation there
Then, what mention of the internal one !

The entire kiln is filled with smoke
The smoke is whirling around wildly into the kiln.–

Like the whirlwind of final destruction of the world,
Nothing else,
Only smoke...smoke...smoke...!
Consequently hither
The Potter–artisan's head is whirling
No mention of how does the pitcher do !

The smoke and only the smoke is
Blocking up the mouth of the pitcher,
The belly, the eyes, the ears
And the holes of the nose as well,
Not the tears but the life-breath; that is,
The vitality, is going to breathe its last;
But
The smoke which is entering inside from outside
Doesn't permit the life-breath to break off;
Due to the pungent smell of the smoke
The nose-nerve of the pitcher is almost dead.
Even then !
Having utilized the full capacity of the nose,
While taking the medium of supplementary process,
After filling the belly with the smoke,
The pitcher observes the Yogic process
Of suspending breath in *Prāṇāyāma,* that is, *Kumbhaka*[75]
Which is a most effective means
In accomplishing the meditation,
Which is the root of the healing tree of asceticism.

□

Does our digestive fire of stomach have
The capacity to digest the fire itself
And not merely the food-stuffs, –

To make this point clear
The pitcher starts eating up the smoke.
During the period of smoke-eating
The tongue of the pitcher doesn't feel distaste
Therefore...
The smoke isn't vomited.
The reason behind vomiting is nothing else,
But the internal dislike only.
It only signifies that
The non-vomiting of sensual passions and dirty emotions
Indicates the presence of deeper inclinations
For them into one's mind.

Little by little, now !
The uprise of the smoke stopped
The brightness of the smokeless fire
Starts gleaming inside the sphere of the kiln.
Even the rosy radiance of the purified gold
Is subdued
By the inward glorious beauty of the kiln–
On this day and by this time
The warmth of the fire has manifested itself
Cent-per-cent.

Through the touches of the fire
The bodily brilliance of the pitcher has burnt off
And
It's getting itself drooped into faintness
While
Its soul being gradually enlightened
Is about to plunge into natural peace…

The inner-feeler of the pitcher asks the
pitcher itself
– What type of touch is it ?
The pitcher replied–it is the purest touch
Its experience
Isn't possible without observing austerities
and penance.
In this very context, even the tongue
of the pitcher
Declares the point, that –
'The fire is fully devoid of the sense of taste'–
This settled opinion held by some of
the wise ones
Is hampered by experience and inference.
When the smoke can be tasted
Why, then
The taste-organ would fail in tasting the fire ?
Yes ! O yes !!
– The flavour can be relished through that
very tongue
Which has risen not only above the instinct
to live,
But also above the fear of death.

The man overpowered by the taste-organ, tongue –
Can never be acquainted with
The genuine taste of any thing indeed,
On mixing the boiled rice with milk
Only the taste of the admixture is felt,
And not that of the milk and the boiled rice separately,
Then, On blending with the sugar candy…too –
The exact taste of all the three stuffs is undone !

The lean and thin nose of the pitcher
Which faints due to the choking by the smoke,
Now, as if supporting the declaration by the tongue
In absence of the sense of suffocation,

Is eager to smell
The fair fragrance of the fire.

The eyes of the pitcher seemed to be closed
They seemed to be blinded due to smoke
Now they have unfolded themselves,
Due to the lustrous devotion of the sublime fire
Due to the receding and cleaning of darkness
Due to the uprise of the reddish *lotus-friend*,[76]
As if the lotuses were burst into blooming.

The first sight of the pitcher viewed
The immutable and smokeless fire.
For some different vision
No other scene was really, found
The viewer extended his eye in all the directions.
The one and the same scene was found all-around
The fire...the fire...the fire…!

□

– The different types of all the timber-pieces –
Where they have been found now, as before !
Having assimilated the fire,
All of them have drunk it deep, indeed…!
Or, to put it otherwise, –
Having given birth to fire,
They were themselves immersed into the fire.

Everything, which gives birth to some particular feelings,
Gets itself effaced by those very feelings,
It is merged therein.
This integration and disintegration of the sentiments

Is naturally self-dependent
And
Having neither a beginning nor an end...!

On seeing the Pitcher
Active to show his developing sensibility
Along with the joy and favourableness of his mind,
The fire itself tells about its own excess,
With a sense of some hesitation, that
" At present, there is no excess in my further movement.

And listen !
To touch the finis of the excess is very far off
...At present, it is something very distant !

My ignition makes one
...Remember the cool water,
My ignition makes one
...Taste the bitter collyrium,
It is a rule that,
In the first step, the woe and hard-work
...Is unkind,
My ignition makes every one
...Drink the water afterwards,
For this reason...to have a sense of forgiveness... the bestowal of pardon–
Is the virtuous conduct of a devotee–
Is to rest into righteousness...!"

On hearing these lines
The strength of the pitcher is invigorated,
The steps of enthusiasm feel a new vitality,
And it speaks out that –

'The attainment of the desired results indeed,
Has been acknowledged the limit of the
endeavours' –
– This saying is retained in my memory.
That is the reason why,
This wayfarer doesn't know
To take rest on the way.
Pray to God–again a requisition
For an unique strength !

Not only the longing for sensual gratifications,
But even that for liberation
Isn't there within this Pitcher
There is no concern for repeated applauds
In the moments of praise.
Let me immerse into the stream of feverish heat,
But,
Even a ripple of sigh
Should never arise
Into this pitcher...in severe troubles.
Let the darkness of the universe should come
And fill its each and every limb,
Each and every nerve–
There is nothing to be worried for,
But, through the sense of a reverse order of words–,
That is to say,
'*Tāmasa*',[77] that is 'ignorance'... '*Samatā...*,' that is,
'equanimity'!

O Lord, listen a bit more...!
It has been bored up fully
With the sway of personality,

And
It has fully immersed into
The power of dutifulness,
Now
Only a silent smile isn't enough,
It wishes indeed,
From your joyous face,
Your holy utterings, O Lord !

– From the compass of consequences
From the fascinating durations
Now it
Desires to keep himself away, O Lord !
Beyond the charms of beauty and juices
Beyond the charms of fragrance and touch
It wants to make its own creation, O Lord !
Having *no* 'alloy'[78a] with it of worldly possessions
Having *no* '*rusted element*' [78b] of alien feelings
thoughts and deeds.
Now, *the* genuine *iron*[78c]
Tries to be only immersed
Into the flames of meditation, my Lord !"

□

On hearing about the earnest prayer to Lord,
The complete identification of the pitcher,
The point of absorption into the meditation,
The point of the path of knowledge,
The fire interrupts to say :
" I remember from time immemorial,
Am acquainted with very many persons
Have moved in the company of saints and hermits !

To observe meditation
And
To converse with meditation
Between these two there is a vast difference
It is not possible to be absorbed in meditation
By simply starting the centres of meditation.

Lo, a new-fashioned depiction
In the context of meditation !
Some lines are as follows :

'Two human beings
Of the modern age
Wish to get absorbed
Themselves –
By the first one
The sensual enjoyments
The drinking of wine
Is selected;
While the other one
Practises
Austerities and renouncement,
Profound self-meditation.
Within a few moments
Both of them
Are freed from their options,
What to say, then ?
The first one is lying alone
Like a dead-body,
While the other one
Has proved his worth
Like that of auspicious Śiva.'

From the gifted thinkers, philosophers
Even the metaphysicians
Aren't generally obtained
Such utterings, mellowed by experience...,
Which reached the ears that day through the fire.

Thinking thus, the pitcher,
For achieving the undeniability of philosophy
And,
The fathomlessness of spiritualism,
Entreats the fire again :
Are philosophy and spiritualism
The two steps of one and the same life ?
Are they connected with the sense of the
adored and the adorer ?
If...they are, then...
Which one is the adorer and which one
the adored ?
Are they connected
With the sense of cause and effect ?
If...they are...then...
Which one is the effect and which one the cause ?
Between them
Which one is expressive and which one silent ?
Wherefrom does the fragrance of meditation erupt ?
Which one smells it
With its clever nose ?
Through whom the liberation is attained ?
Through whom the contentment is achieved ?

This Age ought to hear
Only the thorough investigation of these both !

Hereat, the discourse of the fire starts :
Therefore...you listen :
" The source of philosophy is the head,
The spring of spiritualism flows from
The heart marked with fylfot.
The spiritual life can move on –
Does, indeed, move without philosophy
But, yes !
Without spiritualism,
No appearance of philosophy is there.
Without waves, a tank
May exist, does exist, indeed,
But yes !
There can be no wave without a tank.
Spiritualism is an independent eye
Philosophy is a dependent second-eye,
In philosophy, there is no vision of
the Supreme Soul
'Reality' and 'Non-reality'
Revolve around the philosophy
That is, the philosophy, at times, assumes the Truth
And, at times, it assumes falsehood,
While, the spiritualism, always
Radiates in the form of Truth and
the Supreme Spirit.

The right knowledge of the 'Self' is spiritualism.
The life of philosophy
Is engrossed with various resolves and options.
An extrovert or a versatile genius only
Drinks at the fount of philosophy,
An introvert silent halo of intuition
Sings the Songs of the, path of salvation / Eternal Soul.

The weapon-word of philosophy is–'thought',
The spiritualism is weaponless
Entirely stilled, devoid of thoughts !
The one is knowledge, the knowable too,
The other is meditation, the 'meditated upon' too.

A swimmer swims into a tank –
Not the inward,
But the outward scenes indeed come to his sight.
At that very place, the other one takes a dip,
The inner portion of the tank
Is discernible to him,
The contact with the outer world is suspended."

How excellent, bravo, well done !
What a deep dive is it !
The investigation of philosophy and spiritualism !
And
The fire earns an eulogy from the pitcher.

What happened thereafter, please…listen !
The fire got kindled extraordinarily,
As if accepting the eulogy.
That morning breeze
With a heartening coolness
May well blow outside,

But,
It didn't leave any imprint upon the Kiln !
The ratio of temperature is growing on
The day in and the day out,
There remained no difference
Between the sharp heat, and the day-break.

In these days, where can be found
The time which changes its countenance
In a convulsive manner ?
Amid the kiln, the division of time
Has really come to a standstill
Only, there is a constant flow of unbroken and
indivisible time !

□

In this very context
All of a sudden
A flattering refrain of sound from within the Kiln...
Like that of a wanton wanderer –
...O thou wayfarer, hark !
It has been a continuous flow of a river –
The constant flow of time, indeed,
It glides on and on.
Lo,
While gliding forth
It is muttering, that
" This life of the sentient or the insentient beings
Is gushing off
Is floating away
Into this stream, every second,
Here, no one
Has ever been, shall be or was
Constant - permanent - everlasting –
The flow of the current
Has only been perpetual,
It has really been –

The mystery of existence
Which is still laughing around."

□

O my goodness, what is this hither ?
The period of some sudden agony...!
Wherefrom is being emitted
The voice of humble entreaty ?
Whose voice is it,
For what reason,
For whose search does it set itself out ?

Is it the voice of a male or that of a female,
Does it represent a boy or a girl ?
Definitely, it is not that of a man,
Because, proportionately,
It is resounding into the ears softly enough.
Ultimately, what does it mean ?
Its clarity and display
Has now…been evident, therefore...

" O Mother-Earth !
Isn't it the aggrieved voice of a child, –
Which infuses the heart with compassion
for the offspring,
Reaching your ears ?
The destination still being beyond access,
There is no hope even for some water on
the way !
What about the story of fruits and flowers,
Here…indeed…
The paucity even of shade is sustained –

Don't push me into the jaws of death !
By arousing the expectations for
the future brightness
Don't spread darkness in the present !
Now this heat is beyond forbearance,
The lack of tolerance is
Gradually making its headway into it.
Don't burn off this life
Fetching the cool water, make it drink it !
Re-vitalize it, O Mother !"

When, from the side of the mother Earth,
Even the assurances and blessings aren't bestowed
Then, having remembered the Artisan,
The pitcher said –
" Have all the means of protection
Departed somewhere else ?
Being the doer and fosterer of the pitcher
Have you too have forgotten it ?
Now these life-breaths
Won't be able to honour any one
Without some drinking water.
That is,
Their departure is sure and certain
Now they can no more enter into a fire-test,
Any vow, even an insignificant one,
Is appearing to them as tough as the mount Meru,
The faith has almost been shattered,
No trace of curiosity for future life has almost
left its mark.

Alas, that
Now I am Pondering –

Without quenching our own thirst,
The resolve to cause the others to drink water
Is mere fancy,
Is bare boasting."

Having listened to the entreaty of the pitcher
Almost turned towards weeping,
The liberal, large and troubled heart,
Of the Artisan too
Is pondering
Over its grave condition,
Over the excess of pain of that heart.

And,
To vitalize the pitcher with the life-breath
of patience,
For warding off its hunger and thirst,
The Artisan goes towards the Kiln
With some refreshment
When, at once, the Artisan's deep sleep
is broken,
And that
Dreaming posture is abandoned !

□

Thus,
Where can the dreams be visualized
Whenever they are wished for !
That...is...why, at first,
The Artisan feels like laughing at his dreamy condition,
Thereafter, his eyes
Go on growing grave –

The eyes in which
Not only the elapsed life of the past
But also the present life, like a dream,
Floats in a hazy manner,
And
All the future, the probable, the suspected –
In toto, everything
Reflects as smoky, hoary
And somewhat cumbersome.

After taking repose from the morning prayers,
The Artisan, on stepping out, views –
The golden sunshine of the morn is seen
Which is sliding
Over the cheeks of the Earth;
Before the early morning since the very dawn
His heart has become impatient,
He has to undertake a survey
Of the Kiln today !

The pitcher passes through the fire-test
And
The fire itself is put to an ordeal,
There is not only some hope, but full confidence
About the cent-per-cent results,
Even then, where does the mind keep up restraint,
And…when ?
The dream visualized is, indeed, out of accord...!
On seeing the steps of the Artisan moving towards it,
The kiln itself speaks out on behalf of the pitcher :
" O Mr. Artisan Sir !

The dreams are generally unavailing
To confide too much in them is harmful.

> ‘*Swa*’, that is, our own ‘self’
> ‘*P*’, that is, ‘breeding-securing’
> And
> ‘*Na*’, that is ‘not’, –
> That which can’t secure the sense of our own ‘self’
> How shall it be of any help to others ?
> Connected with the past
> Departed from the intimate associate –
> The mind, entangled indeed with so many worries,
> The threads of awakening are left behind in a
> dreamy condition
> Self-realization is not possible then,
> Even the accomplished incantation
> falls ineffective.”

Thus, having heard the voice of the Kiln,
That Artisan, now,
Approaches nearer the Kiln,
But,
Where is being heard
The shrieks of the pitcher ?…
Where is being asked
The begging from the Artisan ?

Neither the tortures of the pitcher
Nor the entreaties by the pitcher
Only the pitcher itself...there at the spot…then !
Where are the vital life-breaths pained by thirst ?
Where is that sorrow
Where are those bewailings –

Where is that ailment
Where is that face
And where is
That mansion of flames ?
Which
These ears, these eyes
And these hands
Had heard, seen and touched in dreams ?
The dream comes out untrue in the real sense of the word,
The deadly result of the dream passes away.

□

'The well-being of the pitcher reflects our own well-being';
– Having remarked thus, the Potter–artisan
Welcomes joyfully the Kiln,
And
The heap of the dusty ashes,
Which has gathered upon the chest of the kiln
Is removed by him with a spade in hand.
The more the ashes get out of the way,
The more the curiosity of the Potter–artisan
Grows as to
When that proficient pitcher should come in view...

Lo, now it comes to sight !
The hue of the ashes, the limb of the pitcher –
Both of them as one, are together,
These eyes are unable to recognize truly –
After being burnt into the flames gradually,
The body of the pitcher has assumed its shape
As that of a dark night.

The intensive sufferings have been undergone,
The highest disaster has been faced
Despite being caught into the jaws of death
Having fared a narrow escape, the pitcher
comes out safe.
Of grief and pain, of hellish noise and tumult
The Artisan has a feeling,
On having a look upon the body of the pitcher,
Of happy display, of dignity –
On seeing the test-results.
And
On discerning *the fluent essential element*[79]
The Artisan experienced
Neither surprise nor pride,
But,
By weighing a thing on the balance of time
The outcome which is arrived at,
– That too, is fully evident
Upon his mental level !

The future of the pious personality
Shall remain pious, indeed,
But,
The past...history of that pious one –
Shall remain a laughing stock, even after it
concludes –
Impure...Impure...Impure.

□

Today has come out of the Kiln
The safe and sound pitcher.
Like that of the body of Shri Krishna,
A bluishness is emanating from it,

It seems to appear as if
All the jumble of inner vices
On being burnt off
Has emerged out,
There is no protection in life for sins now,
When does a sinner
Make a thirsty being
Even to drink water ?

On the face of the pitcher, there reflects joy as that of a
liberated soul
As if, while swimming constantly, the other extremity
Of the endless, ocean of existence has been reached.
Where is the applied consciousness of the pitcher
Towards its scorched body ?
It is the introspection which is transpiring inwardly....!
When does the large black bee
Is found unhappy ?
Its body too is dark black indeed,
Although it is found always busy with gathering honey !

Only by being into a body
The bodily perceptions aren't necessarily gained,
Illusions aren't born
Due to merely dwelling into illusory worldliness,
The sense of attachment and longing too
Is inevitable for them.

□

The Artisan, having a cautious approach towards the Kiln
One by one, in an orderly manner,

Taking them up on the palm,
Is placing the pitchers on the earth.
Of the Earth was, is and shall remain
This soil.
But formerly it was into the lap of the Earth,
While today, it dwells upon the chest of the earth
In the appearance of the pitcher.
Whether it is outward or inward,
A wave of music is flowing out
From each and every limb of the pitcher,
And
These spheres of earth and sky
Are floating into that song.

Lo, even two or three days only weren't gone
When the pitcher was brought out of the kiln
The gush of noble sentiments within its mind
Is indicating to all that,
There is now no falling down only uprising…
Progressive upgrading, uplifting,
The unfolding of the fortune
Of a new future-harvest...!
Enough,
Now, nothing is beyond its reach
Everything present within…the eye-view !

The true devotion of a devotee draws
Even God towards his side,
That sentiment is –

Alms to a worthy personage, hospitality to a guest.
But,
The personage should be deserving and pious
Should be a traveller on foot, using his palms as
his vessels
A nectar-taker, a liberated soul a great ascetic with
divine powers,
Hard upon himself like a thunder-bolt
For the others, as soft and mild…
As butter…, and
Should be experiencing
His own pain in the pain of the others'
His own playfulness in the eulogy to God.
Free from all snares of sin
Fully, without bondage, like air,
Afraid of dependence,
Like a mirror, devoid of arrogance
Humble like a tree –
Green, grown-up, under perfect fruition.
Like the flow of a river, Towards his destination
Undeterred, unwearied...dynamic.

For whom regard and disregard is similar,
Firm like the Mount Meru, while observing penance,
Like an honest cow while providing functional
consciousness,
Who lives beyond worldly ambitions
Attains excellence only in the
Investigation of Supreme Reality;
Should be the merit–seeker
And not the fault-finder
Who never tells heavily upon
The opposing foes,

Never feels puffed up
With the favourable friends,
And
Never pines for
Fame, glory and gain.

Not cruel, but as fearless as a lion,
No demand from any corner for alms,
As benevolent as the Sun
Never expects some return
Even by mistake,
Who attains victory over sleep and the sense-organs,
Well-intentioned like a water-reservoir.
Modest in diet, benevolent moderate counsellor,
One of those, who are desirous of the jewel of
Supreme Soul;
Who, for the cleansing of his own drawbacks
Should be self-critical,
What to talk of censuring the others...
Whose ears are never eager
Even to hear the calumny of others
...As if they have turned deaf
Despite being
The renowned, the strong-minded and an ascetic
Whose tongue turns mute
In the context of his own applause.

Whose
Winter night passes
On the shores of a sea, a river, or a lake,
Thereafter...

The summer-days pass upon the high hills
Under the shining shadow of the Sun.

Thus ! the pitcher promotes its feelings
Therefore, 'sacred sentiments are the saviours from worldly-bondage'
–This saying by the sages
Has to accomplish the very meaning, indeed,
Hence, it proves its purport…to be valid.

□

Lo, hither...that
The eminent trader of the city dreams that
He, himself
In his own courtyard
With an auspicious pitcher of soil into his hands
Receives a great saint, seeking holy alms.
Wakes up from his sleep, at dawn,
Regards himself as a blessed one
And
Thanks his dream,
Tells the gist of the dream to his family.
One of the servant is sent to the pot-maker
To bring back a pitcher,
The servant communicates what his master tells him,
On hearing it, the Potter–artisan says delightfully :

"Our vital energy sustains us
Our labours prove to be fruitful
And
We come out as successful."

On seeing the Artisan rejoicing
The attendant feels still more pleased,

Holding up the pitcher into one hand,
When he starts examining the pitcher,
Sounding it carefully once and again
With a pebble caught into the other hand...
The pitcher speaks out with a note of surprise–
" Despite the fiery ordeal
Does any more test and inspection still remain ?
Take, take the test !
You are examining the others
Examine...a bit of yourself, indeed !
Take your own test now !
Sounding yourself carefully, have a check-up of
your own 'self',
What voice springs up there –
Listen to it with your own ears !
Is it the absurd crowing of a crow
or
A donkey's outcry in its fifth tone ?

It is compulsory to pass the examination,
Before becoming an examiner,
Otherwise
The one shall make himself a laughing stock."

Hearing this, the attendant replies with courtesy –
" It's true, that
You appear at the fire-test,
But
The test which is furnished to you by the fire,
Is proper upto what extent –
This judgment
Isn't possible without putting you to test.
That is,

Utilizing you as an efficient cause
I'm putting the fire itself to the fire-test through you.

The other point is that
I'm not only an attendant to a master
But
I'm also the owner of some commodities
Essential to life, and their user as well.

Through the business of the things
Through their give and take only,
Their real test can't be undertaken –
The viewpoint being that of monetary gain;
While
According to the customer's view
The true, value of a thing consists in its utility.
That utility indeed makes a man–the consumer –
Enjoy comfort for some moments."
Hence, he has come as a customer
And
After holding up the pitcher in his hand,
The attendant sounds it seven times .
As the first strain
The note '*sā*' swells out from the pitcher
Then, continuously, in a series,
Re...ga...ma...pa...dha...ni...[80]
Having gushed out, unfolds
The unimpassioned destiny regulations full of feelings
Like that of the imperishable strains.
In toto, the sense prevails –

Sā...re...ga...ma,[81a] that is,
All types of afflictions
Pa...dha, that is, the essential quality –
And,
Ni, that is, 'not', –
–Affliction can never be an essential quality of Soul,
It is only the degenerating after-effect contrary
to the real nature
Of the soul, under the bondage of the kārmic nature
of delusion.

The dispositions, produced due to some special
reason are *somehow*[81b] alien,
From a particular point of view, that is '*kathanchit*',
To comprehend, indeed, the sense of these
seven notes of gamut
Is to be rapt with the true music
Is to obtain a true companion.

Where from did the pitcher attain
Such a power, thinking thus, the attendant
Gets an answer from the pitcher
That

"All this craftsmanship is the creation of the Artisan,
The result of genuine devotion and purification,
Special efforts and firm resolve.
And, hark,
This body of mine
Which has turned blackish as a dark cloud
Hasn't...really...burnt away.
Just as
A craftsman skilled in the art of musical instruments
Applies dark ink on the mouth-top of a timbrel,
In the same manner
The Artisan has applied dark ink
Upon each and every limb of my body,
And the different notes of the gamut

Unfold
The mysteries of Nature and Soul,
(*Prakṛti* and *puruṣa*) –
Through the touch and friction of the palm of hand
Along with the middle finger, –
Dhā...dhin...dhin...dhā...[82a]
Dhā...dhin...dhin...dhā...
Different are those bodies different the vital consciousness
Tā...tin... tin...tā...[82b]
Tā...tin...tin...tā...
Why worry for the body...why worry for the body...?
Beat...beat...exactly thus !

The attendant who arrives as a customer
Feels astonished
His mind was enchanted
His body under the magic-spell is wonder-struck
At the figure of the pitcher
And
Upon the amazing craftsmanship of the Artisan.
What to say, if
There is an union
Of the marvel of the Supreme Spirit with the Supreme Knowledge !
The worries of perception, their agonizing effects
Fade away, being demolished, within seconds,
Not somewhere outside–
The wave of the reservoir rests beck into the reservoir itself.

□

The pitcher is examined
Again it is inspected, then...

The attendant selects pitchers
One or two small, and one or two big in size
And
An attempt is made to put the proper money
As the price
Into the hands of the craftsman
When
The Artisan speaks out –

" It is the day of charity to-day
And not that of the give and take, the interchange,
It is the preventive measure for all the miserable days –
The gateway for the auspicious days !

We have to honour now –
Not the shell, but the pearl
Not the lamp, but the flame !
Forgetting the soul, we get allured by the body
Discarding the religiousness, we swing with the money
An unlimited time-span is frittered away
Under this very snare of worldly illusion,
Now only the nearness with the imperishable Soul
Has to be established,
Has only to be composed within our own 'self' !

Somehow or other,
The gold has its value
The silver has its value
Whether it is a particle or forty seras, i.e., a 'mana'
Each and everything, indeed, has its value,
But,
The value of money in itself –

Is nothing at all.
Only the basic object
Is valuable indeed.
Money is really none of the fundamental things
The life of the money begs dependence –
An imaginary existence, it is meant for the others !

Yes ! yes !!
The prices of the other things
May be evaluated by the money
That too, according to the need,
At times more, at times less,
And at times in a formal way –
And all this
Depends upon the rich.

The rich and the poor –
Both of these
Can't evaluate even in a dream
The exact price of a thing,
Because,
A poor man is generally pitiable and inferior,
And,
The wealthy person –
Blind with sensuality, a slave to wantonness !!"

The amount then wasn't granted
Even as a gift,
The attendant, with due respect,
Extended thanks to Artisan in place of money
And
Started on his way home joyfully, with the pitcher !

□

Stepping down from his seat
The eminent trader too, joyfully,
Holds out the pitcher in his own hand
From the hand of the cheerful attendant,
And
He washes it himself thoroughly
With the fresh cool water !

Then, holding the pitcher into his left hand ,
Marks the fylfot, a symbol of one's own 'Self',
By his ring-finger of the right hand
On all the four sides around the pitcher,
With the lovely sandalwood from the Mount Malaya–
Cherishing the only feeling
That everyone should accomplish his own 'Self'.
And
Inside all the four petals of the each of the fylfot,
With the sandalwood, mingled with
Kashmīra–saffron,
Spotted four round drops each,
Which are telling the world, that
All the four worldly courses of transmigration of soul[83a]
Are devoid of real happiness.
In the same manner,
On the head of *every fylfot*[83b]
'*Omkāra*'[83c] is writ large, along with a dot within
a crescent
For the steadfastness of penance and divine devotion.
The meditation of ascetics
More often dwells firmly upon this base.

The throat of the pitcher is adorned
With the two thin streaks of turmeric,
The streaks, amid which –

The covering of rouge is worth seeing !
The turmeric, rouge, saffron and sandalwood
Make the surroundings charming and pleasing
With their odour.

Soft, lovely, having an uniform group
With a green smile –
Digestive for the food-stuffs and drinkables,
Four or five eatable betel-leaves,
Are placed around the mouth of the pitcher.
Like the petals of a blossomed lotus,
Whose frontal tops are peeping outside
And
Amid them, to tickle them,
Is placed a coconut,
On which turmeric and saffron were sprinkled.
On this occasion,
The *Śrīfala* (coconut) tells the betel-leaves, that
"Our body is hard
Yours is the soft one, and
This hardness won't suit you.

Uptil now
This body has really been relishing the softness,
But,
It was, then, the way of the world
Isn't this path contrary to it !
Isn't there the triumph of Soul here !
The relation of this path
Isn't with the body,
The body is secondary, the Sentient Being or
Consciousness is desirable.

There is a resemblance here between the soft and the hard.
And
How tender is
This heart of ours,
Is your external body
Soft in such a measure ?

Enough of it,
peep a bit into us,
The true cognizance of softness and hardness
Is obtained by touching the heart
And not the body."

All the coirs of the coconut were removed,
Only a crest of hair is stretched up overhead
Into which, a blooming open fragrant rose
Has been decorated.

Everybody's crests of hair overhead
Are generally downcast,
But
That of the coconut is upcast.
It might be so,
Hence the offering of a coconut
Would have been termed as the 'bestower of the fruit of salvation'.

" Tell the beads of a rosary in memory of passionless sacred soul–Munirāja',

As if uttering such words
A garland of pure gems of crystal,
Exhibiting transparency,
Has been put around the neck of the pitcher.

Decorated in this manner,
As if attentive in waiting for the sacred guest–Munirāja.

The auspicious pitcher is placed
Upon the eight-cornered seat of sandalwood.

□

According to his daily routine
The eminent trader sets out for the Lord's worship,
Due to the auspicious ripening of the virtuous deeds
By the grace of religiousness, whatever was obtained
– On the fifth apartment of the grand mansion,
Where there stands a special temple,
Is installed
Upon the silvery throne
The dustless silver image of the invincible Lord.

First of all, the adoration of the Lord
Is observed with a sense of deepest faith,
Then, the ritual of His 'anointment' is observed;
The eminent trader applies over his own head
The fragrant sacred water, that is, the *Gandhodaka*
Pure in itself, and instrumental in purification,
With a sense of reverence...and...joy.

Then, after washing his hands with water,
He performs the holy cleansing of the idol
With the help of a clean white piece of cloth,
– Worships the renouncer and passion-winner Lord,–
Free from and unmixed with the segments of possessions
The sins and hypocrisies
The segments of possessions,
Offering eight auspicious substances
With a sense of deep devotion, eager strength
And not under the sway of some worldly gains,

The only purpose, deliverance from worldly
bondage !
The farthest end ...the coast of the ocean of
worldly existence.

□

Meanwhile, a square space with coloured meal or
powders is drawn artfully
By some sportive girls in the courtyard.
The time has almost ripened
For the routine observance of food-taking by the holy
guest–Munirāja
The mention is being made on this very point
Among all the benefactors !

The situation at every street of the city is, that
Facing each other, in the neighbourhood,
Inside their own courtyards
The line of benefactors runs a long way,
Absorbed in expectation of the worthy personage–
Munirāja.

Within each of the courtyards
Generally
Every benefactor stands with his lawful wife.
The only feeling which belongs to everyone,
The only prayer done unto the Lord is,
That
The suitable bestowal of food to the sacred guest–
Munirāja–
Should take place unhampered,
And that
How fortunate, if it could be at his own place.

Lo, after being free from the offerings of adoration
The eminent trader descends in the courtyard
And he also
Stands up with an auspicious earthen pitcher in hand.

Some of them are standing
With the silver-urn holding into their hands,
Some others are standing,
Having folded both of their hands
Into the form of an urn,

Some of them holding the copper-urn
The others with the mango-fruit
Some of them with brass-urns
Some one putting the custard apples on his palms
The others with the pumpkin into their hands
The others having guava into their hands
Some of them holding one jar upon the other jar
The other balancing-pitcher upon his head
Some one standing alone
Putting a banana over his palms
The other one with his hands really vacant
Some one with a platter in his hand.
The remarkable thing is that
All of them are there with their heads humbly bowed,
And
Once and again...at distant places…,
Casting their glances
Are waiting for some sacred guest–Munirāja.

Lo, meanwhile, the arriving sacred guest–Munirāja
Comes within their sight,
And
The cheers of rejoicings
Break out from the throats of the benefactors !

Victory ! victory ! victory ! to those
Whose departures or arrivals are unfixed
Whose thinking is well-disciplined

To the saints, to those who are eminent in merits,
To those who possess an amiable and peaceful
appearance
There be victory ! victory ! victory !

To those who are far away from partiality
To those who are the brave ascetics in their
natural naked form
To those who are the roots of the religion of
compassion
To those whose hearts are filled with the true
equanimity
There be victory ! victory ! victory !

To those who are the coasts to the ocean of
worldly existence
To those who are the pivots of the treasure-house
of salvation
To those who are firm-minded in tolerance
To those who are like waters for washing the
dirt of *Karmas*[84]
There be victory ! victory ! victory !

□

In the meantime...more
Closer comes the arrival of the sacred guest--Munirāja
He crosses many courtyards at the start,
The holy feet of the worthy guest–Munirāja
Are taking large strides forward every minute,
The life-breath of the courtyards left behind
Looks like frost-bitten
There isn't among them the normal rejoicing and bloom !
The sun reclines over the slope
Hither the lotus-grove withers away,
Even then
A ray of hope awakes into their hearts
That the worthy guest may turn his feet back.

The sun may appear the next day also
...It does appear, indeed !
But
While tracking its way
It doesn't take a turn the half-way
Far from returning back...
It doesn't even turn itself to see,
While taking its journey from Eastwards to
Westward,
It has never been sighted,
Arriving Eastward from Westward even up to
this day,
And that is not possible also.

When and how does the worthy guest–Munirāja
Recognizes the benefactors and *the ceremonial*
substances[85]–
– Can't be even detected,
Every thing happens without delay
Like a flash of lightning.

"The arrival of worthy guest within the courtyard,
Then
Without obtaining food and water
Turning back...
– The benefactor is deeply pained on that Score"
Thus, these utterings
Broke out from the lips of a benefactor.
Hastily
He remembered the saying of the Saints, that
Due to the supreme rise of the Supreme
moral merits
The benefit of food-offering is accredited,
The moment of the rise of our moral merits is
there...indeed,
But, according to the proportion, –

It has undergone enough of lightness,
This is what is called rarity, indeed.
No word is issued forth
From the lips of some of the benefactors
Who remain standing as if charmed and nailed.

Some of them...indeed
Become restless because of forgetting the methodical rites,
And
Put their palms over their skull once and again,
It seems as if
They are scolding off
Their unfavourable fate.

" O great saint !
If the methodical rituals have lacked...let it be so,
At least your Holiness should have cast a
glance hither,
We would have felt satisfied with this
much only"
–Thus, one of the benefactors expressed his mind
In a natural manner.

There are many qualities of a benefactor
One of them is the power of discretion,
Lo,
One of the benefactors lost his power of discretion
And
Under excessive feelings of devotion,
On reaching nearer the sacred guest
After going along the way,
Spoke out in pitiable words, that
"He couldn't get in this life
The good luck of food-offering to a sacred
guest–Munirāja.

The worthy ascetics (Munirājas) came across many a times
But, the feelings were not aroused
the sentiments have acquired vigour to-day,
Even on this occasion, if
The visiting should take place but not the holy touch,
The touching should, occur but not the rejoicing,–
The sentiments shall remain famished…!
At what stage, then...
That fulfilment of hunger ?–
The holy meals to-day should occur at our place, yes !
If any fault is found in this context
It shall then...be imputed to me,
And not to you, O Lord !
O thou ocean of mercy, take pity upon me,
Now, show your compassion without delay."

–On this sentimentalism of the benefactor,
The silent Munirāja (saint) turns
His face bearing a soft smile
And
Observing gradually the ground by four cubits,
Goes ahead on his path.
Meanwhile, a line full of hopelessness
Again breaks out from the lips of the benefactor :
" Of what good use are the teeth without
the grams,
Of what good use are the grams without the teeth,
And of what good use are the both of
them...indeed
If they are without a digestive intestine...!"

□

The various types of misconceptions
Are thus committed by the benefactors,
" Yes ! yes !!
This very position may prevail upon us too"
Speaks thus the pitcher (*kumbha*) to the
noble trader,
And
Serves a note of caution to the noble trader–

" A request may be made to holy guest–Munirāja
But no excess should be done,
We can, at this time,
Forget everything else
But discretion.
A sense of due service should be expressed
Through the body, the mind and the word
But not that of indifference.
There should play a tender smile across the lips,
But not buffoonery.
There should be enthusiasm and gust
But not impatience.
The pollen of humility should fall off
From each and every limb,
But there should be no smell of pitiableness.
And,
In this very context
A poem was heard from the saints,
Therefore...hark, it is presented,
It is honoured, and is admired by the wise :

The land is thirsty
The hope for water has awakened –

The vessel of mouth has been opened
The earth is firmly determined
That
The benefactor is not to be waited for
Special review of the benefactor is not to be done
Our own limit
Our own courtyard
Has not to be transgressed even by mistake
Because,
The pitiableness of a sacred guest–Munirāja
Wakes the appearance of pride
In the prideless benefactor,
The pan of sins then,
Gets heavier,
And
In the free and self-respecting sacred guest
The sense of dependence creeps in, indeed,
The ground of dutifulness, slowly and gradually,
Slides downward,
What shall happen then ?
The benefactor as well as the sacred guest–Munirāja
Both of them get overhanged in the void. ...

That...is why...
These dark and blackish
Dense clouds, which
Having obtained the visit of sacred guest–Munirāja
Are absorbed into the search of a holy spot –
To mould their acquired sin
Into the form of meritorious action,
On feeling overjoyed with an emotional heart in ecstasy,–

Produce a thundering sound,
Both the eyes brimming with tears.
The sixty four-fold currents of *the month of Sāvana*[86]
Prostrate upon the feet-spot
Of the worthy...Sacred guest (Munirāja)

Thereafter...indeed...
The earth
Easily, in a natural way
Washes away
The blackness of the cloud,
Otherwise
After the rains
Why that band of clouds,
Would have become spotless ?"

□

The verse was heard from the mouth of the pitcher
In brief and substantial form,
The glorious story of the benefactor
The moral code of conduct was indeed, presented, –
The one, who has forsaken his ideal life,
After showing his face mirrored forth into the ideals,
– The face, on which
Only the false pride of being unstained
Was shining off.
The eyes of the noble trader
Were woke up from sleep,
He exercised self-control upon himself,
All the misapprehensions were cleansed away.

The listening of poetry
Has impressed him deeply.
Again, some hint is dropped with the eminent trader –
The arrival of the holy hermit towards us
Is now cent-per-cent certain.
The more the courtyard
Came nearer,
The more the gait of the holy hermit
Caught slowness accordingly
And
The holy guest (Munirāja) felt that
By arresting his steps from going ahead,
Some unique ripeness of the virtuous deeds
Is attracting them towards itself!

On seeing the gait of the worthy guest –
Being more cautious,
Being filled with veneration,
With the medium melodious voice –
Not too dim
Not too loud as well,
The reception of the holy visitor began :

'O Swāmin!
Salutation to thee! Salutation to thee! Salutation to thee!
Hither! hither! hither!
Please stay! stay! stay!'
Thus the notes of addressing and greeting
Were repeated twice or thrice
Along, with it,
Moving to and fro very slowly –

The large ear-rings of the noble-trader
Are also inviting the sacred guest (Munirāja)
reverentially.

A mansion of fearlessness –
The sacred guest stays up within the courtyard
Unperturbed, unshaken...
How excellent then, nothing remains to be said !
Regarding himself to be fortunate enough
Expressing his sense of blissfulness with the words
'well done !'

'What a blessed one !',
Taking the sacred guest towards his right side,
Keeping himself at a distance of two or three cubits,
From the sacred guest
The noble trader starts making circumambulations
Along with his wife and family members !

□

This scene of today
Is looking, as if

The Sun and the Moon
Along with the planets, constellations and stars
Are circumambulating the Mount Meru,
The three revered rounds were made
With the observance of compassion for all the
living beings.

Again, with reverential salutations,
The nine-fold devotional rituals are commenced :
'The mind is purified
The word is chaste
The body is neat and clean
And
The food and drinks are pure,
Proceed please, O Swāmin (Munirāja) !

Kindly enter the kitchen for food-taking',
And
Without turning their backs towards the sacred guest
The whole of the family moves onwards.
After the inside entry,
Telling about the purified seating
A request is made to be seated upon an elevated seat
The holy guest takes his seat.

An humble request is made to the worthy personage
(Munirāja)
For the holy bathing of the feet,
The request is accepted by a slight move of the head.

Depriving the red-blossom of a *Palāśa*[87] *tree* of
its splendour
The non-abstinence-fearing feat-soles
Of the sacred guest (Munirāja)
Descend upon the silver-platter !
Lo, at that very time
Even the platter expresses
Its affection for the dignity of the Spiritual
Guide–Guru !
That is,
In pursuance of the feet of the sacred guest
It grows reddish like saffron or pure gold.

Holding up into his hands the earthen pitcher
Filled with filtered, heated
Lukewarm boiled water,
As soon as the benefactor
Bends down upon the feet of the worthy guest
At that very moment indeed,
Far away from the pride of cupidity,
Being reflected into the mirror-nails of the saint's feet,

The pitcher (*kumbha*) views its own image,
And
Exclaims to itself, well-done ! 'how fortunate !'

Victory, victory to the great saint !
Triumph to this specific occasion !
The thoughts take a concrete shape,–
The troubles and agonies of the path,
Whatever the impurity which remains behind, –
Every thing is entirely dedicated, here and now,
To self-realization :
'Protect us, your holy feet are
The ship which floats as well as rescues.
O compassionate sage of sages !
Carry us to the shores of the ocean of existence !'
Thus, while extolling the virtues of the Spiritual
Guide–Gurudeva,
Is performed the holy bathing (*Abhiṣeka*) of the feet
Along with their holy cleansing too,
Which is trouble-destroyer and prosperity-bestower.
Everyone, feeling overjoyed,
Applies the fragrant sacred water '*Gandhodaka*' upon
his fore-head,
The eminent trader, along with his family,
Is looking like an Indra, the lord of gods.

In due course now,
According to rituals, according to means,
Under the genuine auspices of the naked saint
(Munirāja),
With proper representation,
Arranging the eight-fold auspicious substances,
With water, liquidized sandalwood, unbroken
white rice, saffroned rice,
With white and saffroned coco-pieces or lighted
lamp, incense, dry fruits –
The rituals of adoration are performed
With five-fold sacred salutations !

Again
With folded hands, the whole of the family
Beseeches the holy guest, that –
" O Swāmin ! having unfolded the posture of finger-tips –
On the right shoulder, that is, *Añjuli-mudrā*
Kindly take food !"

Finding the benefactor skilled at the mode of
serving the food –
Forsaking his right hand with the special posture,
The worthy personage (Munirāja) washes both
his hands
And, for some moments,
Having fixed his deep insight upon the nose-tip,
Absorbs the magnanimous one himself
Into the meditation of such Ārhat Jinadevas,
Who live after being liberated from all delusions
Who are fully free from worldly attachments and aversions
For whom the births and deaths, old age and decay
Can't touch now,
Who can't be tortured by hunger,
Whose life-breath can't be oppressed by thirst,
In whom there is no place of shelter
For arrogance, amazement even for a moment,
In whose presence
The fear itself, being afraid, indeed, flies away,
They are the abode of fearlessness, free from the
seven fears[88]
To whom sleep and drowsiness doesn't encircle,
Always a perfectly vigilant countenance,
No such body, which is drenched with perspiration,
Nothing of the sort of the wearied labours;
In whom, infinite power is evident –
As a result of which
No terror can take them into its fold
Who have attained infinite bliss...therefore

Who are devoid of sorrow, always in the state of
sorrowlessness.
Whose very life is free from worldly attachments,
That is...why...
The sensual pleasures loiter about, keeping away from them;

Those who have neither attachment in belongings nor
any union of saints
Those who are alone–only their own True 'selves'
Whom should they care for ?
They are always fully beyond all worries,
Absolved from the *eighteen blemishes.*[89a]

□

The spiritual or meditative relaxation (*Kāyotsarga*)[89b]
by the ascetic is performed, when
The holy saint stands upon the seat,
After maintaining a difference
Of four and eleven finger's breadth
Between the both of his heels and the toes.

He is the custodian of not only the 'rule of taking food in
the standing posture,
But also the observer of the 'one-meal-a-day'
The worthy personage (Munirāja) folds
Both his hands like a bowl
And furthers it before the benefactor.

'This is the very practice of dependence for
food-taking
Which brings the mind down from the peak of pride,'
Telling thus, this pen investigates appetite

The appetite reveals two aspects
The one that of the body, the other that of the mind.
That of the body is a little, natural too,
That of the mind may be known by mind itself–
How much can it be testified ?
It has been fully of disorders,
It is not merely an appetite, it is a horrible ghost,
Which is not only connected with the past,
But also with the non-existent (future) !
This is the reason why
This living being,
Having accomplished his True Self
Hasn't been really subdued.

So far as the sense-organs are concerned,
They don't feel really hungry,
It seems outwardly
That they are hungry.
When does the tongue desire the taste,
The rose doesn't remember the smell,
When does the sense of touch wait for the act of touching ?
When does the sense of hearing feel feverish
In absence of the sound ?
Even the deaf sense of hearing is found alive.
When do the eyes move a lighted lamp circularly
Before the from of beauty, the formless soul in a religious ceremony ?
All these sense-organs are inanimate,
The inanimate is the material cause of the inanimate
No longing is found there into the inanimate –
The inanimate has no way to tread upon –

Always, every where, all the same
Whether there is darkness or light.

Yes ! O yes !
The perceptive understanding of various objects
Can be attained through the medium of the
sense-organs
For the sensual admirers of worldly pleasures.
The real thing is that
These sense-organs are the windows
This body has been a mansion,
The Soul, while sitting inside the mansion,
Keeps on peeping through the different windows
With the eyes of Desire
And
Perceives the worldly objects.

The other point is that
The sweet, the sour, the astringent etc. –
Whatever the tastes are there, good or bad –
Never ask, that
We should relish them.

Light-heavy, smooth-rough,
Cold-warm, soft-hard
Whatever the touches-good or evil –
Never ask, that
We should perceive them.

Sweet -smelling or bad-smelling
Whatever the odours-favourable or unfavorable–
Never ask, that
They should be smelled by us.

The black, blue, yellow etc.
Whatever are the colours good or evil –
Never ask, that,
We should have a look at them !
And,
Sā-re-ga-ma-pa-dha-ni[90]
Whatever is the gamut, favourable or unfavourable,
Never asks, that,
We should listen to it
Hark…listen !

The sense of touching, tasting, smelling,
The form and the word –
All these are the intrinsic attributes of the matter, –
Are the operations of the inanimate objects... .

The conclusion is that
In the fruition of delusion and Kārmic nature of
discomfort (*Asātā*)
The agony of hunger occurs –
It is the principle behind hunger and thirst.
Only, of it being known
Is not saintliness,
But
Even-mindedness is inevitable along with the
knowledge
The ornament of a saint is really,
The sentiment of equanimity and even–
–mindedness...!

□

Hither, begins the ceremony of the serving of food
With the boiled water into the palms-bowl of the
holy saint;
But
It is strange, all of a sudden,
The holy saint closes up his palms-bowl,
When

At once, from the other side,
The golden urn (pitcher) is furthered ahead
Which is filled with tasty milk,
Even then, seeing the palms of hand interlocked together
The third one shows the silver urn (pitcher),
Which contains the sweet juice of sugarcane,
When
Even that too remains unheeded, then

Comes the turn of the slender-necked crystal pitcher
Filled with the reddish juice of pomegranate
Looking like the rosiness of the young age !
What a surprise !
Even a single glance isn't cast
Upon it by the sacred guest, the hermit !
Being compelled, that crystal pitcher sinks into despair.

Now
More delay is improper,
The holy guest may go back without taking food–
Taking it to be an obstacle (*Antarāya*), he may sit down,
– Such a doubt springs upon the face of the family,
And
Remembering God within their hearts,
Somehow keeping up the steadiness of the mind,
Gathering up his courage fully
The noble trader furthers ahead the earthen urn (pitcher)
With his trembling hands.

Lo,
The palms of hand interlocked together get unfolded
Like a pearl-oyster, floating over the chest of the ocean !
On beholding the bright water-drops of the planet *Swāti* !

Four or five handfuls of water are taken through the
palm-bowl,
Some of the sugarcane-juice too is taken,
Then whatever is offered
Is taken without interruptions.
Not at whatever time, not at sweet will
Without solicitation,
Without any hint,
Only the stomach ought to be hungry
Whatever then the quality of food –
Juicy or rough and dried up,
There is no difference.

The eatables and the drinkables are transferred
From one vessel into the another
Does any change occur into the vessels
At that time...or afterwards...?
Neither any vessel really takes to dancing
Nor does it start weeping indeed
How fortunate ! What a good luck to this
human being
And to this human body
Which is the supermost among all the bodies !

□

Before sowing the seeds
The land, full of holes and pits,
Eroded by the flow of water-currents,
Is levelled by the farmer
By depositing the rubbish, the stone-pieces into it.
Really, in the same way,
The benefactor goes on offering the food...

The saint receives it in continuance,
He has to fill up his belly with it, indeed !
It is duly named as a 'practice of pit-filling'
By the equanimous ascetic–*the 'Śramaṇa' !*[91]

When weed, straw and fodder is thrown
Before a hungry cow
She, then, doesn't cast a supine look
To see the organs and limbs
The decorations and ornaments of her protectors.
Thus, in this very way,
An ascetic too has an attitude
At the time of taking his meals
Which is called 'the practice of pasturage.'

There is no option of this or that type
Whether it is salty or tasty
Of whatever type, there be the water
At once, the fire 'encircling the house'
Is put out in this very manner indeed.

Whether it is tasteful or tasteless
Whatever it is, it should be some foodstuff;
The digestive fire, indeed, has to be pacified !
And
This is truly the 'fire-pacifying practice' of an ascetic,
the '*Śramaṇa*',
–A great practice among all the practices !

The pollen-thirsty band of large black-bees
Sips the juicy fragrance
Of the bunches of tendrils, flowers and fruits,
But, for them,
Never creates any trouble;

Contrary to it,
Through its throbbing touch of hand
Makes them dance
Sings to them sweet songs in its buzzing sound.
In this very manner, indeed,
The delight of the donor too knows no bounds
He feels transported with joy,
By bestowing food-offerings to the holy
personages (Munirājas).
The dense darkness is dispelled,
A new morn dawns into life
And this is...what is really called
The 'large black-bee-like practice' of the saints !

Thus, there are so many practices of a '*Śramaṇa*'
Through which
Are manifested the spiritual splendours –
Which are heard humbly through the Scriptures,
Which have come near and nearer to-day
To be visible before the naked eye.

The result is that
The whole of the noble trader's family
Is filled with great exhilaration
And into both the fair-coloured hands
Of the noble trader
The earthen pitcher is placed gracefully
Like a sapphire set into a golden ornament.

Between those hands and the pitcher,
In the form of mutual admiration,
Some points are exchanged, when
At first, the pitcher utters –

" Having held me up, you have owned me
You have been very beneficent to me
And
I have been fortunate enough as a helper
In this auspicious deed."

On hearing this, the hands too at once add, that –
"No...no, hark...listen !
It is you, indeed, who have done a favour unto us
This task wasn't even possible without you,
In this task the feelings and devotion,
Whatever is there, belongs to you
We do...happen to be...
Only an external cause indeed !"

Below…
Having heard the aforesaid talk
The pitcher in the palms of the other worthy
person says that
" The life of water can never continue to stay
Without a vessel
And
The life of a living being can never be sustained
Without a receptacle, that is, supreme personage–
(saint)
But
The one who takes water with a vessel
Can never be a best personage–(Munirāja)
The vessel of palms-woven-together is regarded
as the best one,
The vessel too is taken to be as the belongings !

The other thing to be mentioned too is, that
The due dates can never be sanctified
Without a holy guest, the saint,
The holy guest is indeed the performer of the due
dates, isn't it !

Even then
He doesn't keep up the dates with him
The due dates really depend upon the time-factor, isn't it !
Modifications take their own courses
They differ from person to person,
To be bound with the chains of dates too
Is to wander within the lanes of worldly existence.
On any account !
Getting bound of ascetics under any bonds
Is to dwell upon the delights of destiny."
Thus went on the discourse about the worthy
personage–saint.

□

Hither,
The unobstructed offerings of food are going on
And this very act as such
Should be accomplished joyfully,
– The eminent trader has attached and
absorbed himself
Into this very sentiment.
Descending from the both of his shoulders,
Clinging around the both of his arms,
– Then, both the ends of the blue
'upper-garment',
– The right-sided end moving towards the
left one
While the left-sided end moving towards
the right one
Thus, fastening around the waist-part –
Are hanging downwards.

It is unable to have an upward look,
It has been fully defeated
By the bluishness of the pitcher –

Feeling a sense of shyness
It wishes to hide itself into the Earth
It doesn't want to show to anyone
Its face, which tends to shrink.

Into the mid-finger of the noble trader's
right hand
There is a pleasant-looking golden ring
Which is studded with the gems of ruby
Whose reddish radiance
Is comparing itself once and again
With the rosy lips of the holy guest, the saint
And
Ultimately, feeling pained due to its defeat
Is touching the feet of the holy guest
With a heavy sense of shyness,
And it is proper to do so –
One gets the desired blessings
Through his devotion to the venerable feet.

In the same manner
Into the fore-finger of the noble trader's left hand
There is a silver-made ring,
The ring is inwrought with a pearl.
It feels distress at
Seeing the unforeseen brilliance
Of the hand-nails of the bowl-palmed ascetic
And
Feels a feverish attack.
That is why it keeps up
Its bloodless bright body;

Both the cheeks of the holy guest, the saint,
Are circular, and well-shaped too, –

Are fleshy, as well as refined also,
Into whose refinement
The golden ear-rings of the benefactor,
Under the pretext of their reflected image,
Compare themselves with the cheeks –

"Are we in any sense inferior ?
We scatter radiance
Like the rising Sun
We are circular and well-shaped too
Are fine-coloured and fascinating
Are purely golden, and not copper-mixed.
Even then,
Between the lustre of the cheeks and that of
this splendour,
Why such a difference ?
What is the deficiency with us ?
Who is acquainted with this mystery ?
Whom should we ask from ?
How, indeed, should we ask ?"

Lo ! an awakening address of the cheeks
To the ear-rings, entangled into confusion :
"At the very sight of you
A sense of attachment is awakened in the on-lookers
And
At the very sight of us
They are filled with a natural feeling of affection,
Even a deeply attached person is lost for some
moments
Into a sense of indifference for the worldly attachment,
Gathered within our hearts,
That feeling of deep affection, having risen up,

Sliding down from the surface of the cheeks,
Transforms into the tender flowers;
Even the stony chest of the foes
Who stand in the form of opposition.
Invaluable utterings have been nourished within us,
And
Only hollowness has been found into you.

There is one thing more, that
Whether life is developed,
Or it may be developing,
Whether there are so many bright qualities,
To compare the 'Self' with the 'Non-self'
Is the cause of discomfiture
Is a symbol of sorry plight too.

And
That very act of comparison
Is, in another way, rivalry;
The rivalry brings out into light
The subtle existence of egotism
Which is seated...far...deep...within.
Then, where is satisfaction to egotism ?
Without contentment, life is faulty,
This is the very reason, why
Scorched by the desire of name and fame –
This blemished life –
Is deprived of the dense and cool shade
Of the natural cheers of triumph, of delightful merits.

In that way, the word 'swa', that is 'self,'
Is indeed itself indicating that, –

‘*Swa*’–that is ‘self’ is the real wealth
‘*Swa*’–that is ‘self’ is indeed *the Law of ‘Divine Desting’*[92] itself as the Creator
‘*Swa*’–that is ‘self’ is the treasure-house of the true virtues
The realization of ‘self’ is the Final Attainment
Then,
Why the comparison of the incomparable ?”
Thus, the disclosure of their hollowness being made by the cheeks,
Those ear-rings of purified gold
Become still more dim and devoid of brightness.

□

Right from the heel upto the head,
The eminent trader has put on the yellow garment,
Full of the lustre like that of a lotus-stalk,
Wrapped in such a clothing
His face has bloomed as a rose,
And
Under the sway of the blowing breeze
The yellow garment is rippling like waves–
The waves in which
The bluish beauty of the pitcher seems afloat
Hence...the yellowness of the yellow garment
Makes haste to drink up
The lovely-looking bluishness !

□

Yes, hither...
All the boys and girls of the household –

Have been ordered to stay within the house
And
Have been pressed to sit down without uttering a word,
Despite it, every now and then,
Through the doorframes and windows
Some attempts are being made to peep out
While pushing one another back or ahead.

It is none of the concern of an intemperate person
To keep up the due limits,
The more the one is forbidden
The more self-willed does he become
Towards the cherished condition of the observance.
In the state of boyhood,
It is not possible to give up the renouncable,
It is not possible to adore the adorable.
Even then, whatever is observed,
It is only forced out of fear !
This very situation prevails here !

To be rescued from the trouble of hair-locks
The eminent trader has kept his head tied up fast.
Even then,
Over the broad surface of his fore-head
A dark curly lock of hair
Springs up to stare, once and again, at
The pleasant scene of the offerings of food
The scene of the attention distracted by the other things,
And
Tells fearlessly
To the eminent one of the personages there present that

" Thou art an ascetic, rich in equanimity,
This noble benefactor is the mine of affection–

Who has attachment for non-attachment;
Both of you aim at freedom from bondage
Then, please tell me, a bit rather !
Why do you throw me into the bondage ?
Now
I too don't like bondage
I acknowledge the point that
My past is wrong,
And
Whose past isn't so ?
It is depraved, old and muddy also
It is decayed, fickle and restless too,
But
The situation to-day has undergone a change
I wish to escape the *wrong habits*[93]
(*Sapta-vyasanas*).

The Sin has arrived to meet moral merits
The poison has come to be dissolved into nectar
O thou mass of light, the Sun !
Listen to the request of Darkness !
O Lord, wake up him for once
Than putting him to flight once and again !
Allot a place for him with you
Efface him or affiliate him with yourself;
The true sign of light is only that
Which enlightens the one and all !
– I show the audacity to add one thing more !
The unlucky is never driven off
By the fortunate ones, O Lord !
They make him the lucky one, the god."

Uttering thus, the lock of hair upon the fore-head
Reverting itself instantly, turns speechless.
And...hither
The food-offerings come to a happy finish,
The holy personage(Munirāja) takes his seat upon a
wooden plank
The mouth-wash is done with the boiled warm water
Having purified with his own hands
The organs-the stomach, chest, and thighs etc.,
Which are affected
By the bits of offerings which sprang up from the
palms-cavity –
The holy saint absorbs himself into the Supreme Spirit
For some moments,
With his eye-lids half-unfolded.

□

The posture of bodily resignation (Kāyotsarga)[94] is completed,
The eminent trader, with his humble hands,
Bestows into both the lotus-hands of the holy guest (Munirāja),
Which are marked with the sign of the assurance of
fearlessness,
The means of self-restraint made of peacock-feathers
That is, '*Pichhikā*', which is
Tender, soft, handy and pleasing.

Not for quenching the thirst,
– But, for cleansing the hands and feet etc.
Before the regular study of the holy Scriptures
And
After being free from the calls of nature
The boiled warm water is filled in *Kamandalu*, that is,
–The 'wooden water-spout', the means of routine ablutions,

The water...which
Can be utilized
For the period of twenty four hours of a
whole day,
After that period which gets polluted.

For touching the feet of the holy guest, the saint,
For getting his pious look
The public of the neighbourhood
Has gathered within the courtyard.
No sooner than
The holy guest enters the courtyard,
When
Even the sky is filled with an outcry of victory.
And, along, with the sentimental public,
The noble trader requested the holy personage, that
" Besides having perseverance for the 'Fundamental
duties of life'
We are optimistic too
We should deserve the blessings soon,
The expectations of sensual pleasures should vanish
soon, it's enough !
We should only follow the path shown by you.
While parting away from us, O Lord !
Bless us with such a short precept
By getting bound with which
We should realize our real existence,
The...needle...which is threaded...
Is never lost –
Anywhere it may get dropped."

On hearing this, the holy guest (Munirāja)
thinks that
Neither is it a proper place nor a proper time
For due exhortations, –

Even then
The inner compassion overflows,
A few words drop out from the lips of
the holy guest
Like the pearls from an oyster :

" From outside
Whatever is being seen
That...I...am...not...indeed
And all that
Doesn't really belong to me.
These eyes
Can't see me
The power to see
Is there within me;
I was...am...and shall be
The maker of that power,
The seer of all
I was...am...and shall be.
From outside
Whatever is being seen
That...I...am...not...indeed !"

Uttering, these words, the feet
Of the holy guest take their way to the
small garden,
The back gets turned towards the spectators...!

□

Following closely the holy personage
Like a shadow
The noble trader is treading the path
With *the wooden water-spout (Kamaṇḍalu)*[95] in his
hand

There is a small garden near the city
Nasiyājī–a glorious temple is there outside within the garden
Whose crest kisses the sky,
The rounded pinnacle is glittering fast,
With its golden glory
The rounded pinnacle indicates that
All the brilliance and splendour of the world
Is erroneous and deceiving also,
It is without the significance of the virtuous path.

At *Nasiyājī*, there is a 'Jina-Image'
Of Nemināthā,[96] very beautiful to look at,
The image is visited
A sense of real self is perceived
The body feels thrilled
A chorus of joy is sung.

The noble trader prostrates once more
Upon the holy feet of the Spiritual Guide
A prelude to return is made, but
The body shows signs of deficiency.

The eyes become wet with tears
The path seems to be out of sight
The feet assume some heaviness
The weeping doesn't get stopped,
Though, an attempt is made to control it,
He starts weeping bitterly
And begins to roll restlessly
At the auspicious and venerable feet.

" Having forsaken the shelter of the Great preceptor's feet
This soul

Doesn't wish to go back, O Lord !
Like a swan leaving away the lake
Mānasarovara.
Even then, it is a matter of sorrow, that
The body too has to go hand-in-hand with
the mind
The impetus of mind is greater, O Lord !
It is clouded with anxiety and uneasiness
Once and again, while talking.
Then, those feet of *mental excitement*
(saṁvega)[97a]
Do not hold up the ground of conduct
Then, what shall it do without support...?

If it is a hill-side river
If it is swollen with *Āṣāḍhī flood*,[97b]
No mention of the tiny forest-creatures,
Even an elephant would lose its existence
Everything would be swept away...!
Our own earned kārmic nature (attached with soul)
Has come to rise as our troubling destiny to-day,
Despite the will, the leading of a religious life,
Has become an uphill task,
And I...?
Have not only become a 'dwarf', but also 'lame'.
The path is very long
How can I track it on...?
The pivot is kissing the high skies,
How can I climb-up,
There is no far-sighted fellow-traveller also...
How should I go ahead...now...?

Should I become a complete optimist ?
Or should I resign everything to destiny ?

Should I relinquish my perseverence (*Puruṣārtha*) ?
O Supreme personage (saint), tell me what to do ?
Should I test myself
On the touchstone of time ?
Should I accept the time
As the supreme ruler
Of all the movements-developments-arrivals,
Stoopings-progress-modifications ?

Each and every substance is independent.
The 'doer' is free –
Is this principle faulty ?
Along with the verb-form 'being'
There is the verb-form 'doing' also...
In the dictionary, indeed !"

On hearing the questionnaire of the eminent trader,
As if a persuading mother to a son
In caressing words,
Having broken his silence, the Spiritual Guide said, that
" The answer to all these doubts is hither
Look at me...here...upwards...!"
And
The upward looking was done
With tearful eyes –
Only a silent posture was met with,
Even a bit of smile wasn't found
Behind the countenance,
It is filled up with gravity,
There is a stillness in the eyes
There is an innocence across the forehead –
Which really seems to unravel the mystery...

'*Ni*', that is, within our own 'self'
'*Yati*', that is, the endeavour
To be absorbed within our own 'self' is the destiny
Certainly, it is indeed the stage of higher quietude,
And
'*Puruṣa*', that is, the 'Soul' is the 'Supreme Spirit'
'*Artha*', that is, 'the attainable' is the real purpose,
Barring the 'Soul'
The forgetting of everything else
Is the supreme endeavour, that is, the right '*Puruṣārtha*'.

The nature of 'destiny' and Supreme Endeavour
Is, indeed, known in their genuine form
Then, at the same time,...
The attributive existence of Time,
Which is only in the form of 'presence'
And not as a 'motive-force,'
Which is neutral, and seated on single quarter,
Hasn't remained concealed, has got unravelled.

The doubts of the noble trader find their answer
Even then...!

□

Like the clouds without brilliance
Having lightness in absence of water,
Without the glory and thunder,
Being, silent after the rains –
– The noble trader is tracking his way home –
With a small downcast face...!

Due to almost the breakage
Of the contact of a wick with the oil
Or –

Like a twinkling lamp
Due to the sharp decline of oil
The noble trader is going on with a slow pace
Keeping up his vital breath within his body...!

Some reasoning too is traversing the mind !
Having lost the capital money,
Returning homewards with empty hands
Feeling worried for the future, –
Like a merchant, caught in dilemma
The eminent trader is tracking his way home...!

The full portion of the clarified butter
Being churned out,
Feeling himself thus his own dryness,
Getting devoid of sensitivity,
Like that of the bare milk
The eminent trader is going on his way home...!

At this time, the wealthy person
Has been experiencing the distress
In manifold ways
Even more than the pangs caused by insult
Before his class-fellows.
The juice-sucking from the cheeks of the bough
On being left completely behind,
–Like a flower fallen into dust
Keeping the departure of intimacy with himself
The wealthy person is tracking his way home–
Along with the poor courage left behind...!

Being aggrieved from the separation of his mother
Continually, –

Sobbing like a child,
The wealthy trader is tracking his way home,
With deeper respirations...!

At the termination of the spring season
Being restless
Like the face of the wild-life
The wealthy trader is moving homewards,
After being excluded from the association of saints...!

In the wide-spread desert
Which plunders greenery,
Which is enveloped with mirage,
Like a thin crawling river
Having flowless and flat shores,
With only some hope of embracing the ocean
The wealthy trader is tracking his way home...!

Which springs up from the lap of the East
Then
Which sets behind the Western Mount
Like that mass of light, the Sun,
The eminent trader is moving homewards,
On being afraid of the approaching
darkness...!

The condition of the wealthy trader
Is similar to that of the moon of the dark fortnight,
Like the verses vacant with the sentiment of quietude
Like the dawn devoid of the warbling of birds
Like the night without the cool moon-light
And
Vacant with a tiny round mark of vermilion *(Bindī)*[98]–

Like the forehead of a woman
Everything is appearing to be dull and cheerless.
Lo,
Rolling down over a slope
Like a boulder
The eminent trader reaches his home...!

□

The whole of the family is merged into
unlimited delight,
It is the result of the offerings to a worthy
personage;
The deserving pitcher too is feeling puffed up.
All of them gather together to take food
But, having looked intently
At the eminent trader's face
Fair-coloured, yet filled with dejection –
Thus adds the glorious pitcher, that

" It is the very significance of a saint's arrival, indeed,
That the end of the worldliness is visualized,"
It matters little if
The one, who makes an approach,
May or may not become at once
A saint, or a person with self-restraint –
There is no rule or regulation whatsoever
But,
He is sure to be a man of self-contentment.
A blessing in the right direction, indeed,
Is a temple in the right condition.

After the right diagnosis of the disease
By the expert doctors –

The patient, who takes the medicine,
Whose adorable deity is true healthiness,
Can never be a sensualist
Sensual enjoyments are, really, the diseases.
And...hark !
It is a marvel of correct diagnosis
And not that of the medicine itself,
The purgation of the disease
Is the result of taking the medicine –
Perfect health is really an invaluable wealth".

What else is added by the pitcher –
Listen ...to it !
" In that way
Leave aside the mention of adornments and
ornaments,
Even the fine thin muslin of Dhaka
Seems to be a burden in old age,
While,
Whether the one is a boy or a young man
A mature person or an old man
Whether the one inhabits a forest or a palace
In the state of all worldly detachments
Even the reception and obligation
Appears to be a burden."

These lines too by the saints
Aren't irrelevant :
" There can be no love
Of the Sky with the Earth
The Cupid's love can never
Condescend to the old age;

It is also an injunction (*Niyoga*), that
A virtuous person can never
Have a liking for wine.
The cosmetics are
Never agreeable to a widow,
The separation with her husband
Is never favourable to a married woman,
Only the rare personages adopt a mode of living
Contrary to the sinful ways of the worldliness,
The colour-stain is never acceptable
To *the saffron dye.*[100a]

□

On hearing the feelings and the words of the
sacred pitcher
The eminent trader felt at that moment, as if
The actual taste of saintliness
Is being perceived by him.

What sense does *the sharpness*[100b]
Of the thorn carry now ?
What purpose do the symptoms
Of the essence now serve ?
Indeed, all the slumbering sources
Of the sum and substance
Do spring up before the eyes...
How fortunate ! good luck !!

The descent of the ascetic has reflected into
The bright mirror of the pitcher,
And –

The obligations are expressed to the ascetic
Through the whole-hearted dedication by the
pitcher.

This-pen too bestows
Some timely sayings:
" If you are afraid of grief
Then...listen!
Develop affection for hard work
And
If you have a liking for egotism
Then...hark!
Be afraid of its climax
Retain tranquillity!
Choose equanimity!
Due to the dignity of the perfected incantation
The distressed perplexity of the eminent trader,
Like the poison pervading a body
Decreases and fades away somewhere.
And the eminent trader says, that
" With an exception to the Lord's worship,
Within this fortnight, keeping in line with the holy guest
(Munirāja),
The earthen-wares shall be made use of,"
And
After stepping down from the silvery seat,
He seats himself upon a wooden slab,
Hearing this, the family also remarked –
'Our sentiments too are exactly similar'.

On perceiving the altered attitude of the family
The golden platters and
The small round jars

The mugs, cups and bowls
As bright as white Jessamine flowers
The platters and the small round jars
Silvery like the full moon,
The water-jugs of crystals and rubies nice and fine,
The dishes of different shapes and size,
The glittering spoons
With a sparkling brightness, –
What is this all happening...?
– Lost in fancies, all of them feel amazed !

Then...hither...what is it that happens !
The brass-vase filled with cold water,
Feeling pained from within,
While drinking the draught of insult once and again,
Being inflammed, gets
Boiled and more pallid.
On seeing the reception of the 'black-coloured' –
At the gate of the 'fair-coloured' –
That hue of the golden pitcher
Grows more reddened,
Which is beyond description through the words;
Loses all control over itself.
Through the mouth-cavity of the golden pitcher
Wrathful wordings are issued forth,
As if some volcano assumes its true shape :

" Even the current day
Hasn't yet ended,
And
So much of regard and reception to a stranger !

Applying the dust over the forehead
And
Throwing away the crown under the feet –
– All this
Doesn't appear to be like a civilized conduct,
The sense of owning our own is something distant
indeed,
Even according to the ordinary formality,
There doesn't appear to be a sense of belonging here,
It is by itself bearing the fruits.

I acknowledge the fact, that
The sentiment of belongingness –
The bestowal of kinship
And
To consider the others at preference to our own self
Is civility, it is the moral duty of all the living beings;
But, this task,
Should take place in due order, and in due way,
– I should disclose this sense a bit more –
The high one does remain the high
The low one does remain the low –
It is not my firm opinion,
The low one may be uplifted,
Through the proper-improper contacts
A change is possible in every body.
But ! it ought to be kept in mind
Through the physical, monetary, educational etc.
Co-operation only
The low one can't be transformed into the high one,
This task can be accomplished
On the basis of the virtuous rites.

If the whey is seasoned with spices
The whey turns not only tasteful
But also becomes digestive,
And
If the sugar candy is mixed with milk, then
The milk becomes tasty as well as strength-giving.
If the method applied is contrary to it,
That is,
The mixing up of sugar candy with whey
May, indeed, be somehow potential
But
The seasoning of milk with spices...really...
Proves the deformation of the mind."
Thus was gradually pacified
The boiling and ebullition of the golden pitcher.

□

The eminent trader hears peacefully
The ebullition of the golden pitcher
With the both of his ears,
Then, in return, he
Wishing for the well-being of the earthen pitcher
Puts forth some points of harmony.

" So far as the soil-dust is concerned,
No one applies the bare dust
Upon his forehead,
Except a silly stupid fellow.
The dust assumes adorability due to its contact with the holy feet.
And –

Those feet are venerable
Where worship is performed by the eyes,
They evaluate the feet
Which cause us to reach our destination
Only those eyes are considered to be the right ones.
The wanton eyes which disregard
The holy feet, get unhappy,
The very word '*Charaṇa*'[101a] itself
Is preaching and instructing
The benevolent eyes, that
Having forsaken the holy feet, that is, the 'right conduct'–
Never wander ! never wander !! never wander !!!
Else-where, at any time !
Not only this much,
By the reverse order too of the syllables
This very sense is inferred,
That is,
Cha...ra…ṇa, na...ra...cha...[101b]
– Having forsaken the 'holy feet', that is, 'the right conduct'–
Never be rapt ! never be rapt ! never be rapt !
Else where, at any time !

O God !
I want to understand that
What atoms have gone into
The making of the eyes –
When they are begotten or are sore,...then,
They are troublesome!
When the eyes are 'lost'...then,
They are distressing !
How far and how long I should relate,

When the eyes fall in 'love' or are 'drowsy' ...then
They afflict pains !
Where is happiness there within the eyes ?
These eyes –
Are the mines of troubles
Are beaten by worldly pleasures
That is the reason why
The saints, the self-restrained saintly persons
Do not trust these eyes
And
While always keeping their eye firmly upon their feet
Move on with an humble look
...How fortunate !

Even then,
The point of sorrow is, that
The eyes are placed above
And
The feet below !
To seek the shelter of the high-ups indeed,
Is proper and salutary –
– By holding such a firm opinion out of ignorance,
With an idea of becoming venerable,
Some particles of dust
Take refuge into the eyes.
Their venerability remains indeed a distant affair,
Even their free movement
Is sacked...alas !
Now, it becomes impossible for them
To be free from the confinement of the eyes

They lose their very existence
While struggling with their eyes
Constantly from within
And
Those particles of dust...
Come out in an ugly form,
Assuming the shape of a hateful bad-smelling,
Horrible filth.

All this effect
Which has been produced upon us
Is that of an ascetic, who is rich in equanimity"
Having said thus in the end, the eminent trader
Would have just started taking food, when,
Again, from the side of the golden pitcher,
The ironical wordings were used –
" O listen !
The ascetics of funds have been found frequently
The ascetics of sense and sensibility are rarely seen,
And
What purpose is served with that equanimity
Which doesn't possess even the competence
That should infuse at the right time,
A sense of fearlessness into the terror-stricken,
That should give refuge to the shelterless ?
What a mockery is it ?
Without being afraid of the recurrent births and deaths
Having held his hand high as an assurance of
protection,
Having impersonated himself as an ascetic,
In view of blessing a shelter-seeker –

A Challenge thrown, gallantly at the battlefield
By the perseverant one like Rām,
Against the one who treads the path of injustice –
An enemy like Rāvaṇa,
Can proclaim the advent of the First Age-*(Sat-yuga)*[102a]
In the Iron Age–the *Fifth Yuga (Kali-yuga),*[102b]
Can bring down the heavens;
Hereupon...over the earth.

The one who toils is a 'Śramaṇa'...the saint
sinvolved in austerities !

Even a maddest jackal too
Won't like even to touch –
– Eating up is something of a distant affair –
The reddish cheeks
Of such an indolent destitute."

However, even now
The ebullition of the golden pitcher wasn't
pacified,
The noise of bubbling up and down,
The cooking of the *mixed heap, that is*
(Khichaḍī)
Went on continuously
And
More anger in the name of the saint !
" Who asserts it
That
The guest-saint had impartiality within himself ?
He was really an idol of partisanship,
Even the display of impartiality
Wasn't ten percent –
The view point of impartiality is a distant affair.
In whose vision, even now –

There remains the difference between high
and low

The golden and the earthen pots
Aren't still alike
He can never be rich in having equity !

To sustain attachment for the one, indeed
Is to evince repugnance for the others,
The one, who harbours attachment and malice too,
Can never be a saint,
And
Through the adoration of a so-called saint
The worldliness can never come to a close
On the contrary, a genuine saint shall be put to
mockery...

These words are bitter, but true,
Let the truth be welcomed !"

Then,
Having a look of derision upon the
eminent trader
The golden pitcher utters that
"As a householder–
This person, a so-called saint,
If he has been brought up in scarcity
If he has been surrounded by the ghost of
privations –
– Then, how can he well be an enjoyer
Of the invaluable things ?
That is the reason why...
Having disregarded the vessels of gold etc.,
He has welcomed the clay only, –
Like a Lord of penury, that is, a penniless person.

□

Without being profaned by
The bitterness of the golden pitcher,
The water filled inside the earthen pitcher,
On obtaining fame due to the donation to the holy guest
Says, with a sense of calmness that
" There is no water within you
Your foot is stained
With the mud of sin, entirely unholy,
You are devoid of the acquaintance with moral
merit (*Punya*),

That is why...
The worship of the pious is not agreeable to you
The piety is named as 'hypocrisy' by you.
In whose eyes, the black water too has been accumulated
Can this sight be seen by him.
Your sinful eyes
Have drunk up the ailment of jaundice
Otherwise, how is it
That your body looks pale ?

The praise to others pricks you like a thorn
You have flown into a rage
Due to the welcome-reception of the earthen pitcher,–
Only that shall come out which lies there within,
Having yourself taken the rice boiled in whey,
While you are making the others take the
milk-food–
If a belch is felt...it would be sour indeed !

You are gold
You boil up instantly,
The clay is not gold
But –

Certainly, it vomits the gold,
You are the disgorgement of the Earth !

Till today
Neither it has been heard, nor seen
And nor it was read, that
The seed sowed into the gold
Had ever flourished
As a plant
After sprouting, flowering and fruiting.
O thou golden pitcher !
The one who feels a deeper sense of pity
At seeing a life of pains and penury
Only that wealth of feeling has been
regarded invaluable.
What is the use of the wealth of feeling
Which is poor in compassion ?
The clay itself drenches with pity
And
It moistens the others too.
The seed sowed into the earth
With the help of proper air and water
Bears fruits a thousand times more,
On being strengthened and filled by
nutritious substances.

In the natural characteristics of the Earth
Even for a short period
The visibility of even a very little difference
Ends the faith within the vital breathings of the world.
That is
It indicates the advent of universal destruction.

O thou golden pitcher !
One thing more, that –

Had you been really one of the higher caste or colour
Then...indeed...that
Rare vision of the Sun
Why wouldn't have been feasible to you daily ?
May be that, like a day-blind, an owl
You feel afraid of the light,
That is why...
You are buried
Into a very distant...interior part of the Earth.
It is probable that you relish the taste
Of hell, the low1er underworld,
The one, who falls in company with you,
Generally takes to the path of misery –
It is not irrelevant to say so.
At the very sight of you
One perceives the actual presence of bondage,
You are a bondage-bound mortgage too
For the 'self' as well as the 'non-self.'

You are the foundation-stone of a dependent life,
You are the impenetrable, inaccessible
Fort of the capitalism,
And
An endless series of restlessness !

O thou golden pitcher !
Obey, at least once, what I say
Be grateful in this life
Extend immeasurable honour to Mother Earth,
Only remember the name 'Mother', 'Mother'
now !"

□

On seeing the courage of the water
Being thwarted, hereafter,
This pen is filled with endeavour
To add something more, that
"O Thou golden pitcher !
To sing songs in praise of the meritorious is
something distant,
You want to hide your own faults
By blaming the blameless ones !
To express anger against a saint,
To make fun of equanimity
To insult the eminent trader...
Etcetera, etcetera; all these
Are your unpardonable offences,
Even then, making all of them secondary,
I not only place before you –
The majesty of the Earth,
By citing two examples
Lo, I wish to tell...
How much value and importance is attached to
you also,

A lamp as well as a flambeau, that is, 'Maśāla',
In an ordinary manner,
Both of them are the devices of light,
But,
Both of them are separate in their qualities and
attributes.
Having taken a bamboo-piece of one and a
half or two cubits
The rags of cloths are fastened
Very tightly
Placing the one upon the other
At the one of its ends, –

There is a catch-space at the lower end,
Enough, it is a flambeau (Maśāla),

The soil is rubbed
Upon the face of the flambeau
Because, it is uncontrolled.

Flambeau emits light
But very trivial !
The flames of fire flow from it
Like the reddish tongue of a devil,
Those flames can't be termed as brilliant light.
The flambeau is extravagant also,
Its mouth has to be filled
With the oil once and again –
The oil, which is edible and dear, indeed !

Yes ! O yes !!, now and then,
When it is time for recreation,
The bearer of the flambeau,
– Having flung his hands...into the...far-off sky
– Having filled his mouth with kerosene oil,
Blows at the face of the flambeau,
Then...
Within moments, the oil being burnt off,
Gets lost and disappears into the empty space
In the form of smoke similar to blackish clouds.
And
The flambeau appears to be
As fierce as the fire-pool at the time of
annihilation
If even a minor negligence takes place...then
It may create an uproar, extensive harm.... .

The flambeau can't be put out by blowing a puff
The very life of the extinguisher may, indeed, get
extinguished,

No devotee, at the time of his devotion,
Can sustain the meditative retention and resolution
While keeping an eye upon the flambeau,
– The fickleness of the flambeau is indeed the
reason behind it,
'If the aim is unsteady, then
Even the tranquil mind of an expert meditator
Shall become fickle, indeed
There are so many such other
Flaws too, with the flambeau !
How many instances should be quoted, –
Adding thus..., this pen
Turns towards another example.

The lamp is full of restraint
It grows by pushing its wick up,
And
It subsides also by reducing it.
The lamp filled to the brim
With the low-priced kerosene oil
Takes to its own course,
Burns bit-by-bit in fragments,
Doesn't guttle the oil altogether,
The lamp is frugal
Like an ideal house-holder !
How regular, how desireless !
Even a little child
May move on lovingly with a lamp
In his tender hand
And not with a flambeau.

It is more illuminating
Than the flambeau,
Hot, rude, devastative –
That kerosene oil too
Moves itself into upliftment
On obtaining the affection of the lamp.
The lonely, strayed wayfarer,
Frightened and surrounded with darkness,
Feels secure at the very sight of a lamp.

It is heard that, in the cremation ground,
Flambeau is held high into the hands of the ghosts,
At the very sight of which
The eyes of even the undaunted get shut off.

Lo, the reddish glow of the lamp
Seems to be fire-like, though it is not fire,
It is an illumination which enlightens itself
and the others
Which is without fluctuation,
On seeing which, with unblinking eyes,
The attentive cognition (*Upayoga*) of the devotee,
In a missionary spirit
Gradually advancing on and on
From the corporeal to the spiritual,
Makes itself concentrated within moments
After being fully free from all restlessness.
Then, then what ?
The subtle realization with entirety !

There are many characteristics of the lamp
How far should I go on describing !

There should, indeed, be some beginning and
an end also !
Well, then,

O thou golden pitcher !
You are really like a *flambeau*,[103a]
With an foul intention
And
The earthen pitcher
Is like a guiding lamp–
A destroyer of darkness
Valiant and good-natured as *a swan*
(Haṁsa) ![103b]

□

The golden pitcher
Felt itself disgraced
On being compared to a flambeau,
This one-eyed pen
On the pretext of my admiration
Executed this despicable deed,
Through it, I am also proved to be guilty;
I have been used as an efficient cause in
defaming the others,

In this manner
Reproaching himself...
The Earthen pitcher drew a deep sigh
Then,
Started a prayer to the lord :

"These impoverished fortunate ones
Have experienced subjection
Throughout their worldly existence.
Now, –

When shall be perceived
That feeling of supreme self-existence...?
Is that possible or not
In the near future ?
Tell me without delay, O Lord !

Before attaining the Lordship
Praising the one
While punishing the other,
Upgrading the one
While degrading the other,
The one is prosperous, the other poor
The one is worthy, the other worthless
The one is comely, the other-ugly-a monkey s–
Why is it so ?
This disparity in merits
Is agonizing to him, O Lord !
It is all beyond his comprehension
And
On being compelled by this reason
He has to close his eyes.
It shall be so kind of you
It shall be an act of benevolence
If there is equality in every quarter, My Lord !"

□

Being irritated by the request of the
Earthen pitcher
The crystal ewer added, that,
"O thou the sinner !

The Lord doesn't feel pleased
Through a sinful prayer,
That happiness of the pious Lord
Is based upon the abandoning of sins.

I have passed through the ordeal by fire –
Having uttered so once and again,
Whosoever
Wants to prove himself sinless –
It is not only an ordinary sin
But a heinous crime.

There is so much storage of sinfulness in you,
That, for ages –
it can't be burnt away
By setting it on fire,
Can't be dissolved by washing it off.

In the days of universal annihilation
Not only the water,
But the fire also was showered
Upon you, once and again !
Even then,
Thine blemish should have been...somewhat lessened ?

And hark ! indeed !
It doesn't matter, outwardly,
Which seems to be enveloped into the
blackish cloudiness–
That wooden piece of acacia tree too
Looking like the moonless night in the dark
fortnight of *Sāvana* (month)[104]
Passes through the ordeal by fire, and,
In the very first attempt, without frequent
repetitions–

Makes her life
Free from all sins.

That is why...indeed,
She befits, when changed into
The bright beauty of the silver-like ashes."
On hearing this, the Earthen pitcher interrupted,
That

" Despite the ordeal by fire
The coals produced by the acacia tree
Are even more blackish too, among all the other coals
Why is it so ? Please tell me !"

Lo, the ewer answers thus :
" O thou dullard, arrogance-blind, listen to me !
Due to obtaining lesser heat of fire, indeed,
Than in the proportionate ratio,
The wooden pieces, not being burnt to the finish,
Assume the shape of coal,
Otherwise
They are really moulded into the shape of ashes.
In the transaction of this affair
Either the fire itself is at fault
Or
It is the fault of the water-remnant inside the wooden pieces,

But,
The wooden pieces are not to be blamed at all,
Even such an ordinary thing
Isn't known to thee ?

Out you go, anywhere you like !
Even to hold an extra conversation with you –

Is to welcome the defaults...!"
And
The ewer instantly twists her face
Away from the side of the Earthen pitcher.

" If to have even a talk with me
Is a sin,...then...don't converse,
If to have a look at me,
Agonises you, then...don't see,
But
Whatever decision about sinning
Has been taken by you at your own behest,
It is repugnant–
I want to tell you only this very thing.
At least, do give your ear to it !
...Then, try to weigh it !"
And
The Earthen pitcher starts to relate thus :
The perception of the 'self' in its genuineness
The perception of the 'non-self' in its true reality
Is the true knowledge
And
To dwell joyfully within one's own 'self'
Is the 'fruit' of true knowledge.

A relisher of sensuous pleasures
A slave to various *worldly objects of enjoyment*[105] (*Bhogas/Upa-bhogas*)
A waiter to sense-organs
Further more...what furthermore ?
The very slave to his physical body and desire-body
Wishes to become an owner of the worldly objects inimical to 'self',

This is the very sin, indeed...
The father of all the sins !

O thy ewer !
Have a bit of look at thyself too
How is thine mode of life and tendency ?
Thou becomes whitened,
While the milk is filled into thee,
Then, it remains unknown –
Where does thine transparency disappear ?
Thou becomes yellowish
By filling in *Ghī*, that is, clarified butter
And
By coming in contact with the sugarcane juice
Thou befits the greenish lustre, of greenery
On taking over the grace of emerald !

Due to the different contacts,
Thou changes within seconds
Thine gesticulations, hues and views,
Like a lustful nymph,
Thou acts and reacts
Due to the power of alteration.

Not only this much,
The objects lying near thee
Which
Look blackish or yellowish
Greenish or rosy–
Thou assimilates
Their distinguishing attributes;
Thine lustful desires know no bounds...

Thou hast kicked off
Even the caste and community, ah me !
There remains for thee
Nothing like modesty and regard !
Thou can't name it as equanimity
Nor an unlimited competence !

To be influenced by the others,
And
To influence the others –
Upon the both of these
Even the shadow of equanimity doesn't fall.
Mere passions are running
Through thine each and every nerve.
It matters little that, from outside,
Thou appears to be made of crystal,
–Looks as if rippling, bright and fluid,
O Thou fraudulent ewer !
How long thou can keep it a secret ?

No more of gabbling now
The heron[106] has taken a lesson
From this very nature of thine !

Now how should I introduce my own nature ?
Whatever is there, it is open"
The Earthen pitcher spoke thus,
"When was this pitcher introduced to the
veil indeed ?
In the name of a cover,
Only sky has remained stretched over it,
Eagerness and safety, everything
Remains under its this very shade.

If there is any sin with me I should hide it
then...,
I should gather the means to get it concealed,
That freedom of the others
Is never sacked, on their joining here,
Nor is our own effaced by any one.

– No dye and polish tell any effect upon me,
My condition always displays fully the complete
uniformity
It is indeed named as equanimity
For the accomplishment of this very equanimity
The great sages and seers, the saints and hermits
Take refuge with the Earth,
That is,
Practise perfection in sleeping upon the Earth
And

A friend to equanimity, the liberation –
Chooses the devotees of perfect calmness moving
upon the Earth,
– Not the gods, the demons,
And the beings moving under the water and in the sky.
O Thou ewer, do you understand the point !
Thou hast taken the Earth to be crazy,
O Thou a petty puppet of sins !
And
The Earthen pitcher sinks into deep silence...!

□

In the form of a 'doll of sins'
The ewer gets an address,
On hearing which –

That Juice of pomegranate filled into the ewer
Gets a bit more reddened.
Doesn't a true attendant feel painfully restless
On beholding his master's disgrace in his presence ?
The very shaking of the foundation
Is the shaking of the supportable.
And
The Juice adds in an excited voice that,
" The quantity of the eminent trader's decorum,
The asceticism of an ascetic,
His beauty of equanimity and genuine contemplation,
Is how much and due to what reason –
We know it all.
Even a touch at the water on shores
May indicate the depth of it."

And hither
On a blue-black seat made of rosewood
Lying in the glittering silvery tray
The saffron-coloured porridge –
Stuck into which
A Spoon, under the pretext of keeping its head in upside–
down-posture,
Is trying to hide its bashful face
Due to its uselessness,
In support of the pomegranate, speaks out
That
'You have given a true analysis about
an ascetic.'

And
On being neglected by the Saint,
As if weeping with the tearful eyes
In the guise of the *Ghī*–that is the clarified butter
being in excess.

In the hope of obtaining the shelter of a saint
The fragrance of the ghee, that is clarified butter, comes
Upto the nose of the saint.
No sooner than,
An attempt of entering the nose is made, when
By undergoing a kick of purgative method,
And having taken back on its heels.
She returns to the clarified butter, and tells, that
" The shelter of a saint is without a blessed approval–
A dreadful sight is preserved there internally,
–That nose is the destructor of happiness,
I wish to stay really here, without any complaint,
Now, don't send me back there !"

Lo, hither...again
The saffron too, joining its head
Expresses wonder, that
To grant shelter to the shelterless is indeed
something distant,
He didn't get even a glance strengthened by smile.

Remain no more dark-black as before
Whose hair on head,
Having adopted the appearance of ascetics
Who have passed their years and ages

Still, there appears to be absence of asceticism–
They have forgotten their righteous sentiments
In spite of their head being intact.
Where has that life of the high-headed elevated
thoughts
Remained impressive ?
Now, no indication even of uprightness
Is found there within the body, the mind, the
consciousness.

The opportunity has slipped away
Into the unbounded jungle of the past.
I accept,
That since time immemorial
The knowledge truly lives upon *knowledge*,[107a]
The knowable, in fact, exists within the
knowable,[107b]
Even then
Not only to know,
But to be also one with the knowable,
is the nature of knowledge,
So...what is the harm
In looking into this side ?

It seems that the knowledge of the so-called saint
Should have felt alarmed with the knowables,
In such a condition, certainly,
A life opposed to one's temperament and equanimity
Is sliding towards conflict,
Towards doom,
And not towards immortality.
And, hark !
The saffron adds in his sharp tone :
" Non-sliding of the life-time, indeed,
Is the freshness
And
The sailing on in a boat !"

□

In this way,
A debate goes on
Between the Earthen pitcher and the other
vessels– (characters)–

The point of conversation became secondary
Gradually
The Earthen pitcher
Is made indeed a laughing stock
Generally by all the *vessels (characters)*,[108a]
All of them take it to be as worthless.
Mostly, this is the very outcome
Which is obtained through the majority,
– Even a worthy person is included in the class of the worthless

And then,
There appears no sin in the homage to a worthless person.

The different types of eatables,
Like a wicked and dissolute person,
View the equanimity of an ascetic
In the form of only a farce,
And
Disregard openly
The eminent trader as well as the ascetic.

By this time, hither...
All the family-members have finished their meals,
'The experience of to-day is only an experience'
Neither that of privation
Nor that of worldly existence,
In fact, only
The purpose of taking meals has become known,
Having become an ascetic
After discarding the sense of taste,
On absorbing oneself into the adoration of the adorable
'Even that liberation which exists away, at distance of *'Yojanas'*-[108b]

Seems to be speeding towards the perfect accomplisher
Like the sun-rays rushing towards a lotus.
For a few days
The state of debating among these vessels
Like the glare of lightning,
After passing through fits and starts
Appeared to be pacified from outside
Flashing and disappearing at intervals.
The internal situation is different
It remains really alive
Like the warmth of the potter's kiln
Almost in each of the bodied living beings, in one
and all !

The resolve of *the bright half of the lunar month*[109a]
Comes to a finish joyfully,
And
The dark half of the lunar month[109b] arrives.
Having disposed of their routine programmes
The whole of the family goes into the lap of
sleep,
But,
The eminent trader turns sides once
and again while sleeping
The sleep spares no grace upon him,
And
The night is not coming to its fall,
It seems to be prolongated.

The body of the eminent trader, from heels to head,
Is getting heated up like a griddle
The watery element has almost burnt off
That...is why,
Despite the weeping
At interval –

The flow of tears has stopped
Into his oblong eyes
And
His inner affliction
On being obstructed, is getting suffocated inwardly.
The ratio of inflammation into the eyes
Is growing due to the repeated winking of the eyelids,
By the slow blowing of the breeze
At first, indeed,
The fire gets aroused,
Then, it really gains momentum for blazing up.

> Though there is such an arrangement that,
> Through the windows,
> In the bed-chamber of the eminent trader.
> The slow and cooling
> Air enters every moment,
> But,
> Due to the blaze of the heated breaths
> Emitting from the mouth of the eminent trader,
> The whole of the atmosphere
> Changes really into a very hot state.

The sense of grace seemed escaping
From the compassionate skull,
And
The forehead of the eminent trader became blood-red,
To sit up at which
An obstinate mosquito
Who lives upon blood,
Is feeling perplexed, and is descending not to sit.

Because,
On reaching the skull soon
The thirst of the mosquito gets doubled,
The whole of the body gets fully heated up,
The throat gets thoroughly scorched,
Both the wings become feeble,
And
The eagerness flies away somewhere !
And that mosquito,
On the pretence of humming
Wings himself off while uttering, that

> " Oh, the creed of the rich happens to be forceful,
> Their favour falls upon miserliness,
> Nothing is attained on visiting them,
> If something is obtained at random
> According to *the maxim of 'the crow and the palm –'*[110]
> That meeting is found to be mixed with salt
> The thirst is just doubled within moments.

At first, in the form of prostration,
I did their feet-adoration,
Then
Eulogized them through musical recitations
Along with harmonious modulations of voice
At the entrance of their ears.
Even then, I have to pass through this sorry plight !"

> On hearing a calumny against the eminent trader
> By its friend, the mosquito –
> Thirsty for a blood-drop,
> In the form of honorarium –

While circumambulating the eminent trader
The bug tells, that –
" What to say, O Friend !
You have indicated towards the right direction
At the right time,
You have furnished a definition
Of a proud, greedy and miserly one,
This night of error
Which came down since long past,
Which went on into long futurity,
Has been effaced by you,
When do the other living creatures
Except the human beings
Accumulate the possessions for them
In their life-time ?

I too acknowledge the fact that
There are some objects useful to life,
A house, a housewife, *Ghī*–(the clarified butter), the pots etc. –
– They are surely taken under possession,
That is why the saints
Have granted *the wedding-rite of marital hand-taking*[111]
As the protector and promoter
Of the religious culture.
But it is a pity that
The greedy and sinful persons
Turn even the marital hand-taking (ceremony)
Into the life-taking (formality).

Generally, the attendants are asked to serve
In an improper way,

And
The disbursement of salaries too, improper
indeed.
– Such persons tell themselves to be
The progeny of Manu !
The magnanimous human beings !
On hearing the name of donation
The symptoms of paralysis come up
Into their liberal hands,
Even then, whatever is bestowed
Or is caused to be bestowed
In the form of one or a half drop
It is indeed with a sense of ill-will.

The obtainers of which are unable to digest it properly,
Otherwise
Despite being red, why is our blood
So much bad-smelling ?"
And, without being displeased, that bug,
Desisting all expectations of being rewarded,
Having left the task of circumambulation,
Says to the eminent trader, that
"Don't try to confer dry temptations,
A self-dependent life should be lived up,
Offer away the watery libations
To the skill of cunningness !
Pay, homage
To humility which is the mother of eminence !
The sky should be contained
Within the largeness of decorum
And –

The life should become an example of liberality !
Without any pretext–
The troubles of the others should be removed !"
In the end, its view
Is added thus by the bug :

" I am a minutest portion, and not a '*mana*',
[i.e., forty seras]
I am not property, therefore,
I am not, behind some body's death – ,
The cause of battle.
I am not indebted to any body
I am not strong too,
Nor am I living upon or wish to depend upon
The strength of somebody else !
I exist...that is all...
I want to live after this manner.
Neither I have any magical incantation nor any
mechanism
Nor any conspiracy.
The whole of my life is self-controlled.
I am not an impostor,
I am never intent upon finding fault with others
Surely, I live inside a hole !"
And
The bug enters into
A very small opening.

Having heard a genuine discourse
Through the impartial tongue of the bug,
The heart of the eminent trader is filled with joy,
And
Gets somewhat trained also !

□

The withering away of night
And
The flowering of the dawn
Came to pass at a very slow pace.
The moments of expectancy,
Happen to be very long indeed, isn't it !
And that too
At the times of trouble...
Then, there remains nothing to be said !
In that way,
The hour of happiness
Which is *like a limitless ocean,* that is,
'*Sāgaropama*' [112]even
Gallops away with an unmatched speed,
It is not known, when
How and where
Does it pass away ?

It is a reference about a day-break :
The specialists in the science of medicine,
Each one of them surpassing the other in experience,
The physicians of world-fame
Have arrived for the treatment of the eminent trader,
Among whom
There are even such prudent experts
Who
Arrive at a right diagnosis of the disease
By having only a keen look at the patient's face;
While...some others
By discerning, indeed
The colour and shape of the tongue,
Still others, through the throbbing of the pulse

And
By the comparative degree of redness of nails and eyelids
Diagnose the disease.
There has arrived one such physician also
Who, having achieved the maturity of supreme
auspiciousness
In his life
Has achieved success
In the uncommon and rare of voice-understanding
Which was accomplished through a long devotion;
Who is well-versed in the mystical and the ritual
formularies,
Who is a senior expert also
In the science of death-symptoms.

All of them examined the eminent trader
Through their respective pathies,
He appears to be arriving at the condition
Of intermittent semi-delirium-stage,
The motions of the body
Seem to be clouded with drowsiness
But, the gestures of speaking come almost to a
stand still !

Step by step, all of them
Took their own decisions
All of them were unanimous in their opinion,
That

The ailment of feverish inflammation has
caught the patient
There has been the addition of the mental
distress to it,
In one and the same direction
With one and the same speed –
The gratification of desires has been fulfilled;
And...

The physicians said thus –
He shouldn't feel worried so much,
In a small measure
One should take care of one's body too,
The *salary*[113] is indispensable according to
physical needs,
The rest, as truly desired, is also absolutely necessary.
Only through the process of suppression
No activity bears fruitfulness,
Only by repeating the word 'Spirit' or 'soul' over
and over again,
By mere thinking and reflecting
Nothing can be achieved !

To go against the Nature
Isn't the way to real devotedness.
Without heart-felt inclination –
The cherishing of mere indifference to worldly pursuits,
Isn't the triumph of real devotion,
'There exists no regard without a sense of fear'
It shall be better If, with this maxim,
One more line should be added that,
'There can be no way without devotional affection –
And, without the devotional ways and means,
There can be no true song,'
Of our own triumph–
– Of the accomplished eternal truth.
It is true that
the '*Puruṣa*' Is the pleasure-seeker, or Enjoyer
And
The 'Mother–Nature'- '*Prakṛti*'- is the 'Enjoyed'–
Through which the pleasure is sought,...

When the Enjoyer (*Puruṣa*) relishes the juicy essence,
The Nature (*Prakṛti*) too, in the guise of the tongue,
Enhances the tastefulness of the juicy essence
By fondly sprinkling
The saliva over it.
The playful personage, the seer,
When visualizes the sportive scene fondly
With his eyes
Widely opened,
What, then...?
The Nature, free from passional vibrations,...
While removing the obstruction of the eyes–
Through the pretence of eyelids,
Seems as if rubbing them off gently, every moment...!
The *Puruṣa* being even an ascetic
The Nature (*Prakṛti*) acts as His supporter;
She goes on assisting
Upto the peak of accomplishment,
She goes on extending a helping hand, indeed,
To the worker shelter-seeker
While herself being ever-active, self-dependent !

It is not improper also to say that
Whatever actions and reactions
Occur in the *Puruṣa* –
– Moving, quivering, pulsating, –
The expressions of all these,–
The index of the *Puruṣa*'s life
Is based upon the Nature, indeed
– Nature, that is, The *Prakṛti–Female Prakṛti*[114]

In the dissolution of the 'pulse'...!
The very life of the *Puruṣa* ceases to exist...!

In the end,
It is also worth knowing that
The passions do not dwell within
the real Nature (*Prakṛti*)
The fragrance
That is, the sweet smell, certainly resides
therein.
Under the different foul conditions,
The *Puruṣa,* being a slave to passions,
For the satisfactions of his passional feelings
Closes his eyes
Like a wearied traveller
Under the shade of the Kārmic Nature, that is,
Karma-prakṛti,
And
It is something indispensable
For the *Puruṣa* at that time...!

The usage of *tamarind*[115] may be a
different thing,
Even the very remembrance of it
Makes the mouth to water –
Not that of the healthy one,
But that of the person pained by thirst.
It is indeed natural,
But
The point of surprise really is, that
Despite entering into the mouth of the eater,
The mouth of the tamarind itself
Never...begins to water.
Yes ! o yes !
The *Prakṛti*–Nature...then
Seems to be flushed with
Blood–red–fondness in the *Puruṣa* !

This is the very insanity of the *Puruṣa*,
...The foolishness,
Who, under pressure,
Has been a slave to his passions
Since ages bygone !
And
This is the very purity and mercuriality
Of the *Prakṛti*–the Kārmic Nature indeed,
Which, without being disabled,
For ages
Being self-disciplined –
Rains down in showers,
And,
Having liberated the *Puruṣa*,
From a deformed costume and excitement,
Compels him to be naturally self-disciplined,
Makes his path excellently genuine !

The *Puruṣa* and the *Prakṛti*–the Kārmic Nature–
–The world is, only the name of
The playful performance of the both of these–
–To say thus, is a stupidity, the mere exaltation
of delusion !
The real player is the Supreme Personage
Puruṣa Himself,
And
The *Prakṛti*–Kārmic Nature, is only a toy !
It is not a fun and frolic
To let oneself become a toy,
It is something of a special sportsman !

□

You have well-acquainted yourself
*With the Prakṛti (Mother Nature) and 'The Supreme
Personage',*[116] *Puruṣa.*

The knowledge is acquired, the mystery revealed –
'*The Puruṣārtha of human existence*[117]
Can't bear fruitfulness to The Mankind
Without attaining the favourableness of the
Kārmic Nature/Mother Nature' –
On hearing this, the family accepted it
In the form of a finding issued forth by the physicians.
And
Entreats with due humility that
" The eminent trader should recover his health soon,
The illness should be remedied –
Such a treatment should be administered.
The prescribed course of dieting
Shall be followed cent-per-cent,
Whatever is suggested by you
Is, therefore...altogether acceptable.

Don't worry for the remuneration, please,
It shall be offered
With due regard and honour,
Like a lady-in-waiting
Who is found always prepared
As a delicate beauty of a shadow...!

In that manner
That insight of the physicians
Doesn't turn towards the remuneration,
It ought not take such a turn, –
– Like the intellect of a chaste
Noble virgin, who leads a life of dignity,
Despite this
The sway of the Iron Age (Kaliyuga) itself is also
there, indeed –

The life remains unable to accomplish its objectives
If it becomes capable of going ahead
It finds itself unable to remain firm.
We have been hearing
We have also been observing indeed, that

> The reckoning and amassing of money
> Only
> Has become the purpose of all the various arts.
> The means of livelihood, fie...fie...
> Are emitting the smell as that of an animal's
> diseased tongue –
> The nose has been accustomed,
> And
> In this matter, it is regretted, –
> The eyes express nothing at all.

What the real purport behind a word is, –
– Carries no sense now !

> The, word *'Kalā'* [118] itself indicates that
> '*Ka*', that is,–the ' Soul' with happiness'
> '*Lā*', that is, 'to bring'-'to give'
> There may be any art –
> The life is flowered with happiness, peace
> and prosperity
> By each and every art,
> There is real joy neither in the money itself
> Nor through it !"
> Having heard the utterings relating to art
> Through the words of the family –
> Which is far away from sensuous greed and
> ardent desire
> The group of physicians becomes wakeful,
> On seeing which, the family too –

Brings enough of change
Into the discussion under reference
And
Makes some entreaty when,
The earthen pitcher meanwhile interrupts :
" So far as the prescribed course of diet is
concerned
Really...
All the medical sciences
Are uniform in their opinion, indeed –

If the prescribed course of diet is correctly
followed...then
The medicines are not really needed,
And if
The prescribed course of diet goes unheeded,...even then
The medicines are not needed.

In spite of this, if
The references to medicines are required,
Then, hark !
Not only the immediate bodily ailments,
The ailments of the Sentient Being too,
since time immemorial
Which
Exist in the form of birth, old age and death,
Take to their heels within moments,
'Śa' (श), 'sa'(स), 'ṣa' (ष)–[119]
These are the three mystic seed-syllables,
That colossal tree of the freedom from disease
Flourishes through them !
At the time of their pronunciation
With all its might and main –

The breath has to be inhaled
And
Has to be ex-haled through the nose
In the form of the rhythmic tone of '*Omkāra*'.

This '*śa*' (श)–that is in its three-fold entity- [*śakāratraya*] –
Is offering its own introduction, that
'*Śa*' (श)–that is,
The pacifier of dirty emotions (*Kaṣāya*),
An indicator of *Śaṅkara*–the Supreme One, causing bliss
beyond doubt,
The abode of perpetual peace...!
'*Sa*'(स)–that is,
The companion of all
– Which takes the whole of the world in its totality
within its fold,
The world in its reverse form
The means of innate happiness
The incessant source of equanimity...!
And
The graceful play of '*ṣa*' (ष) is remarkable.
The syllable '*ṣa*' (ष) makes its appearance
When the stomach of '*pa*' is cut across –
'*Pa*'[120]– (प), that is,
The sinful and the auspicious actions
Which result in worldliness,
Through which, being under delusion, the *Puruṣa* (Soul)
goes astray,
That is why
The syllable '*ṣ*'(ष), which remains beyond the grip
of all actions (Karmas)
Bi-sects the belly of the sinful as well as the
auspicious deeds.
This is explained as the inward dimension,
Now pay heed to the outward...dimension too...!

The Earth is the Mother of the past,
The Earth is the Mother of the future too.
The Earth is the Mother of sentiments,
The Earth is the Mother of majesty too.
The Earth is the Mother of sensibility,
The Earth is the Mother of possibility too.
The Earth is the Mother of mansion,
The Earth is the Mother of mountains,
The Earth is the Mother of all the living
beings on earth.
The Earth is the Mother of hunger,
The Earth is the Mother of all the
groundwork too.
The Earth is the Mother of birth,
The Earth is the Mother of prosperousness too,
And
The Earth is the Mother of all that is
self-existent too
Through all the three courses of a time
Through all the three worlds –
The Earth is there in the background of everything.
Nothing else is seen except the Earth
The Earth...the Earth...the Earth...the Earth
Hither, thither and everywhere...the Earth !
The lexicographers in the prime of the Era,
Have said : *'Bhū Sattāyam'*, [121]
That is, '*The Earth behind all existence*' !

And listen,
The essence of the Earth is 'Soil'
That is why...
This maxim is humming : 'The soil, the water and
the air,
Is the panacea for a hundred ills'

This remedy is, indeed, independent
It is not wasteful but economical.
Through its usage
Adverse reactions of any type do not appear,
Within any corner of the body or the mind.

□

The heart may get excited to have a touch –
– The dark black soil, soft like saffron,
Filtered in such a manner –
Is mixed up with cool water in accurate quantity,
Having kneaded it well,
It is turned into one single lump,
After moulding it into a cap
At first,
It is plastered around the eminent trader's head
For the sake of warding off the delirium.

The manner
In which the hot iron-ball,
Fallen into a vessel full of water,
Absorbs the water –
From all sides –
Similarly, the soil-cap too
Starts drinking up every second,
The heat pervading the head.
The more the proportion of the heat
Goes on decreasing,
The more the dawn of awakening
Manifests itself in the same order.

Look here,
Through the subtle vibrations of the lips
The inference is reflected that
The effort of pronouncing the holy symbol –
'*Omkāra*', is gaining ground.

In that manner,
The adoration of '*Omkāra*',[122]
Which is the winner and protector of the three
worlds,

Is going on inwardly,
Which is the resultant of a long-continuing devotion.

The tradition of the 'supreme-power-of-speech' *(Parā-vāk)*[123]
Beyond the range of comprehension
Remained formerly unheard-of, unknown
According to the conventional scriptures
It has been acknowledged attainable 'by ascetics *or*
Yogīs',

Having originated at the very root-base,
that is *(Mūlodgamā)*[123 (1)] it travels
Upto the navel, with face rising upwards,
Due to it being motivated by the vital wind !
Then, that very 'voice'
After circumambulating the navel,
Manifests itself as an 'appearance of
a particular measured Sound *(Paśyantī)*[123(2)]
Which, like a vibrating wave of splendour,
Goes on singing into the well of the navel *(Nābhi-kūpa).*
But,
It is totally without any syllables,
It remains beyond the comprehension of the literates
Who, being merged into the discussions of the mundane
world, *(Vipaśyanā)*[123(3)]
Are very far away from temperance.

Again that very 'particular measured inner sound' that is (*Paśyantī*)
Rises up towards the liberal heart
Enters the lotus-heart to move it,
Emits forth the sweet-smiling utterances
Through each of the blooming petals,
Tickles them like a mother !
Into the mid-heart –
Is now called the 'mediatory', that is, *Madhyamā.*[123(4)]

And, we should know, that
Not a nourisher, but a young child, indeed –
Who is untouched by the vices,
Can know the nature of the 'Mother'.
Then, that very 'mediatory' now,
Starts its journey
From the inner world towards the outer world,
According to the 'purpose' of the '*Puruṣa*', that is, the mundane soul !
The 'purpose' the '*Puruṣa*', that is, the mundane soul !
Is found almost of the two types –
Based upon the difference between ''vice' and 'virtue' that is (*Pāpa-Puṇya*).

> The purpose of the speech-functioning
> Which is performed by the great worthy persons
> Is, indeed, to accomplish the welfare of the others;
> And
> The purpose of the speech-affair
> Operated through the sinners and their misdeeds
> Is to escape from the well-being of others-oppression.
> With the help of the palate, throat, tongue etc.,
> When that very central sound or 'mediatory' comes out–
> – Which becomes the part of the hearing by all,
> Is called '*Vaikharī*',[123(5)] that is, the speech in general.

Why the naming of the speech
Emanating from the mouth of a sensualist as well as
that of a saint
Is done in one and the same way –
No such suspicion should be entertained.
It appears to be similar
But, really, it bears no likeness.
Here, in view of a worthy person
There is the difference, not only in its purport,
But, there is difference in the usage of wordings also.

The utterances emerging from the lips of a
virtuous person
'*Vai*'[124(a)] that is, certainly
Are '*kharī*', that is, genuine
–Which is the accomplisher of happiness and
prosperity.
Doesn't the outpour from the clouds
Take the form of a sugar candy
On getting recourse to a sugarcane ?
And
The speech coming out from the mouth of a
wicked person
'*Vai*'[124(b)] – that is, certainly –
Is '*Khalī*', that is, fraudulent and sinful
Without substance and troublesome,
Doesn't that very out pour from the clouds
Envelops itself into bitterness
On reaching the root of the margosa, that is the
Neema tree ?

Hereat
In place of the Hindi syllable – '*lī*'
The Hindi syllable – '*rī*' has currently been used
Due to heedlessness or ignorance,

Basically, indeed the Hindi syllable – '*lī*' – is really
under usage
That is, the word is '*Vaikhalī,*' indeed.
Nevertheless...if
The text '*Vaikharī*' is taken for granted... then
We interpret it
In a different way, that
The Hindi syllable – '*kha*' –
Denotes void, nothingness !
Therefore
Having left the syllable – '*kha*- aside,
On joining the remaining two syllables –
The word '*Vairī*'[125] – that is 'the enemy' – comes into being,
– Those utterings of the wicked persons
Act as an 'enemy'
To our own 'self' as well as that of the others !
Hence
It is proper to acknowledge the word
As '*Vai-khalī*' or '*Vairī*' – That is, an enemy
...Let the just be !

□

In a natural mood,
With accurate pronunciation
The eminent trader eulogizes the Supreme
Spirit.
The family holds discussions with him,
The physicians are also introduced –
He tells the experience of his agony,
But
Due to ceaseless inflammation –

The eyelids are not vibrating at present,
They have not regained still the capability
Of beholding the light.
Even the tender rays of the jewels
Appear to be the sparks of fire,
On looking at the unwinking eyelids
The sacred pitcher again says that –
" There is nothing to be worried for,
Leaving aside the heart-area only
The soil can be experimented
Upon any organ of the body.

It may be a wound filled with ripe or
raw blood,
It may be internal or external injury,
It may be unbearable ear-ache,
If the skull is being split with fever,
If the nasal ulcer is there,
If the nose flows due to cold
If it bursts due to heat,
And
If the severe headache is half or full –
The usage of the soil shall be beneficial
In all these conditions.
In as much as
The bones of hands and feet, if fractured,
May be set again..., without delay,
By plastering with the soil !
The work may be taken up..., as before,
Within a few days !

How far can be depicted the dignity of the Earth,
Where is such a balance,
How to weigh ?
With whom should the Earth be compared
Hereat ?
The significance of weighing and valuating
Isn't based upon the money-matters,
But
It carries with it the attributes, the characteristic
qualities."
Only such words by the earthen pitcher were
enough when
The two small balls weighing two *Tolās*[126] each,
Prepared with the Soil
Were placed upon both the eyelids –
After moulding them as fried cakes,
And
Within a few minutes, the signs of success
Were noticed by the physicians !

Hence, continually, with a gap of twenty four minutes,
Upon the lower part of the navel also,
With a stop-gap, turning upside down,
During the day and the night –
Repeatedly for six or seven times,
This very experiment was duly conducted.

The group of physicians, on being impressed
By the fruitful treatment through the soil,
Finalizes its opinion
About the diet and drinks,
In conformity with the sacred pitcher, that,
After boiling up into an earthen vessel,

Then cooling down the milk fully,
It has to be served to the patient as a drink,
To a considerable extent,
Having congealed the milk
By adding rennet into that same vessel
proportionately,
And extracting all the butter
After churning it with a churning-stick,
The pure and simple butter-milk has to be served.
As bright and white as a pearl –
Delicious, digestive, endowed with goodness,
Millet of Karnāṭaka
Crystallized into porridge,
Which is not too watery,
Has to be served with butter-milk
Before it is the noon-time,
Warding off the evening hours –

Because
The sun-element, at *the (sandhi-kāla),* that is,
twilight-hour,[127a]
Is found in its termination
And
There comes into being the rise of the 'dual-element'
That is '*Suṣumnā*'-[127b] which
Has been regarded as the suitable time
For meditation and devotional austerities.
The presence of sensuous element at the time of *Yoga*
Is the reason of ailments,
And
The presence of some disease at the time of
worldly pleasures
Is the cause of sorrow.

Then..., at what point of time –
That continuation of sorrows ceases to be...?
When
The flow of the time-stream glides far...and
far away,
Then, and then alone...somehow...
May bless the dark blue shade of the *Aśoka Tree !*[128]

□

After a few days, not only partially,
But wholly, all was cured and improved,
The vagaries of inflammation were shattered
Through this fruitful experiment.
As the fancifulness of the fair mood of a poet,
On beholding the vividness of stanzas,
Is pacified on its own accord
After shrinking within itself !

The holy books say, we should learn, –
The true value of the medicines
Is the cure of the ailments.
Any medicine, whatsoever it be,
Never carries less or more value with it,
Even then
The belief of the rich and the wise
Holds the sway which goes contrary to it,
And which
Is found resting upon the costly medicines only.
The eminent trader
Is an exception to it.

The group of the physicians was honoured,
It was rewarded according to its services,
And
The medical practice based on non-violence
Should survive for ever, –
Keeping only this very fair objective in view
With his eyes wet with tears of joy,
Showing due respect with humble submission,
–The eminent trader himself, with his own hands
Placed into the hands of the group of physicians
A huge amount of money bearing nine digits
And
Acknowledged himself obliged
At the favour bestowed by the group.

Turning towards the eminent trader,
The group, while departing, asserted that
All those surprising events
Were really caused by the Earthen pitcher
And its cooperativeness also,
They were only instrumental cause to it, the treating...agents.
And
Expressing their thankfulness,
They bade the final good-bye with a sense of gratefulness !

□

'Once again, before us,
Has turned back the hour
Of self-aversion
Of humiliation.'

–And saying thus
The golden pitcher, feeling some compulsion,
Sinks down into cheerlessness,
Like an inactive jungle-dweller
Fallen from the Faith in Soul !

Once again, an opportunity has arrived,
These well-bred ears of noble descent
Have still to hear
The songs of repute of the ill-bred folk !
And even that too
From the mouth of the wise
Surrounded with the greed for money.
Oh ! what an agony is this,
It is unbearable,
Let me indeed, drive the nails into my ears !

That beauty of Truth
Is appearing to be somewhat blurred;
The ruddiness of dusk also is about to sink,
Once again, a scene has appeared
Before these sacred eyes.
Regarding as the holy ones, the wicked
Are being seated over the high throne.
And
Those, who have repealed the sins,
Are being termed as hypocrites, impostors.

This nose did not cherish such a hope
Nor did it believe that
Once again, towards this direction –

A dry wave shall arrive moving fast,
The bad smell of the moral degeneration of humanity
And
Having polluted the tender nostrils
Shall make them numb...!
Despite all this, the fury knew no appeasement
The golden pitcher adds something more
With a grave countenance clouded with worry
That

"It should be ascribed to the influence of the
'Kalikāla',
that is, 'Iron Age',
Or, even,
A glimpse of the gloomy future, –
If
The world is becoming averse
To the usage of the original things !
And
Is becoming prominent in the consumption
Of the worldly things, phew !

The gracefully glittering
Garlands of gems and jewels
The chains of charming pearls,
With countless curves of carvings –
The broadly dazzling diamond-necklaces
Producing rustling and rattling sound,
The dumb-like corals
Making a parrot's beak ashamed of its beauty,
The pieces of sapphire gladdening the eye –
– At the very sight of which
The bluishness of a peacock's neck takes to dancing,–

The topaz scattering saffron
The transparent crystals,
Despite being flame-like reddish –
The rubies, a heap of tranquil rays...
– Not only coolness is obtained by us
Through all these things,
They also help in healing up
The fatal diseases,
Like diabetes, cough, asthma, tuberculosis etc.,
And, generally, the life remains secure
From the adverse effects of the planets too,
But today !
Only the glass and rubbish are being honoured.

– The pitchers, jars and platters of gold
The mugs, cups and plates of silver,
The copper jars, boilers, big cooking pots,
Which protect from the watery flaws,
The huge shallow brass-dishes, kettles,
And other such things etc., the original utensils,
Are being sold,
And even the rich and the wise are buying
The most inferior and harmful utensils.
In the market today, with due regard,
At every step, only the steel
Strikes the eye of every one.
Inside the jail even,
The criminals are enchained
With the handcuffs and fetters only of steel
Around their hands and feet. –

How far one should go on relating
And...hither
Around the wrists of the young boys and girls too
Only the bangles of steel are found.
Does the science really go this way ?
Is this, indeed, the development ?
Enough of it,
The gold has gone into a deep slumber now,
Wage a war with the iron...weapons, fie !

Hark ! listen !
A bit more, the glory of the 'Iron Age', that
is– 'Kaliyuga' !
In the moon-lit night –
Having taken the clean cool water
Fallen off from the moon-stone gem
And having rubbed off into it
The sandalwoods from *the Mount Malaya,*[129a]
When besmeared as a balm
Upon the forehead and the navel-spot,
Has been regarded as a boon
For pacifying the ailments of inflammations.
It is also heard and experienced too that
Having mingled and dissolved the camphor
in due quantity
Into the instant fresh
Pure and fragrant *Ghī*-(clarified butter) –
Massaging with soft fingers upon the
'*Brahma-randhra*'–
That is, the *suture,*[129b] on the mid-top of the head,
And

With the effective oils etc. (like almond oil),
Massaging by the expert massagists

Over the back-bone part
Has been regarded as a proven remedy
For curing the inflammatory ailments.
Having discarded these proper treatments
Advised by the experts, –
It is the lack of wisdom, indeed,
To apply the paint of soil and mud !

Something similar has been happening
In regard to the diets and drinks too –
The taking of tasteful strength-giving milk,
The taking of food prepared by *Ghī* (clarified butter)
Which provides vitality and energy;
Prepared with curd, the victuals etc. –
Which ward off the untimely death,
Which produce gentle peaceful sentiments,
– Such tasty, diverse foods have been given up,
That very situation has resulted
In the prevalence of inflammatory ailments
By which, even the eminent trader has got himself
encircled,
And
The usage of whey without substance,
Along with the porridge of millet devoid of vitality
Is to extend invitation to poverty.

One thing more has to be added that
Spend the money frugally, and not extravagantly
Never, indeed, spend it wastefully,
Not by mistake, even in a dream.
And
Non-spending is the...best...indeed !
–This is a general notion, which
Doesn't touch the genuine nature of things.

The reason is that
From the real point of view,
Every object contains within it
As much of expenditure
As much of income it does provide,
And
It furnishes the income only
In proportion to the expenditure incurred.
There falls the difference
Not even of an iota of time
Between the income and the expenditure
So that
One may get a breathing gap for hoarding.

Here at,
This very regularity of getting and spending
Has been regarded as unending,
Well, then, in such a condition,
Where does the question of
Prodigality and extravagant expenditure
remain ?

Can our 'especial endeavours'
Bring change into 'essential reality of things' ?
No, no, never.
Yes ! Oh Yes !
Our polluted minds may feel
A sense of affecting a change.
And,
This is the very root of the world – 'egotism'.
The conclusion drawn from it is, that
A well-established doctrine can't be of our own accord–
We may simply adopt it as a doctrine."

While moving towards the end
Like a lamp flaring up
Due to unfiltered oil in it
– The golden pitcher, out of excitement,
Makes so many comments
Upon the eminent trader, including his family,
Upon the penal of physicians in their absence,
And
Upon the Earthen pitcher even,
Out of envy-jealousy-malice-pride
Strong incitement etc.–
But it
Has been ineffective indeed upon this side,
All really remains the same as before.

In that manner,
What is exactly the capability of anger !
How far shall it stay before forgiveness ?
The one who is bitten by a snake
May even pass away
And may not, indeed,
He may even get himself poisoned
And may not, really,
But
That snake, after biting,
Slips certainly into a swoon.
What else,
The golden pitcher has to face the same condition,
– Its shadow is falling upon
The other small jars of gold and silver,
Tiny in size and shape, lying near-by it.

For some time, the sway of
The peaceful quietness prevails,
Then, brimming with gentle sentiments,
The earthen pitcher itself
Says to the tiny golden-jar
That,

" O Thou tiny jar !
Where is thou appearing to be
In thine...past form ?
Thou art indulging to-day,
In imitating only the yesterday !
Thou hast not retained now
Thine past potness...!
Where is that tender loveliness
Upon thine cheeks !
It seems as if
That sweet nectar of thine lips
Hast almost...faded...away somewhere !
The body has been lying alone
In the absence of wisdom,
As if artless and uneasy,
With a shabby appearance
O Thou tiny jar !
Where is thou appearing to be...
In thine past form ?"

□

On hearing these sarcastic remarks from
the earthen pitcher
On finding itself to be a laughing stock,...

–Finding itself insignificant and neglected
Gets Filled with the feeling of revengefulness,
Heated and suffocated from within, the golden pitcher !

Lo,
the conspiracy to finish
The eminent trader along with his family !
The day and the hour is affixed
To invite the terrorism.

It is certain that
the terrorism is procreated
When prestige gets indeed hurt.
Over-protection or over-exploitation too
Brings the similar results,
Then
The aim of life becomes, not to make amends,
But the sense of retaliation...to take revenge !
Which is
Dire ignorance, the lack of far-sightedness,
Not only fatal for others
But also for one's own self !

In this matter, secretly,
The golden pitcher holds discussion
Among its friends and followers.
No member of the family
Smells this vulgarity, –
That nose of the civilized ones
May remain hungry, but
Doesn't, even by mistake, or in dream,
Feel inclined towards the bad-smelling.

The large black bee and the fly
Can't be one and the same
Only due to both having smell-liking.
Leaving behind the flowers filled with sweet odour
The large black bee never sits upon
The things like
Sewage-urine-phlegm-flesh etc.,
–On being caught wherein
The dullish fly dies.

□

To-day, the gang of terrorists shall arrive,
Along with the storm of disaster at mid-night.
And hither,
A huge problem raised its head
Before the Golden pitcher, that,
One more section of dissenters
Has been formed within themselves.
It has dishonoured the taken decision
It has declared it as injustice, incivility,
Its co-operation and support
Has not been consented.

The group has asked
Not to put up frantic dance of injustice
Upon the altar of justice.
The directress of that group –
Is the bright ewer of crystal,
It
Is under the sway of the Earthen pitcher !

By and by
The wisdom of the ewer
Has come to be understood by several persons,
And
The side of the ewer
Is gaining favour without any effort.

The big and small jars of silver
Jumping up with some shinings,
The big and small spoons
Misled by the cunning conductors
The copper vessels, growing red in face,
As if tied up out of malice,
The thirsty cups and plates...
Appeased and mixed up with the royal
arrogance.
Nourished under the fondness of the others,–
Hence caught into the sway of delusion,–
Of such type, –
Almost all the utensils,
Which
Were sniffed by the snake of partiality,
Bow themselves at the feet of the ewer,
After discarding the golden side.
Lo now
The ewer says : " O Thou Golden-pitcher !
The one, who is advancing towards the
Mother-existence,
Who is ascending the stairs of equanimity,
Into his deeper insight –
The pieces of gold, as well as those of the clay,
Are one and the same,
And, really, such is the true state !

Hence, take advantage of the opportunity
Don't see with a view of insistence,
Now, you step down
From the Vehicle of pride !
Get yourself prostrated at the feet of those,
Who are prideless, despite being the divine souls;
And get yourself through the shoreless sea
of sins !"

□

Lo, when the effect of the ewer was
To tell itself upon the doer of terrible deeds–the
golden-pitcher !
In the context of Sītā's liberation from bondage,
Where the sharp-witted Mandodarī's[130] address
Did remain influential,
Where the arrogance of Rāvaṇa did become insignificant ?
So contrary to it,
The golden pitcher arrived at the position
As that of a cauldron, full of boiling oil,
While four or five drops of cold water fall into it.
Horrible show of the uncontrolled fret and fume !
Then,
With sharp excitement,
The roaring of the Golden pitcher !
"I shall spare none of you,
Upon you, the showers of mercy
Aren't possible as yet,
You will have to face just now
The hour of annihilation."
Now, what else remains to be asked !

There is every probability of an approaching mishap,
Taking place before the affixed hour, indeed !

Lo, hither...
The ewer too
Drops a hint to the Earthen pitcher
And
The Earthen pitcher cautions the family,
Everything in a hushed up manner, but
Secretly active !

Let the innocent public of the neighbourhood
Shouldn't get itself entangled,
On falling into the trap of this whirlwind –
– With this very fair intention
The Earthen pitcher advises the eminent trader, that
" You have to start off, from here
At once, with your family,
The delay may prove to be fatal."
And,
Through the back-way of the palace,
The whole of the family runs away abruptly !

No one knows their whereabouts
Not even the ewer itself,
Indeed, the condition isn't fit to be leaked out !
'Someone may well be reliable, but,
Upto the ears of the newly-acquainted,
The confidential matter, the complete matter
Shouldn't reach at this stage'
And
The eminent trader holds the Sacred Pitcher-guide
Into his hands, –

The sin-fearing family follows him !
Every now and then, turning aback, all of them
Cross over the town and the town-gate,
Then, on entering the dense forest, they
disappear !

The various types of fine trees
Kissing the high sky
Are standing with open umbrellas,
The ground is the winner of the weariness
It looks graceful with rich greenery
The shadows have spread a carpet over the ground.
The tiny and huge shrubs and bunches
Laden with flowers, fruits and foliage,
As if scattering smiles
Upon the toiling and wearied way-farers.
Those charming creepers
Embracing the trees from feet to gullet
Seem to be calling and enticing the visitors,
And
Are asking the passers-by, walking constantly,
To take repose for a while.
Thus...the whole of the family, taking a breath of
fearlessness,
Sits down, for some time,
At the neat and clean dry ground devoid of creatures !

On being drenched into perspiration,
The bodies of the family
Feel harmed and hurt by grief –
The minds of the family,
On getting the touch of the cool wind,
Feel together a sense of peace.

Which received the nectar of love
From the lips of the flute-player
In a hereditary way, through ages,
– That row of bamboos
With its fleshy arms, –
Imitating the arched gateway
Which keeps up the auspicious and keeps off the inauspicious,
Prostrates at the feet of the Earthen pitcher –
Regards itself as the most blessed one.
And
In the form of the drops from the eyes,
Showers the bamboo-pearls.
Bright enough like swans, Supreme Swans, that is, great ascetics.

Meanwhile, hither...
On being harassed by a flesh-eater lion,
A group of alarmed elephants
Running in search of fearlessness,
All of a sudden,
Is seen when advancing towards their side,
The family addresses thus :
'Don't be afraid; come brothers !'
And
Gives them an affectionate call.
Hurrah ! how excellent, then !
At the feet of the family
The group experiences a breath of unique peace–
Like that of a child sensing dauntlessness
Into the singular lap of the mother
Then, –

Making fun of the bamboos,
Crossing over the bamboo-pearls,
The group offers its valuable heap of pearls
Before the Earthen pitcher
In all humility !
That is why, perhaps,
These pearls are well-known
By the name of elephant-pearls.

Under the favourable atmosphere of quietness
While staring at each other,
Some moments pass, when
Both, the elephant-pearls
As well as the bamboo-pearls
Transmit their respective brilliance
Into each other
To a great extent –
At this hour, the long-deserted intimacy
Is being put to test.
But,
That discriminative gifted intellect
Is left as if without a tongue,
The sense of melancholy resting upon
'Ownness' and 'otherness' has almost faded away,
The sense of difference between 'ownness' and 'otherness'
Has almost crumbled down.
All else remains without any remnants,
The residue is only
The splendour…! the lustre...!! the light...!!!

□

When the wrong notions get vanished
All the labours get disappeared
The body recovers its health
The mind feels overjoyed.

Still the path has to be covered up in advance
So...the family, having stood up, just starts, when
A roaring sound is heard from behind
–Which, having emanated from the mouth of a gang of persons,
Deafens the ears;
–Which lives upon violence and is aggressive.
" O thou, the cowards, stay back !
Whereto and how far shall you go on fleeing ?
Abandon now the attachment to your own bodies.
O thou, the sinners, stop !
You have to bear the consequences for your sins,
O you, the hiders of ill-gotten money,
Under the garb of religion !
Tell us the exact truth,
How much money you have plundered
How many lives have been ruined by you !
Remember all those things within your conscience
You should embrace death within moments now !"
And...
On turning round, when the family looks back...then
A gang of terrorists comes to their sight,
With the force to wound and kill even the elephants !
– Who carry weapons into their hands,
Who are blowing them once and again through the space,

Causing the flames to wake up
Like a flash of lightning, and –

Hither, the eyes of the public get closed;
Those who are frequently munching their lips,
Who are being enveloped into anger,
As a result of which, the blood
Is dripping from the lips;
Whose body is well-built
Whose mind is stubborn
By whom
The lower edges of the '*dhotīs*'[131]
After being folded up,
Have been fastened tight around their waists,
Whose loins draw almost no parallels
With the waists of lions,
Like banana trees are their thighs –
Whose fleshiness
Is laughing loudly.
This is the very reason why
From a distance do not appear the knees,
Which are thrusting themselves into obscurity.
The hair on their heads
Are dense, curly and dark-black
Which are hanging down upto the shoulders
Appear to be like dreadful black serpents.
Who have a broad chest,
– Into whose sturdy shins
A network of nerves has swelled out,
Like the roots of a Banyan tree into the Earth
Whose agitated eyes
Are emitting fire
Like a jasper.

The surface of whose fore-heads
Bear triangular marks of saffron
It seems as if the very third eye of *Mahādeva*
Is gazing, on getting opened.
The gang is about to move in the *Rāhu*[132a]–like way
With its black body, from top to bottom.
By whom
Only a glimpse being shown,
Makes even the cruel death feel shivering !
Like the tails of the young horses of Kathiyawad[132b]
Who keep up blackish moustaches,
Raised upwards
And twisted with excessive arrogance.
– On beholding whose robust
And strong arms,
Even the strength of the glorious Sun
Becomes insane.
– The arms, around which,
Fastened with black strings
The lemon-fruits are tied up,
Ultimately, I should rather say, that,
Within whose each and every limb
The lack of mercy is really filled up.
–The face, indeed, follows the heart !, isn't it !

Generally, the bouncing bodies
Are built-up by the suppression of mercy,
That is why, these lines from the saints say :
"O Thou embodied soul !
The bouncing body, radiant with splendour

Isn't the aim of life,
Thou couldn't attain the spiritual incorporeal status
Upto even this day
Due to thine corporeal attachment.
On seeing the merciful civilians
Being attacked
By merciless villains –
It is difficult to safeguard against the blows of the swords
To save the family from such assaults, indeed
Is inevitable, the prime duty of the *Āryas*
(civilized people)"
Pondering thus, the group of elephants,
After taking the family amid itself,
Pitches there, after encircling them from all sides.

□

The roaring of the elephant-ring
Resounds across the vast sky,
The firmness of the Earth gives way,
Even the campus of the mountain-ranges too
Experiences the endeavour,
The birds flying all alone
Being terrified and losing all sense of direction,
Enter the nests of the others,
The deep slumber of the pythons
Is broken all of a sudden,
The wakeful ones suffer from fever,
Forgetting its right path a sect of deers
After going astray, stops before a lion,
Even the snake-holes, huge in size…indeed...

After returning to dust
Fall down upon the Earth,
And
Emitting poison, the savage serpents
Coming out with a whizzing sound,
In whose eyes, the wrath
Is dancing frantically,
Having raised up their expanded hoods,
Having erected themselves upon their tails,
Start gazing at the obstructive element!

The serpents come to know at once
The root cause of the havoc.
The family is found to be flawless
Which
Is engaged into the holy remembrance of its God,
The group of elephants is found furious
Which
Is occupied with the protection of the civilians,
And
According to the *Pāriśeṣya-nyāya*[133](final judgment)
Based upon the axiom of residue
The remaining group is found guilty
Which is
Seeking indulgence in devouring all.

No more of enquiries, then!
The leading serpent told each one of them, that
"No one should be bitten,
No one should be put to death
We have to provide simply a strong
pushback to the foe.
There is a penal code
For warding off the violent rudeness –

I acknowledge,
Death-sentence is the ultimate one
Of all the punishments.
Through the capital punishment
The others may indeed learn a lesson,
But
For the one, who is being punished,
All chances of his progress are lost forever.
The penal code may accept it or not,
To punish a cruel criminal
With cruelty,
Is really a crime in itself,
It is to stumble from the path of justice."

□

Now
The terrorism is surrounded from all sides.
Wherever one looks at, there...everywhere
Countless male and female serpents –
As if, from the lower regions, the king of
serpents (*Nāgendra*)
Ascends upon the Earth with all his
retinue
To favour the fallen and the down-trodden.
It is the first Incident that
The terrorism itself
Feels terrorized,
It is in the position of retreat,
It was black since its very inception –
On beholding its hour of death-at-hand,
It's face grew still more dark-black ! –

The force of terrorism
Is becoming inactive by and by.
Like that of a powerful elephant
Entrapped into a morass !
While cleaving off the earth,
When does a river, gliding upon a slope,
Holds conversation with a mountain ?
What else,
This is the very condition of the terrorism,
And
Entering into a dense forest, it has hidden itself.

" Make no mention of creating havoc,
Go on mounting the struggle !
Make no mention of defeat,
Go on achieving excellence !

And...hark !
No mango fruit grows
Upon a fatally twisted branch,
Even if it grows at all
It doesn't get ripened,
And
Within the opportune time,
If it gets ripened, then...
The eater shall not relish
...That mango fruit !
Due to the campus being defective indeed !"
Uttering these words, from among the snake-community,
A couple of a male and a female serpent –
" Don't count us as
A male and a female serpent, O Thou fortunate one !

The history of the past ages
Is the testimony of the fact, that
This lineage
Has tread under its feet, has crushed
Not even a single life, till today,
For any reason, whatsoever...
Because,
We have remained without feet, indeed !
It is the reason why the saints,
After so much of thinking and understanding
Have meaningfully named us
'Uraga'...,[134] that is, a crawling reptile, a serpent.
Yes ! yes !
If someone puts his feet upon us
If someone teases us...then...
We never spare them.
We have never trodden anyone under our feet,
For detestable selfishness,
Contrary to it, those,
Who have been downtrodden,
Somehow,
–After gliding upon our bosoms
Having reached by their side
We have embraced them,
We have fondled them with affection,
We have treated their wounds gently.

With our fondness and humility
The story of each and every particle has been filled in,
The sufferings of each and every atom have been effaced.

We haven't bitten even the thorns
We have embraced tenderly even the thorns,
Because they are the exploited ones.
The flower sucks up the juice and the pollen
Filled into every branch,
Even the fame too is pillaged by the flower,
As a result of which –
All the remaining part, on being dried up,
Appears indeed as the residue in the form of thorns !

One thing more has to be added by us
That
Only the high-ranking ones, for the sake of
their status
Crush the others under their heels,
Take upon the way of sins and hypocrisy.
We pray to God
To let us remain without high titles or
footing !
Whatever high offices are there –
All of them are the receptacles of disasters,
That poisonous serpent of temptations for
high position
Shouldn't sniff at us even in future
–Only this sentiment is sustained by us, O Lord !"

On hearing about the tendency and the methods
Of the high positions and the position-holders
From the mouth of those who have no footing,
The family stands motionless.
The four-footed herd of elephants too
Becomes benumbed like a machine,
And
The feet of all get frozen like snow.

On beholding the herd of elephants
Sunk into depression, along with the family,
Out of humility, the serpents say :
" Please forgive us ! please forgive us !
We beg your pardon !

In that way,
We don't talk so frankly
The point of lapse is something peculiar,
The complete sense couldn't be expressed.
Listen to what remains, we tell it
In plain and simple words that
Whosoever they may be, almost all the incumbents
And those,
Who hold public offices etc.
Who have been posted in places of authority,
All of them are of the same sort, indeed –
It is not the whole truth.

There are some such feet also
For whose adoration
This life has been yearning
Since times gone by...since long,
Today has arrived that very hour –
This heart is throbbing with joy !"
And, at the very outset,
The holy feet are sanctified
with eyes, filled with the tears of joy,
Along with hundreds of prostrations.

Then, the hoods of the male and the female serpents
Were fully expanded –

They erected themselves with a sense of
homage –
Wherein set and secured
From among the finest of all jewels,
The quiet, mild, radiant
Originally unique and rare
Jewels were offered.
And
The community of serpents
Considers its life to be blessed, the most
fortunate one.
The serpents present salutation
The boastfulness is vomited,
Outwardly, the show of beating,
Internally, fondling and friendliness goes on.

The charming touch of mildness, –
This is such a
Radical and supernatural
Abstractly visual
Creation of audible poetry;
Who he is, the creator of it,
Where he is,
Why is he keeping mum ?
The great personage with the versatility of sentiments,
Who becomes the life-conduct of the prominent
personalities !

□

Having rushed forth from that very quarter,
The terrorism, once and again,
Keeps on peeping through the bushes
And
At this unexpected event –

Keeps on staring with the fixity of condemning it.
Once more
Its alarm has been filled up
With sulkiness–with oppression
And
With the unrestrained hotness
Which originated from its defeat.

Except this
What else can that frail-faced do
In front of those who are powerful !

And
The seven lemons
Are consecrated by accomplished spells !
Across each of the lemon
A needle, fastened with black strings,
Has been pierced through.
Then,
Into the empty space
The fruits are tossed up
With a wish of dark gathering of clouds.
There remains no need for expectations
After the application of the spell,
The outcome is obtained instantly,
It is the result of concentration.

The applicator of the spell
May be well-intentioned or ill-intentioned
No rule is applicable in this context.
It is enough that he should have controlled his mind !
This is the very rule, this is the very mission,
And this is what happened.

The dense assemblage of clouds
Starts swimming across the firmament,
The empire of darkness seems to be overspread
The glimpse of the earth becomes rare –
Only the foot-steps can sense
Whether the Earth is alive or not,
The night of the *rava-rava hell*[135]
Seems to be travelling up through the space,
The merger of the diversity of colours is taking place,
The blowing of terrible winds takes a start
In whose clutches is hidden the total annihilation.
The steps of the mountains stumble
And
The turbans of the high hill-tops
Drop down upon the earth,
A mutual tussle erupts among the trees
There is some friction, some twisting-sound,
Not only of the touchable
But even the contact with the untouchable starts up,
The difference between the soft and the hard disappears,
The roots of the stronger trees are shaken,
Many of the trees start learning
'*Śīrṣāsana*'–the posture with the head upside down,
The bamboos offer prostrations
And begin to cling to the bosom of the Earth.

The heavy thundering of the clouds
Bitter and disagreeable in its sound
Assumes such terrible proportions that
The sense of gladdened dancing is indeed
something distant–
That flock of peacocks –

Strikes dumb in its cackling,
The lightning, which angers and frenzies
the clouds,
Dazzled at intervals,
Like a fickle frail woman –
Crossing all limits of dignity and propriety !
And
It starts raining in torrents.
No mention of tiny or huge drops is there,
It is an experience like that of a huge waterfall
– The Earth is getting drowned into water,
The excessive wrath of the watery sway
Is spreading all around like a very thick
covering of clouds.
When the dusk does creep in
It can't be traced,
When the darkness does befall –
Who would tell it ?
Whom should it be referred to ?
And
The thundering of the clouds goes on gathering up,
The swelling of lightning continues
The hailstorm is in vogue at intervals
The cold-wave gains momentum
The hours after hours, that is, '*Praharas*'[136a]
roll away,
Well then, in such a situation
How one would take to slumbering indeed !
And, to whom would it be desirable ?

For the experience of fruitfulness-for enjoyment and usage,
Not only the objects of enjoyment and usage, that is,
[Bhoga-Upabhoga][136b]

But also the suitability of time and place
Is, as well, expected.

□

Under this terrible situation of total
devastation too
The protection of the family
Goes on without interruption,
By the herd of appreciative elephants.

'The getherings of clouds have become lean
and thin
The dark moments have passed away
Otherwise, why the rosiness has spread out
Over the distant...Eastern horizon !'
And
The family has gone up to the river-bank.

Due to rains, the fresh water
Has flown into the river,
The river-current has gained momentum and flow
Like a charming young frenzied woman
Away from the fear of worldly commotions and
calm emotions !

Now, a serious problem
Is confronting the family,
Gradually,
Its gravity and eminence
Is being overshadowed by timidity.
And...Lo !
The family's conscience feels inclined to say, that,
– Come ! let us turn ourselves back from here.
No sooner the preparations to return are made than –

The sacred pitcher adds :
"No...no...no...
We mustn't return !
Not at present...never indeed...
Because even now
The terrorism hasn't subsided,
A struggle has yet to be waged against it –
It is firm in determination,
Steadily adamant upon its own fixture.

Till the terrorism is alive,
This Earth
Can't take the breath of peace,
These eyes, now
Can't see the terrorism,
These ears, now
Can't hear the name of terror,
This life too is firmly resolute that
That one (terror) or this one (peace) –
Here, the existence of the one shall remain,
Now, don't welcome the delay –
The river has to be crossed, indeed.
– Has failure-emptiness been writ large
Upon the fate of the sacred pitcher ?
–Has there remained any worthlessness, flaw
In the observance of austerities with self-denial,
By the sacred pitcher ?
The feeble faith
Shall inhale pure breathing,
And
The muddy breath shall gain
A prosperous sweetness of smell.

Don't sustain now
Fright-surprise-bashfulness !

Fasten my neck
With the tip of a cord
And
With some gaps in-between
Covering up behind one-another,
All of you get lined up
With the cord tied closely
Around your own waists !
Then
Jump off into the current
With the forceful enunciation of *'Omkāra', that is 'Om'* [137]

Despite all this,
Due to the hitch of the family being unremoved,
Some more utterances come forth
From the lips of the sacred pitcher, that –

" Here
By whom the bondage is liked ?
Freedom is agreeable to me also,
That ...is...why
I don't like to be kept
Under anybody's bondage
Nor do I like to keep anybody
Fastened by me.
We should know,
fastening others is a bondage in itself, indeed !
Even then
From the arbitrariness myself

I wish to escape
The arbitrariness myself,
I try to avoid as far as possible –
And
If the avoidance is there possible or not
I try to save others –
Save them, to the best of my ability.
Here,
To whom the bondage is gratifying ?
Freedom is agreeable to me also."

Lo, this time
The utterances prove effective
Like the medicinal powder – *Lavaṇabhāskara,*[138]
And
According to the indications of the sacred pitcher –
–Having tied up the sacred pitcher with his lean waist,
Like that of a lion,
The eminent trader jumps off
Into the fast-flowing current of the river.
At once, the whole of the family too
Follows suit,
The base of the Earth is left behind
The feet become supportless.
The cord tied up with the waists, indeed,
Is the means of protection, the life-string at the moment !
And, the sacred pitcher...
Is acting as a huge ship,
It has submerged almost entirely, –
Only the mouths and the heads
Are appearing at the surface.

By this time, the whole of the family
Feels the last jolt of coldness.

The natural heat of the body
Is gradually decreasing
The dynamism of the blood
Is turning averse by and by
The hands and feet have become inert
The rows of the teeth have started a crackling
sound
And a little of sliding
Into the river occurs when
The tiny and the big fish
Are sportfully playing
While jumping off the water-surface,
The lean and thin tails of the snakes
Which glide in a zigzag way
Are easily coiling round
The circular shins of the family.

So many
Shy-natured tortoises too, being unrestrained,
Having touched the tender-fatty
Thighs of the family
Pose disappearance all of a sudden.

In whose terrible jaws, like those of a tiger,
Huge and deformed
Sharp rows of teeth are glittering,
Whose blood-thirsty reddish tongues
Are rushing forth once and again, –

Whose tails, full of venomous thorns,
Are held high-up –
Such flesh-eaters
Gigantic crocodiles,
While busy with the search of their eatables,
Have started holding their heads up
Around the family.

Some other watery creatures also
Of various types, with cruel attitude,
Appear to be anguished due to hunger,
Even then,
On beholding the tranquil posture of the family,
They seem to have almost forgotten
To take up a new experiment of disturbance
Which is their basic cult;
Their attitude seems to be
Changed from top to bottom,
–The very purpose of eating has been
abandoned, indeed.

And, as if,
At the very vision of God,
The sense of chanting a hymn
Has sprouted into an adorer's heart,
–The sense of the worthless and the beneficial,
The power of distinguishing the 'Reality' from
'Illusion,'
The turning towards the dutifulness–
So, the life of the watery creatures,
Has thus felt an awakening in different ways.

□

But !
There developed a reverse movement in the water
There are two elements–the insentient and the sentient
Both of them possess their own characteristics–
On obtaining the light
On acquiring the reasonable motion
The very development springs up within the 'sentient'
While
The 'insentient' maintains the status quo.
The 'insentient' is ignorant
Is assumes one-sidedness, obstinacy
It is inwardly static...distressed !
It can't rely upon its own self.
Due to the tendency of the aquatic animals
Due to their state of confusion,
The river flowing in spate.
On being a little more boiled, adds :

" Despite being dependent upon me, indeed,
You go against me !
You want to lead a life
You wish to take a re-animating medicine,
And
You forget your mother
In spite of being a frail child !
Go away ! remove yourself ! You shall be miserable,
You shall not get sweet love anywhere,
You shall have to take the sip of repentance only
The memory of nectar shall inflame your heart !

You have got yourself mixed up with the land-farers
You have been deceived by the cheats and the wicked–

There is indeed nothing to tell you
You are an object of pity;
Only they have to be taken notice of
Who...
Play tricks against the innocents
Who are jealous of even the water-deity."
And
The fretfully angry... river,
With its countless hands of waves,
Starts slapping upon...
The tender cheeks of the family.

"Adorers of the Earth, O you knaves !
Whither shall you go now ?
Go off, hide yourselves under the ground...,
Still beneath...of it !
O Thou sinners, go to hell underneath !
O Thou chiefs among the hypocrites !
Don't display your faces before us.
Showiness is your life
Which is eaten-up by the time,
Which is like a winged serpent –
Aimless, pitiable, poor !
Having lived,
Upon a place like the earth,
You have brought under your control
The others, as well as the other's wealth,
In the form of accumulation and confiscation
You are seized by chronic diarrohea !
That is why, even for a moment,
I take a halt nowhere.

Even after encountering the worldly wealth
I haven't, even in dream,
Taken their possession.
And
To show my magnanimity
I have not bestowed it to others
Out of any selfish motive, for gaining fame or public superiority,
That…is why...indeed
The saints assigned us a meaningful name–
...Nālī !..., that is, *neither taken !... Nādī*, that is, *nor given...!*[139]

Those who conduct themselves contrary to us,
Become pitiable.
– Some ascetics of feeble conduct
Have attained a true sense of right direction
Through this saying –
'The rolling waters and the roaming ascetics'
Well, in this wide world,
What else can be that ideal
Better than this one !
Now into this ideal,
Try to have a look at your own face,
And
Identify your own 'image' and your own 'self' !"

□

On hearing the utterings
Full of rude and foolish views of the river
Absorbed in self-praise,
– Without being excited –

The eminent trader has his own say, that
" If you
Had not obtained the base of the Earth
What course would have been adopted by you !
You would have crossed even the infernal regions of
hell !

The Earth owned you
She kept you closer to her bosom
The gods conferred no compassion upon you,
The sky granted no shelter to you,
You were younger then,
You had fallen down upon the mountain-top
Every one was laughing at you
When you were shedding tears !
You were severely injured,
You appeared to be fickle, simple;
Now you have become poisonous, serpentine !
Only the artifice has become your strength,
Having leapt over everyone
You are galloping away, now.
O Thou, the ungrateful ! O Thou, the executor of
sinfulness !

Don't indulge thyself into earning more sins.
All the world, indeed, is indebted to Earth
You, too, have to repay the debts,
Having held the Earth within your bosom
You have to amend, by heart, your doings."

Ah me ! whose misfortune it is !
– That of the eminent trader, or that of
the river ?
The good intention of the eminent trader
didn't really gain ground–
Even by the criticism of the trader,

The eyes of the river feel no awakening
Contrary to it, that river
Turns more reddish in colour :
" You talk of infernal regions of hell !
O you, the scoundrels !
Now, your extinction is not far off."
And
A move towards the swirl-direction
Where, being drawn from all sides,
Each and every thing disappears
After joining the flow,
Where
Circumambulating itself,
The upper water-level is gushing downwards,
The lower water-deposit is rushing upwards
In a very fast motion,
Where, the watery existence
Is bursting into a loud laughter
After engulfing the Earth-element within its fold;

Whereat
Some beasts, some deers
Some the violent; others the non-violent,
Some of them under swoon, while the others awake;
Some the dead, others the half-dead –
– Over the faces of all of them,
An instinct-to-live is still lurking,
Due to their being a morsel of untimely death, –
All of them, under some compulsion,
Are being carried away by the current.

Before the eyes, from the frontal flow
A huge-bodied elephant
Being set afloat, passes off,
On whose back is seated
An aged lion,
Afraid of its terrible future !
And
On being drawn into the swirl,
Whirling round once or twice,
Disappears within the belly of the whirlpool;
Whereat,
Whether one is strong or weak,
Every body's power fails to prove its worth,
– A sacrifice of all the forces !

□

On seeing the happening taking place,
And feeling worried –
Lest the patience of the family
Should come to a decrease,
And
Lest its mind
Should detract from its fixedness –
– The sacred pitcher challenges the river :
" O Thou one, with sinful steps, hark !
This family has really crossed over to the
other side,
Is not into the current mid-way,
Whosoever takes shelter upon the Earth
The Earth makes him reach the proper end–
It is the rule of the Earth...its vow ! –

Even the word '*dharatī*'[140] in its inverse order,
Carries this very sense–
'*Dha...ra…tī*', '*tī...ra…dha*'
That is,
That which wields the coast,
Or, that which carries the shelter-seeker
To the proper end–
Is truly called the '*dharatī*'–that is, the Earth.

Listen a bit more !
By the usage of the syllable '*tha*'–
In place of the syllable '*dha*'–
The word '*Tīratha*'–comes into being–
–That which absolves a shelter-seeker from sins,
Hence...the '*Tīratha*'–that is–a place of pilgrimage !

Well, then, how can you
Drown us now,
And also mind it that
Now
You can't set us afloat
On any pretext, we shall not be
Carried away along with the outflow !

When the river of fire
Has been crossed over by us,
And,
Not by facing a defeat
But by having a loving affinity
With the grand limits of devotions,
We have arrived at this point,
Even then, you claim
Your capability of drowning us ?

We had already decided, that
We shouldn't serve and admire
The upper surface too much,
Because
Upon the outward level
We shall remain swimming how long,
The arms shall, indeed, get fatigued !
Those, who feel satisfied
Only with viewing the waves,
Have been often found sinking
...Hereat...on the upper surface !

O Thou down-bound, sinful stream !
This Earthen Pitcher abounds with the capacity
Of wielding even a sea within itself –
Because, we have ever been a part of the Earth !
The meaningful task of a sacred pitcher
Is really that of holding the water only,
And...hark !
The word *'dharaṇī'* [141] itself
In its reverse order, signifies
– Dha...ra... ṇī nī...ra...dha,
That which sustains the water...so...*'dharaṇī'*, the Earth,
That which supports the water... hence...*'dharaṇī'*,
the Earth !

□

As
A sapphire among the gems
A blue lotus among the lotuses
The bliss of virtuous and moral conduct,
among all the joys –

The Mount Meru[142a] among the mountains
The Milky Sea [The Kṣīra-sāgara] [142b]
among all the seas
A heroic death (*Vīra maraṇa*)[142c] among the
different deaths
A fish–pearl among all the pearls –
Are regarded excellent,
Exactly so
The virtue among the virtues is 'gratitude',
On beholding the sacred pitcher adorned
With such gratitude
A highly valuable pearl-gem
Is bestowed to the sacred pitcher,
By the one 'Huge fish', being pleased at it.
'Let this insignificant service be accepted, O Lord !'
– Having uttered so, the fish vanishes into the
water.
A special characteristic of this pearl is that
The gentleman who obtains this one,
Can get a smooth way
Through the very deep waters,
And this is what happens at once !

After crossing without effort
The swirling current in spate,
The sacred pitcher, with a faint smile,
Makes the eminent trader remember,
Along with his family a pithy saying, that,
'Even a pearl is obtained without asking,
While no alms reach a begging bowl'
And, O the eminent trader !
This reward is the outcome
Of the renunciation of passions and observance of
austerities.
By the self-confidence of the sacred pitcher –

By its high-spirited life
The river gained a strong impetus,
The bewilderment of the river generally subsided
It got itself filled with a sense of dedication !

And
Speaks out in an humble polite manner :
" I apologize for my arrogance."
And
Devoid of splashing waves,
Starts to flow being resolute and grave,
Like a female hermit, long-initiated as a disciple,
Free from *coquettish gestures*[143a]and
deformed sentiments[143b]
Observing silence with the eye-lids cast down !

□

Almost half of the journey has been done,
The group of travellers is feeling
As if the very destination is proceeding towards them.
A sense of gladness reflects upon the face of the
sacred pitcher
Like that of an uncommon pupil,
Hardworking and humble,
Getting through in first division.
The family, too, is being puffed up, while

The terrorism repeats itself–
The same is the colour, the same the
behaviour –
There appears the same sarcasm in every limb,
The same is the idol, the same the faces
Those very virulently twisted moustaches,
The same is the mien, the same the method–

The same is the fraud and force, the same the commotion
The same are the curly black hairs
The same is the forehead of the cruel death,
The same is the intoxication, the same the condition
Each and every direction is now trembling with fear,
The same is the tongue, the same the belt
None could keep it under his thumb,
The same is the voice as was heard before
The same hearing, the same is the mania.

The same is the breath, the same the distrust
The same is the devastation, the same the horse-laugh,
The same frantic dancing is there
The same devilish deeds are there
Those very are the scarlet eyes
Which are gazing more and more
The same is the body, the same the forehead
The same is the foot, the same the hand
In each and every hidden blow, the same is the company,
The same are the cheeks, the same the lips
The same is the redness, the same the blood
The same is the sentiment, the same the trickfulness
Everything is the same, nothing anew
The heart is the same, without a touch of mercy.

And, to the river,
Begins a request by terrorism :
" O Mother ! O Thou deity of water !
Tell us please
If, even an offender, –

Is redeemed by thee ?
The fostering and supporting of saintly souls
Is appropriate...is our duty,
But do thou confer thy affection
Upon the sinners as well ?

" If not
Then, let them...be...drowned –
Having taken the support of the earthen pitcher,
Who admire the Earth,
Who want to reach the other end !
There is no limit to their sinfulness,
They breed no love in their hearts for virtuous deeds,
Their desired assets are
Wealth, glory, sensual pleasures and properties,
Even then...you will extend co-operation to them
Your bright history
Shall become a laughing stock,
The faith shall receive a setback
Then, what to talk about others,
A question-mark shall indeed be placed
Against the life of all others, indeed.

In the like manner,
You have nailed into the wood
Even the deity of fire –
The fire, that creates trouble and inflammation,
Which burns itself
And sets others to fire.

Then, ever and anon,
Having seen it appearing in the form of
glittering forest-fire
With your invincible strength
After changing the fire into *lāvā*[144]
It has been caused to enter the infernal
regions of hell.

And,
It is still
Under your sway !
Well, then,
What has this happened to you today ?
O Mother ! O Thou deity of water !
Let it be made known to us.
We have no idea, whatsoever,
Thou hast undergone so much of change !"

On hearing this, the river now speaks out
That
" To whom you are asking to drown,
Without them, here
Nothing else shall really be achieved
Except the privation only.
What, indeed, is the value of a sheath
In absence of a sword ?
What is the use of the objects of pleasure
Without their consumer ?
Whatever goodness the Earth musters up,
Is sustained through such persons
And through the social workers similar to
these ones.

What fate a crest shall face
In absence of its foundation-base

What fate the flower shall face
In absence of the soil –
Need not be indicated.
Now
The force will not be misused
The dedication has been completed,
The energy has been turned into adoration
The sense of magnanimity has sprouted into the heart"
And
Having said 'enough of it' –
The river slides into silence.

□

Due to the silent gravity of the river
The firmness of the terrorism
Isn't affected by pain or dejection.
Stillness for some moments...again !
That very sullen activity
Towards...the...fixed end.

And,
It is a proper policy that,
After joining the battle-field,
The force of friends has not to be recalled;
Contrary to it, the forces of the foes,
Have to be attacked all of a sudden.
Dependence on others is a sign of sorry plight,
Through it, the sentiment of heroism is harmed;
Not only this much,
The madada (Help)[145] extended by the friends
Really becomes pride-promoting

Which acts as darkness
Obstructing the path of triumph.

Now, the terrorism
Almost feels
As if the success is about to touch its hand
Nothing of a mirage
No deception !
The fortune almost favouring.

And
The assessment of the situation is done
The boat gains a bit of momentum
Only the gust of wind
Shouldn't just go against –
This very idea prevails there.

On reaching the spot, at last,
The terrorism, posing as a path-barrier
After confronting the family on the way,
Speaks out with a boisterous laugh :

" Now set aside the option of crossing over
to the other side
Tender your resignation to life.
You have to get yourself acquainted with
The Pātāla Loka, that is, *hades* [146]
– The hypocrisy and sinfulness ripen in this
very manner !"
And
The pelting of stones is taken up
In a blind manner against the family.

"– Receptions should be extended to me
Charming luxuries
Excellent things I should get –

Your firm opinion is full of such (*Tāmasatā*) that is
malignancy,
Well, then tell us,
Where is your faith in socialism ?
– I myself, ahead of all,
The society afterwards !

Hark, at least
Look into the true sense of the word indeed !
The word society means '*Samūha*', – that is '*a social group*'[147]
And,
'*Samūha*', that is, 'a group' carries the sense–
'*Sama*', that is, 'rational', '*ūha*' means 'thinking' –
That, which is the foundation of good moral conduct.
The sum and substance is that
Away from advertisement and propaganda
The life of those having exemplary conduct and
thinking
Is indeed socialism,
You will not be a socialist
Only by crying aloud the slogans of socialism."

Such vulgar words
Are being hurled, that
At once, on hearing them
The spark of anger would flare up,
And
The sense of self-respect would get painfully
restless;
Due to the pelting of stones
On being deeply hurt,
The heads of all have almost turned dizzy
The streaks of blood have run down –

The blood-streaks by which
The current of water seems to be reddened–
The two female-friends of the similar thinking
Seem to be displeased at terrorism.
Except the eminent trader,
The whole of the family, under some yoke,
Is passing through the bitter sufferings.

□

Often the feet are held back
As and when they come across the right conduct,
And
Often the eyes feel humbled
As soon as some covering comes before them,
This living being, under some dull comprehension
Sometimes,
Having mistaken a cord for a snake,
Desists from sensual pleasures,...then...sometimes,
Having mistaken a snake for a cord
Gets absorbed into the sensual enjoyments.
All of it is the majesty of delusion, –
This majesty of delusion
Can't be put to an end
So long as shall remain alive
The ignorance of our own 'true self'.

Yes ! yes ! even under such a situation
With forbearance and courage,
Having moved ahead of all,
The struggle of the eminent trader
Is really going on against the terrorism.

For the safety of the sacred pitcher
Having taken the sacred pitcher under his abdomen
He has couched himself with his face turned
downwards.

He has been bearing with self-restraint
The unbearable consequences of his Kārmic results,
Due to the recollections of the happenings in
the forest !

This *'Upasarga'*, that is, calamity, goes on recurring
From a distance of seven or eight cubits only
In a brutal manner.
The attempt to split the sacred pitcher,
Whose strength makes one tide over to the other end,
Gets foiled once and again –
Due to whose strength
The vital life-breaths have been rescued,
The attempt to cut off with weapons the cord
Tied up around their waists
Doesn't succeed even for once;
On beholding the severe austerities of the sacred pitcher
Which passes through the stream of fire,
It seems, as if the very deity of water,
With his power of *Vikriyā*[148] *(-ṛddhi)*, that is,
transformation
Creates a safety-and-halo-ring
All around the family !
Or
It might be
The marvel of the fish-pearl also.

Any way whatsoever,
Now, by the terrorism,
The defeat of its own side –

Is being felt at hand,
Along with it
The magnanimity of the opposite side
Also unfolds itself upon its mind.

Consequently,
That strength of its body
Begins to behold all the family, along with the sacred pitcher,
With a sense of hesitation,
That strength of its mind
Starts roasting itself
With the heat of anger,
And
Its force of utterance indeed...
Brings itself to its knees
Before the whole of its surrounding atmosphere.

But
Its very power of trickery
Has not yet ceased to exist,
There still remains that very old habit
Which is strong as before,
That is...why...
The terrorism, holding into its hands
Such a network,
Wherein huge fish
Can be ensnared with ease,
Is just ready to throw it upon the family, while
The devotee of the Earth –
The wind, finds it detestable to look at,
And –

What else…
The wind assumes the form of total annihilation,
the furiousness increases, the mercury that is
temper goes high
On seeing which, even the power of
a Supreme Emperor (*Chakravartī*)
May feel absolutely confused,
Such is the nature of this violent cyclone !
Instantly, in the very first jerk,
It throws the network off the group's hands,
Into the farthest empty space
Hence...it seems as if
An attempt is being made to ensnare
Even the radiant Sun itself
Who swims according to his own will
Across the clean ocean of the sky,
And
This jolt being stuck,
The feet of the group become groundless,
The group whirls down headlong
After so many bodily twists,
Inside their own boat,
A darkness prevails there before them,
Their eyes get closed up
The beatings of hearts get lowered,
They fall under a swoon
Due to some depression in blood-circulation.
But the moustaches of the group, indeed !
Without feeling fainted
Remain twisted up unfainted as before !

How can the existence of life be guessed
The vital breaths seem to be departed.

With the utter swiftness
The face of the group
Is found averse to vitality and lustre,
The foam peeps through the mouth
Like a sea-coast laughing with the Earth,
And
The boat too starts wavering,
It is not known, as to how many times
It circumambulates itself
Within a few seconds !
The life-breaths of all, along with the boat,
Almost to sink down...!

□

Within no time, when the cyclone
Went on proceeding...
Towards mischief and harmful blows,
For putting an end to this excess
A hint is dropped, with a reproach,
Through the sacred pitcher –
Like an attendant, the wind also,
Regarding the service to the revered master
As a source for the happy life,
Restrains itself at the hint shown by the
sacred pitcher.
And
After three circumambulations of the family,
The boat returns to its previous position.

Due to the mishap being postponed
The surroundings all around, indeed, appear to be
delightful –

The way, in which
The swoon of Lakṣmaṇa receded
Through the sprinkling of water
By the beautiful palms-cavity of '*Viśalyā*'–[149]
On getting the cool touch of water-particles
Leaping up from the river,
The swoon of the terrorism is broken.
Then, no mention of it !
The terrorism again, like Lakṣmaṇa,
Is boiled with fury !

"Capture ! capture !
Stop ! stop !
Do you hear or not
O Thou, the deaf !
Die, or
Support us,
O you takers of the world to hell
Into a chasm !
You aren't, indeed, the one who salvages
anybody from sins !
O Thou, the measuring scales of sins !
Hark ! hear !...listen for a while !

Now don't indulge in amassing wealth,
Look-after the public welfare !
And
Under the sway of greed,
Whatever has been hoarded in a blind manner
Carry out its proper distribution –
Otherwise,
Among the poor –

The ideas of theft arise, have arisen.
Don't practise theft, don't do stealing –
Such preachings are
Only a religious farce,
The superficial civilization...a formality !

The thieves are not as much the sinners
As those
Who give rise to thieves.
You are yourself a thief
You patronize the thieves
And
Also the originators of thieves.
The virtuous persons
Never conceal their faults,
They don't even feel like concealing them,
On the contrary, they bring them to light.

Rāvaṇa had abducted Sītā away,
Then, Sītā had uttered thus :
Had I
Not been so extremely beautiful,
Rāvaṇa's mind won't have been profaned,
And
In the gaining of this beauty and grace,
Only my own Kārmic fruition is the reason behind it,
This –
The Kārmic bondage with my soul –
Is really due to my own good or bad feelings !
In such a condition,
To declare only Rāvaṇa as a culprit –

Is to vitiate still more
My own future-forehead !"

□

By the repressive threatenings of the group,
The heart of the family gets terrified
Except that of the eminent trader,
His firm resolution
Seems to be perspiring !
His will-to-live gets strengthened
And he,
On beholding the untimely
Termination of life,
Would have just felt compelled
For thinking about his surrender, when

The river at once adds,
" Don't be impatient !

The surrender by the truth,
And that too,
How before the falsehood ?
O God !
What type of era has ushered in ?
Shall the Falsehood be the ruler now ?
Shall the Truth be a slave to it ?
Ah me, the defeat of a diamond necklace today
In the market of jewellers !
Alas ! before the dazzling of the glass
Is at the point of death, –

The brilliance of the diamond !
Now
A chaste woman shall follow
An adulteress, as her female attendant.
In the eyes of falsehood
The truth may be untruth,
And
The untruth may be truth,
But
Has even the Truth itself
Lost all sense of discernment...
Between the truth and the falsehood ?
Has even the very Truth also
Lost all confidence in itself ?

Having ridden upon the crowd's back
Shall the journey of Truth go ahead now !
No...no, never... .

All these things
Have now become unbearable
Over the Water, on the Earth and into the Sky.
– This shall be opposed with all might and main,
Till the body breaths its last,
Such an event shouldn't take place
This current shouldn't budge
From its settled path,
Shouldn't give way, shouldn't give way !"–
Making such utterances while being angered,
Gliding and sliding, while being agitated,
The river
Causes the boat dance about.

On beholding the condition of the boat
Which tilted every minute on either sides,
The terrorism remembers
The magic spell at heart, when
At once
Descends there a group of celestial beings
Who bow before the terrorism humbly,
– A request with folded hands is made for
doing service.
" Let the reason behind calling us be
known, O Lord !"
... Is spoken.

While waiting for the instructions,
Some moments slip away, when
The celestial beings speak out
In the very posture of salutation :
" The mystical power of magic spells, O Lord !
Has its own limitations !
The work has to be performed within those limits,
...by us !

We are feeling ashamed to say that
We are fully incapable
In performing the incidental task,
Hence we ask your forgiveness.

Thus,
O Lord !
You would have indeed compared
Your own strength with their strength !
As we arrive here
We feel that
We are standing like fawns

In front of a lion;
In such a situation,
The question of struggling doesn't arise at all,
To seek the shelter indeed with the family
Is to obtain the rudder,
And
To tide over the end of the endless.

It is certain that
All the other types of activities
Shall really prove to be as our assaults and defeat,
Despite this all, if
The idea of retaliation is there
...Then, hark !

In comparison to water
It is difficult to bind the fire
And In comparison to fire
It is more difficult to bind the air.
But,
It is not at all possible
To bind really...the blue sky,
The governance of water
Can never be effective on clarified butter,
– The clarified butter knows to sit upon
the water,

The poison can never
Leave its mark upon gods,
And
The ink can never take drones, i.e., the large
black bees,
Under its sway."

So many good sayings
Lines full of inspirations
So many instances, illustrations
The recent and ancient views
And those
Most rare experiences
Are related by the celestial beings.
They all get affixed somehow
Into the mind of the terrorism,
But,
How they would get digested at once !
Enough of time is required
For the task of assimilation,
At once, before the very eyes indeed,
The views may change
But not the ways,
The momentum of foul emotions
Takes some time, indeed
In keeping itself under restraint !

□

Lo, where is so much of time !
The event has to take place–
So...for its occurrence,
Only a short period remains
Every thing...enough of it...
...Entirely at a finish !

The girdle around the mid-boat drowns
Whereat, it is written thus –

'Victory to terrorism
Down with socialism
End to partisanship
The Divine knowledge be triumphant.'
On beholding this scene
The self-confidence of the group
Gets a sudden blow,
The atmosphere of the fall of thunderbolt is created
The idea of the celestial beings comes true
Ah me !
...Being suffocated with repentance,
Being perplexed and overwhelmed with grief
The terrorism speaks out with the choked throat
That
" There is no shelter
There is no boat
Without you, here, for us,
Forgive us, forgive us
O Thou, the Incarnation of Mercy !
A serious error has been committed by us,
It shall never be repeated,
Let us be trustworthy !

We have been encircled by perils
Please do the favour of...saving us now,
We have been pierced by the thorns
Be kind enough...to scatter flowers;
We are, indeed...*the culprits,*[150] that is, '*Aparādhī*'
We pray for the '*Supreme Wisdom*'
Hence, show us the path which is genuine
Kindly make no more of delay !

Mischief is the nature of an offspring,
Even then, the grace is indeed conferred upon
Her progeny by the mother,
The offspring may be her own or that of the
others –
When does the mother's existence
Favour their torture or harassment ?–
...Please tell us !"
While uttering thus, the group's mouth would have
closed
When
" The sooner the intellect is about to move
From the outer fold towards the centre,
The sooner the pace moves
Towards the sense from senselessness" –
–Pondering over thus, the eminent trader says that,

"Don't make yourself look too much poor and pitiable
brothers !

The tree,
Which is fresh and flourishing
Which stands in expectation of a wayfarer
With its flowers fruits and branches–
To ask for a little of shade
From it –
Isn't it a reason to make us laugh ?
Having prepared food with the six prominent tastes,
By someone whosoever has been invited someone –
With courtesy and request,
Can't...he serve him
Water to drink ?
Well, you tell me yourself !

Now remains the question of a mother...so –
On some occasions
Due to a particular reason,
In the eyes of a mother too,
Excitement and uneasiness
May be reflected, actually reflects;
should also be reflected.

But, till to-day,
The thrusting of anger
Into the sublime lap of a mother
Has neither been heard, nor seen –
The lap-in which the moments of joy
Of a child pass naturally.

Let us further see !
The generosity and beneficence of a mother
Since ages gone by...since infinity
She stands, holding beside her bosom,
Two jars
Filled with milk,
– Always keeps fostering the babies
Feeling troubled with hunger and thirst,
And
Fondling the frightened and the forlorn,
Brings them secretly
Closer to her heart.

□

When, once and for all, the mother
Has been adopted, indeed, as the mother one, –

Why then, once and again,
She be tried and tested ?
Therefore, now,
Don't peep through the eyes of the mother
And
Don't be a culprit
Try to become the one with the Supreme 'wisdom',
Not the one with the 'Proud intellect'
'Don't be a 'slave',
But
Make yourself liberated !"

Only these very words from the eminent trader
Are enough, when
The suspense, suspicion of the group ends
And
The group jumps into the stream
From the drowning boat
Like a child, feeling no hitch
Into his mothers lap !

The family wafts the group away through the water,
Like a mother, an idol of affection,
Holding at once a child up in the air,
Each and every member of the group
Is supported regardfully
By the every member of the family,
And
The new living beings regain a new life !

Lo, now takes place...
The complete submersion of the boat –

The end to terrorism
And
The auspicious beginning of (*Anantavāda*) i.e., infinite happiness !

□

Ahead of all is the Sacred Pitcher,
Which is free from pride and self-conceit,
The Sacred Pitcher is followed
By the two rows of nine persons each
Which,
Being mutually dependent on each other,
Are proceeding
Like the off-springs of one and the same mother,
– As if one soul...
With separate bodies.

The lines of benediction
Are coming forth from the lips of the sacred pitcher :

" Here...the life of each one
Should ever be blissful,
The shade of happiness be overspread –
Each and every inauspicious sentiment
Should vanish –
The life-creeper of all
Should be fresh, flourishing and smiling,
The flowers of virtues should flash upon it,
The expectations of the nose be fulfilled
It should get perfumed from top to bottom
...It's enough !"

And, hither...how is it
A sense of restlessness manifests itself into the shores !

The reception of the Sacred Pitcher has to be
done by it,
The radiant brilliance of the rising sun
Seems to be constantly entangled
With the lively waves heaving incessantly
As if
While taking a bath
Out of shyness, it has been shrinking
Like arrogant ladies
Wrapped into rosy *Sāḍīs.*[151]

The surroundings all around
Get filled with religious fervour,
And
The keenly eager river-bank
Comes Near and nearer, indeed.

At first, affectionately,
Accepting the reception by the river-bank,
The Sacred Pitcher kisses the river-bank.
There is the rise of foam inside the bank,
Within whose white wakefulness
There is the mingling of rosy brightness of
the sun,
So, it is appearing, as if,
Having taken in its own hands,
A garland of roses
The river-bank itself is standing in ovation.

All of them, after crossing over the river,
Avow a breath of delight.
The foot-soles of them all
Come in touch with the rare dust of the Earth–

Then,
Each other mutually loosened the cord
Tied around their waists,
When
The cord speaks out :
"You all pardon me,
You suffer for my sake.
That lean and thin waist
Of yours,
After being rubbed and worn away,
Has become as if more reduced and sliced"
Then, expressing its gratitude,
The family at once adds,
That

"No...no
O Thou humble-hearted one !
O Thou benevolent to others !
It is the sequel of your grace
That...
We have ferried over the tide.
It is today
That we come to know properly
As to what is the ability of a certain one,
What is the extent
Of a certain one's scope.
'This considered opinion seems to be faulty
That the *material cause*[152a] only
Is the originator of an action–
The grace of the *efficient cause*[152b] also
seems to be inevitable.'
Yes ! O yes !!

The material cause, indeed,
Gets moulded into action–
It is an irrefutable law,

But
In the process of it getting moulded
The assistance of the efficient cause too is necessary,
It shall be better if it is put the other way, that
If the material cause has hereat
Any super-friend, then...it is
Certainly the efficient cause,
Which assists its friend
In a continuous and regular way
Till the destination is reached."

And, once again,
Casting its respectful glances towards the cord,
The whole of the family,
Having filled the Sacred Pitcher with the filtered water,
Takes some steps forward, when
That same old spot comes into sight
Where that same Artisan, pot-maker !

Has arrived to gather the soil !
The Sacred Pitcher, along with family,
Bows respectfully before the Artisan–pot-maker, When
The memories get revived–
As if, on feeling the touches of the wind,
The reservoir starts rippling with waves.

□

The overjoyed Earth utters –
" The Mother-entity feels happy, my son,
On seeing your progress
On beholding your pride-winning humility.

'The coming events cast their shadows before'–
Isn't this saying told by me, dear son,
At that time, when...
You follow my instructions
Thus
You come in contact with the Artisan pot-maker
Hence
It comes to be the initial *(Sarga)*[153a] flow/canto
Of a creative life.
– There should be a sense of dedication for him,
With whom the contact is established–
At whose feet you give up
The sense of your egotism,
So,
It comes to be the second (*Sarga*) flow/canto
Of a life full of creativity.

After the dedication
The dedicated one has to go through the acid tests,
And...hark !
Hard and frank reviews are made;
You pass through the fiery ordeals,
With zeal and courage
The calamity *(Upasarga)*,[153b] which
Is endured by you
Really,

It comes to be the third (*Sarga*) that is flow/Canto
Of a life full of creativity.
After the tests
Comes out the result indeed,
'*The nasal sign of dot', that is,(Anuswāra)*[154a]
dependent on others,
That is, a mere dot of the life of a letter of the alphabet,
Has been made by you
An above-rising, supine symbol
In the form of a 'self-dependent sign of colon, that is,[:]–
Hence
It comes to be the last (*Sarga*) that is flow/Canto
Of a life full of creativity.

Like the *(Sanskrit) root-word, 'Sṛj'*[154b] with
various prefixes,
In a natural way, indeed
After suffering various 'calamities',
You mould yourself
In the form of a 'naturally discreet conduct,'
So
It comes to be a classless completion–Final
Beatitude
Of a life full of creativity."

□

On hearing the feelings of the Earth
All of them, along with the holy Pitcher,
Cast their glances of gratitude
Towards the Artisan–the pot-maker–
When,
The Artisan–the pot-maker utters in the posture of
courtesy–

" All this
Is the kindness of the Sages and the Saints,
I'm only a petty attendant
Engrossed into serving them,
Nothing more."
And
Draws the attention of everyone
Towards an ascetic, free from all worldly attachments,
Seated on a stone-pedestal
Under a tree
At a little distance,
...When, at once,
Joining respectfully, along with circumambulations
All of them offer their salutations
At the adorable lotus-feet of the highly adorable one.
The sacred feet are sanctified by the holy water –
The fragrant water of sanctification is applied
reverently upon the head.
Then, each one of them,
Waiting for the grace of the Spiritual Guide, (*Gurudeva*)
Like a cuckoo, that is *Chātaka.*[155]

Before some moments are emptied out, when
The happy countenance of the Spiritual guide
(*Gurudeva*)
Starts bestowing the *Prasāda*, that is blessings,
The hand of the holy protection rises high,
Wherein resides the sentiment –
'There be the attainment of eternal bliss.'
At this, at once,
The terrorism adds, that–
" O my Lord ! –

The entire world, indeed,
Abounds in sufferings,
There is joy here, but it is sensual –
And that too transitory !
This was...really...felt by us,
But
The genuine faith is lacking
In the eternal happiness;
Yes ! yes !!, if,
After attaining the eternal bliss,
You, yourself
Can make us see that blissfulness,
Or
Can tell us about your own experience,
Relating to that subject,
...Then...

It is possible, that
We too, being fully confident,
May own a perfect dedication
In our lives, similar to that of yours,
Otherwise
The idea approved by the mind shall remain unfulfilled,

Hence,
'The idea at your inner heart be accomplished' –
Please bless us with such an utterance,
It shall be a great favour done to us."

□

On hearing the considered opinion of the group,
The Saint says with a tender smile –

" Such an occurrence is impossible
... Listen to its...cause ! I tell...
My Spiritual Guide (*Gurudeva*) has asked me
That
The word should be given
To anyone, never indeed,
Because, a vow has been taken
By you, before your *Gurudeva* - the Spiritual
Preceptor;
Yes ! yes !
If some (*Bhavya*) that is, fortunate soul,
Who is innocent, and has gone stray,
Wishes to get some guidance for proper direction
In a respectful manner–

With an idea of his own well-being,
...Then...
Deliver a discourse to him
Through beneficial, moderate and sweet words,
But,
By mistake even in a dream
A vow should never be made
To anyone at any time.

The other thing to be mentioned is that
The complete uprooting, indeed,
Of all the shackles
In the form of the body, the mind and the speech,
Is *Mokṣa,* that is, the Final Salvation,
Within the stainless state of this Final Salvation,
Resides the Eternal Bliss
Which –

On being accomplished,
How it is possible to return
Here, in this world –
– You please tell me yourself !

The milk passes through the process of development,
Then, in the end,
The clarified butter, that is, (*Ghī*) reveals its playfulness,
But
Is it possible that
The clarified butter (*Ghī*) changes back
In the form of milk again ? –
– You please tell me yourself !

On seeing the facial appearance of the group's feelings,
The Saint further adds that –
" All the same, if
You,
In the context of the (*Śramaṇa Sādhanā*), that is, the saintly austerities
And
In relation to the eternal bliss,
Are feeling no faith–
Then...again, now
I tell you something ultimate,
that,

From the point of view of right conduct,
– And not from that of the particular place,
At present where I am,–
Observe me, after reaching thereat,
Only then, you shall have
A genuine recognition of mine,
Because
On seeing beneath from a big height –

A sense of giddiness prevails with me
And
The guess of a great height from beneath
Is found almost erroneous.

Hence, indeed,
Have faith in these words
Yes ! O yes !!
The faith will beget true perception,
Surely it will,
But
At the final destination, not in the way on !"
And,
Rapt into the Supreme Silence
The Saint...
And
As if staring unwinkingly
At the surroundings
...The Silent Earth.

□□□

The Silent Earth

Brief Explanatory Comments

Canto First

Page No.	Comment No	Comments
8	1	***Swāti (period of Swāti)*** – An auspicious constellation or conjunction of the star Arcturus. That is the *Swāti-Nakṣatra,* within the galaxy of luminous stars. It can be seen with the moon in the beginning of rainy season.
15	2	***Kārmic nature and Mundane soul*** – The English terms '*Kārmic nature*' and 'Mundane Soul' have been used here to indicate the Hindi terms '*Prakṛti*' and '*Puruṣa*' respectively. '*Prakṛti*' carries here the sense of deeper faulty combinations and the subtle intrinsic transformations created with the mundane or wordly 'soul' by the foul emotions, thoughts and deeds. The term '*puruṣa*' denotes here a mundanc soul.

23	3	***The 'True Reality', that is, 'Tattva'*** –According to Jain Philosophy, the True Reality consists of seven fundamental aspects of life and world. They are – (1) The Soul (*Jīva*), (2) The Matter (*Ajīva*), (3) The influx of *karmas* or actions (*Āsrava*), (4) The bondage of soul through good or bad '*karmas*' (*Bandha*), (5) The effective check upon the bondage of '*karmas*' (*Saṁvara*), (6) The process of acquiring freedom from the 'bondages' previously incurred (*Nirjarā*) and (7) The final 'Salvation' or 'Emancipation' of Soul from all the 'bondages' or shackles of '*karmas*' (*Mokṣa*).
28	4a	***Kumbhakāra*** – The Hindi syllable '*kum*' (*ku*) denotes the 'earth' or 'Soil', The next Hindi syllable '*bha*' denotes 'fortune'. Thus, the Hindi word '*Kumbhakāra*' means here the 'fortune-maker', when taken as a whole.
28	4b	***Omkāra*** – This Sanskrit word '*Om*' – taken in the form of '*Omkāra*' is the most ancient holy incantation or '*Mahāmantra*' (Seed syllable).
37	5	***An Epicurean*** – given to the worldly or sensual enjoyment.

38	6	***Yā...da da...yā*** – These Hindi syllables, taken reversely, denote '*dayā*',– that is, pity or mercy.
40	7	***Gadahā*** – The Hindi word '*gada*', that is, 'disease' plus '*hā*' that is, 'healer'–*Gadahā* (an ass). Thus the word '*gadahā*' denotes here–'the healer of ailments or disease.'
41	8	***"Parasparopagraho Jīvānām"***– The maxim means that 'All the living beings have a sense of mutual favour',–Chapter 5, *Sūtra* 21, from the famous Scriptural Book in Sanskrit '*Tattvārtha Sūtra*' by Acharya Umāswāmī, an ancient Jain Saint–*Acharya* of India.
42	9a	***Yoga*** – The profoundly religious and abstract-meditation of the Supreme Spirit, as the only way to Absolution. The eight-fold Yoga, that is : *Yama, Niyama, Āsana, Prāṇāyāma, Pratyāhāra, Dhāraṇā, Dhyāna and Samādhi.*
42	9b	***'Yogaśchittavṛtti Nirodhaḥ'***– That is, perfect self-control over the agitated state of mind and sensuousness is '*Yoga*'.
43	10	***Ārṣa*** – This Sanskrit word means here the holy Texts, written by the great sages (*Ṛṣis*) of the past ages in India.

57	11a	***Rāhī*** – The Hindi syllables of the word '*Rāhī*' (the path-finder) put reversely as '*Hīrā*' (the diamond).
57	11b	***Rākha*** – The Hindi syllables of the word '*Rākha*'(the ashes) put reversely as '*Kharā*'(the genuine).
59	12	***Kumbhaka Prāṇāyāma*** – An Yogic posture in which, breathing is suspended by closing the mouth and the nostrils for a few minutes by the right hand.
64	13a	***Crooked knot*** – Possession, property, belongings and the inner crookedness for other things of worldliness.
64	13b	***Perfect asceticism*** – The state of perfect renunciation; absence of desire or possession or sensual enjoyments.
70	14	***Dharma*** – True religiousness, high morality and genuine righteousness. In other words– right faith, right knowledge and right conduct.
75	15	***'Dhammaṁ Saraṇaṁ Pavvajjāmi'***– This sacred expression in Prakrit Language means– 'I am seeking the shelter of *Dharma*', – that is, the true religiousness and observance of genuine righteousness in life.
77	16	***Bondage of 'karma'***– '*Karma*' is

		the '*Kārmic* molecules' produced by our fair or foul feelings, thoughts and deeds. They inflow into and bind a soul; and in their various kinds and degrees, go on binding and dropping off from the mundane (worldly) soul continually.
82	17a	***Mahābhārata*** – That is, Greater India–The word '*Mahābhārata*' here may also carry punningly the sense of 'Wars'.
82	17b	***Vasu*** – It is a Sanskrit word which means here 'wealth', riches, gold and money-matters etc.
85	18	***Mount Malaya*** – The name of a mountain in the South of India–(Malābāra province) –famous for its (Sandalwood) trees.
86	19	**Note** – In this explanatory comment, some special Hindi word–usages are given in brackets, with their English synonyms : (1) Ailments (*Vyādhi*), (2) Mental agony (*Ādhi*), (3) Possessions (*Upadhi),* (4) Means of subsistence (*Upādhi).*
87	20a	***Sallekhanā*** – A genuine religious vow, in which, one takes the approaching death willingly and peacefully, with deep sense of Supreme Renunciation.
87	20b	***Lābha...Bhalā*** – The Hindi'

syllables of the word '*Lābha*' (that is, 'gain') put in reverse order as '*Bhalā*' (that is, 'well-being').

88 21 ***Samādhi*** – This Sanskrit word denotes profound or deep absorption of thought into the aim or object of meditation, especially with concentration upon the 'Soul'. It also means the eighth or last stage of *Yoga-Sādhanā* or the perfect devotion to *Yoga*.

Canto Second

89 22 The Hindi word '*padon*', – That is *feet* – It is used here in two senses– (1) 'feet', the lower part of the leg.

(2) The poetic stanzas or expressions. So, it is a Hindi figure of speech'– *Śleśa*– susceptible of a double interpretation in rhetoric.

98 23a ***Rāhu*** – Among the nine astrogical planets, the eighth planet, which may create some calamity by its odd presence in a person's horoscope. *Rāhu* may be pacified by devotion to God.

98 23b ***Bālī*** – Bālī was the son of the king Sūryarāja of 'Kiṣkindhāpura' related to 'Vānara Dynasty.'

		According to Jaina tradition, Bālī was the elder brother of Sugrīva, a great warrior, and father of Aṅgada. Bālī renounced the world, and became an ascetic, who attained 'Final Liberation' during the war of Rām and Rāvaṇa.
105	24	***Khammāmi, Khamaṁtu me*** – Full couplet – "*Khammāmi savva-jīvāṇaṁ, savve Jīvā khamaṁtu me, Mitti me savva-bhūdesu, vairaṁ majjhaṁ ṇa keṇavī*". – Mahavira Swami– Quoted from '*Muni Pratikramaṇam*' from the book– '*Dainika Kartavya*'–page 176.
112	25a	***Haṁsā*** – The Hindi word '*Haṁsā*' is used as a symbol for the 'great pious Soul'.
112	25b	***O Body*** – Thou still inflameth the 'Spirit'– the expression carries the sense that the 'Soul' is conditioned by our past worldly actions, while transmigrating to future births and re-births.
119	26	***The eminent conduct*** – That is, '*Samiti*'. It carries the sense of the careful routine observances practised by an ascetic or a saint.
120	27a	***Proper establishment of conduct*** – That is –'*Yathākhyāta Chāritra*'– The natural conduct, when all the illusory 'karmas' are subdued.

120	27b	***Eternal State*** – The perfect state of 'everlasting blissfulness' of the 'Soul', after attaining the Final Emancipation, that is, *Siddhāvasthā.*
122	28	***The functional kārmic world*** – Actions for which the mundane soul is responsible in its earthly or worldly existence.
123	29	***The functional kārmic nature***– '*Karma*' is the subtle 'kārmic matter' which inflows and binds a 'Soul' through its activity, and of which the 'kārmic body' is made. Functional kārmic nature is the 'kārmic impulse' or the vibrations set in the soul by the operation of 'karmas.'
124	30a	***Knowledge*** – The understanding of a mundane or worldly soul.
124	30b	***Absolute Knowledge*** – Absolutely perfect knowledge, that is, the accomplishment of the power of–'omniscience' by an ascetic through his true observances of penance and austerties.
126	31	***Yoga*** – The philosophic sense of '*yoga*' is the union with the universal 'Soul', by means of deep and abstract meditation and perserverence in perfect devotion (*sādhanā*) by the ascetics. But, here, yoga carries the sense of the genuine and subtle vibrations caused by the actions

		and reactions of mind, speech and body upon the innermost consciousness.
129	32a	***Don't bow...the body*** – In our journey of life, one should not feel entangled with the transient and superficial charms of worldliness. We go steadily ahead with a sense of equanimity full of spiritual vigour.
129	32b	***'Having accomplished...stay in rest !'***– Really, on the basis of true spiritual force, the perfect journey of life can be achieved. But, even with the help of money-force and other forces of worldliness, the non-meritorious become meritorious. Hence, never stay back upon the immature and unqualified ways and means.
130	33	***The 'Puruṣa', the 'Nature'***– The Sanskrit word '*Puruṣa*' has been used here for 'Male Nature' and the word 'Nature' (*Prakṛti*) for the 'Female Nature'.
131	34	***The sentiment of heroism***– Chiefly 'bravery-in-war' The other heroic sentiments are also there – (1) Bravery in religiousness, (2) Bravery in mercifulnees, (3) Bravery in charity and (4) Bravery in oratory or speech.
133	35	***Kaṣāya*** – It is a Sanskrit word,

		which is used for foul or dirty emotions. The deep-rooted emotional feelings of human heart, that is, anger, pride, prejudice, fraudulence and greediness etc., are the foul or dirty emotions.
138	36	***'Puruṣa' and 'Prakṛti'*** – The Hindi word '*Puruṣa*' denotes here the 'Soul' while the 'Prakṛti' carrieshere the sense of deeper Kārmic combinations created with the 'soul.'
140	37	***Rām*** – This word here is symbolic of the 'True spiritual self' or 'Soul'.
141	38	***Eminent cause*** – That is, (*Upādāna kāraṇa*)–It is also called *'material cause'*–the material out of which anything is formed. It is internal cause. *Apparent cause or efficient cause*– Hindi word for it is (*Nimitta Kāraṇa*). It is the external helper of the eminent cause.
143	39a	***The Functional kārmic nature*** – Nature here means the functional 'kārmic nature', that is, the *'Karma Prakṛti.'*
143	39b	***The Supreme Being***– This word is used here [under reference] to indicate '*Parama Puruṣa*', that is, the 'Divine Self.'
145	40	***'A bondage-free naked observance'***

– That is, 'Pāṇipātro Digambaraḥ'– These words mean that a true ascetic, whose both the hands placed side by side – (the right hand-palm placed over the left hand-palm) – slightly hollowed, are used as an utensil for taking food-stuffs in a holy standing posture with nakedness.

146 41 ***The usage of Seven-moded delibrations*** –That is (*Saptabhaṅgī-nyāya*)– It is a style of analysis or logical expression under Jaina philosophy.

(*Anekānta*)– The Principle of inter preting one and the same thing in various ways with different styles of presentation.

151 42a ***'Why does the man of to-day...his head up-side -down'*** – The sense of these two lines here is that the man of today, due to his immature or imperfect knowledge without True Faith, has gone astray of the Right Path.

151 42b ***The Prime Brahmā***– The very first 'Tīrthaṅkara' that is, (The great prophet) – Ādinātha Swāmī.

160 43 ***Om*** – (*Omkāra Mantra*) is a highly sacred and mystic syllable, which is accepted in almost all the religions of India. It is also a symbolic representative (*Mantra*) for holy chanting of famous

		'*Ṇamokāra Mantra*', to meditate upon the five great Jain Ascetics– i.e.,*Arihantas*, *Siddhas*, *Āchāryas*, *Upādhyāyas* and all the true Ascetics–saints.
161	44a	***The four life-cycles of births and deaths*** – That is, the cycle of – (1) creatures of hell, (2) animal world, (3) human beings and (4) gods.
161	44b	***The wheel of the world*** – That is, the five-fold reversal of the world, that is, (*Pañcha Parāvartana*) – (1) the material world, (2) region, (3) Time-factor, (4) Sentiments, (5) The course of births and deaths.
167	45a	***The digit 9*** – The sacred number– The digit '9' is a 'muttered prayer' of the immortal incantation– *Ṇamokāra Mantra*, through its nine repetitions.
167	45b	***The digit 99*** – Which is a despicable number, symbolises the fraudulence of the world, which is a merry-go-round of 99.
168	**46**	***The number 63*** – The number 63 denotes the sixty three great grand personages referred to among the Holy Scriptures, that is, the *Śalākā Puruṣas*; they are as follows : 24 Tīrthaṅkaras, 12 Chakravartis, 9 Balabhadras, 9 Nārāyaṇas, and 9 Prati-nārāyaṇas– Total = 63 .
169	47	***The origin of 363 creeds*** – It came

		to exist through the grandson of the first Tīrthaṅkara Ādinātha, Mārīcha. In the course of his life-cycle, Mārīcha ultimately became Mahāvīra Swāmī, the last Tīrthaṅkara.
172	48a	The Hindi syllables *'Hī'* and *'Bhī'* have been translated as 'only' and 'also' –respectively.
172	48b	**For the Hindi words *'Anekānta'* and *'Syādvāda'*–** the English terms used are 'Relative pluralism' and 'Assertion of Probability'. For *Anekāntavāda*, the term used is the Doctrine of Absolutism.
173	49a	**Note** :– '*Hī*' and '*Bhī*'– See page 172 (back page) for comment No. 48a.
173	49b	***Rāvaṇa*** – The well-known king of Lanka, who carried away Sītā by forceful cheating, and was killed in war by Lakshmana, Rām's younger brother.
175	50	***Salve*** – Some healing ointment for wounds and sores.
177	51	***Heat...heat...heat...***–The expression signifies the terrible atmosphere of the summer season.
178	52a	**The Hindi syllables of the word (*Nadī*)**– The river– put in reverse order form the word (*Dīna*), that is, the 'inferior'.

178	52b	**The Hindi syllables of the word (*Nālī*)**–The canal–put in revese order, form the word (*Līnā*), that is 'immersed'.
181	53	**The Hindi word '*Rasanā*', [that is tongue]**– When put in reverse order as *nā...sa...ra*– means 'without head'.
184	54	***"Utpāda-Vyaya-Dhrauvya-yuktaṁ Sat."* (The entire Entity is imbibed with birth-decay-fixity)**– An axiom (*Sūtra*) by Acharya Umāswāmī– '*Tattvārtha Sūtra*', chapter 5, sutra 30. Eng. Translation– Existence is characterized by origination, disappearance and permanence–'Reality', Page No. 99, *Sūtra* No. 30– by Prof. S.A. Jain, M.A.L.T., South India, Tamilanadu.

Canto Third

195	55	***Vanśa*** – The Hindi word (Vanśa) provides here a double meaning :– (i) The posterity or lineage. (ii) The bamboo-stick. The word has been used here punningly.
199	56	***Sāḍī*** –A fine long garment, wrapped around the waist by Indian women, enfolding the legs upto their heels, along with their heads too.
200	57	***Palāśa tree***– A kind of Indian tree,

having beautiful red blossom in the month of March.

202 58a The Hindi word (***nārī***), used here punningly, carries here triple meaning– (i) a lady (ii) *na+ari* = not-a-foe (iii) *na+ārī* = unlike a handsaw.

202 58b The Hindi word '***Mahilā***'– used here punningly, carries triple sense– (i) *Maha+lā* = that is, the one who brings a great festivity in life. The remaining clarifications stand self-explained by the saint-poet himself.

203 59a+b The Hindi words– ***Mahilā and Abalā***, that is, a lady and woman– have been used, through a play of words, with different meanings. Both these words have been used here punningly. The special meanings of these words stand self-explained by the saint-poet himself.

204 60 The Hindi word ***'Kumārī'*** that is, 'virgin' has been used here punningly upon the syllables '*Ku*' + '*mā*' +'*rī*' = *Kumārī*. The Hindi figure of speech used here is '*Śleṣa*', that is, 'play-of-words'.

205 61 The Hindi words– ***Strī***, ***Sutā***, ***Duhitā*** mean respectively– 'lady', 'daughter' and 'married daughter'. They have been used through a play-of-words, with different meanings assigned

to them.

206	62a	***Valid Testimony*– (*Pramāṇa*)** – Authority, by means of which we test the direct or the indirect knowledge of the 'self' or the 'non-self' in all their aspects simultaneously.
206	62b	The Hindi words– ***Jñāna***, ***Jñeya***, ***Jñātā*** are translated here as = The knowledge, the knowable, the knower. And '*Jñeya*'-'*Jñātā-Sambandha*' means here = The knowable-knower-relationship.
207	63	*The three cloudlets* are symbolic of the three types of coloured feelings or emotions : (I) ***Śukla leśyā*** – (curd-like white emotions) (II) ***Padma leśyā*** – (Light red lotus-like emotions) (III) ***Pīta leśyā***– (golden-colour-like yellowish emotions), these three coloured emotions are taken to be as auspicious.
215	64	***Omkāra*** – See the comment No. 04b –on page 28.
227	65a	***The three dense clouds***– That is, the three foul or 'inauspicious' coloured emotions– (1) the black– like a big black bee (ii) the blue– like a dark blue serpent (iii) the grey or dirty white-coloured– like that of a pigeon.
227	65b	***Ghana***– The Hindi word '*ghana*',

		that is, 'cloud' may also denote another sense, a heavy hammer, punningly.
229	66	In the Hindi word ***'Jala-dhara'***, the syllable '*Jala*' has been taken in the sense of 'Jealousy' in place of 'water'; '*dhara*' means 'to hold', Thus, the full sense, carried here, is–jealousy-holders.
230	67	***Payodhara*** – This Hindi word carries the sense of '*Payaḥ*'– that is 'milk' or 'water', and '*dhara*', that is 'holders'. Thus, '*Payodhara*' means here 'milk-holders' or ' water-holders'.
234	68a	***Lāvā*** (An English word)– The burning fluid, gushing out of a volcano.
234	68b	***Rāhu*** – Among the nine astrological planets, the eighth planet, which may create some calamity by its odd presence in a persons horoscope. *Rāhu* may be pacified by devotion to God.
240	69	***Chātaka*** – A special sweet-voiced Indian bird, which drinks only the rain-drops, under the conjunction of *Swāti*-star.
242	70	**The race of Rāghavas** – The race or family of an ancient Kshatriya King 'Raghu', who was the great-grand father of Lord Rām, the famous ruler of Ayodhya.
245	71a	***To acheiev Supreme Reality* or *to***

		be a True 'Self' – The Hindi '***Yathākāra***', that is, an *'Absolute Realist'* or the one who expresses the True (Supreme) Reality, and not a mere relater.
245	71b	***Tathākāra*** – This Hindi word indicates the one who wishes to be a 'perfect ascetic', and not a story-teller or a mere preacher.
251	72	***Hanumān*** – Hanumānjī is described as a great hero in the famous Epic 'Rāmāyaṇa' by the saint-poet Tulsidas. He is also depicted as a supreme character in the old Jain Epic '*Padma-charita*' by Āchārya Raviṣeṇa in Sanskrit epic.

Canto Four

274	73	***Navakāra Mantra*** – "*ṇamo arihantāṇaṁ ṇamo siddhāṇaṁ, ṇamo āiriyāṇaṁ, ṇamo uvajhāyāṇaṁ, ṇamo loye savva-sāhūṇaṁ*" – The holiest of the Jain Mantras or incantations, which pays homage to *Sarvashri Arihanta, Siddha, Āchārya, Upādhyāya* and all the *Sādhus*– Ascetics.
278	74	***Āsāḍha***– This fourth Indian month '*Āsāḍha* ', falls almost within the stretch of the seventh English

		month–'July', when the rainy season begins in India.
279	75	***Kumbhaka Prāṇāyāma***– This Yogic posture is observed in three stages respectively– (I) *Pūraka*– to fill the belly by inhaling the breath deeply (II) the suspending of the breath, as far as possible, with fixed-mindedness. that is, *Kumbhaka* (III) *Rechaka*– the exhaling of the breath slowly.
282	76	***Lotus-friend***– The friend of lotus-flower– Sun. The lotus blossoms by the friendly touch of the rising sun.
284	77	The Hindi word– ***'Tāmasa'***– That is 'ignorance', – has been used in the reverse order of its syllables to signify —*'Samatā'*,–that is 'equanimity.'
285	78a	**Having *no alloy***– Used for Hindi word– ***'Saṅga-rahita'***, It carries here the sense of having no worldly possessiveness.
285	78b	**Having *no rusted element*** (used for Hindi word ***Jaṅga-rahita***)– It carries here the sense of having no war-like sentiments.
285	78c	*The genuine iron*– (*Pure Iron*)– It symbolizes here purified 'Soul'.
297	79	***'The fluent essential element'***– (used here for the Hindi word **Dhārāvāhika**

tattva)– "*Utpāda-vyaya-dhrauvya-yuktaṁ sat*"– *Tattvartha-sūtra*, chapter 5, *Sūtra*-30 - by Āchārya Umāswāmī – defines 'sat' as follows–Existence–(Sat) – is characterized by origination, disappearance (destruction) and permanence. –From the Book 'Reality'– an Eng. Translation, by professor S. A. Jain, published by– Jwalamalini Trust (Regd.), Venkataramana Iyer street, Venkatapuram, Madras, 600053, Tamilanadu, South India.

304 80 **The basic notes of the Gamut**– The basic notes of the musical gamut, that is ***'Saragama'***, in Hindi are– *Sā, re, ga, ma, pa, dha, ni.*

305 81a The Hindi syllables– ***Sā, re, ga, ma***– (The musical notes) –if taken together, mean–'All the griefs'– Here, the letters of musical gamut have been taken punningly.

305 81b ***Somehow*** (that is ***Kathañchit***)– This Sanskrit usage is an indeclinable word, which expresses the sense of 'assertion of probability' from a particular or relative point of view.

306 82a The Hindi syllables, that is ***Dhā...dhin...dhin...dhā*** – have been interpreted mystically to hint– different are those 'bodies' /or 'salaries' [Punningly–interpreted] – different the 'Vital consciousness'.

306	82b	***Tā...Tin...Tin...Tā***– have been interpreted to hint–"Why worry for the 'body', why worry for the body".
309	83a	*All the four worldly courses of transmigration of soul*– The four worldly courses or conditions of all the living beings are :– (I) Hellish creatures (II) animal kind (III) mankind (IV) gods or celestial existence. They are the four courses or modes of existence.
	83b	*Fylfot*– A kind of equal-armed cross, that is, **'*Swastika*'**, It is taken as an auspicious religious symbol.
	83c	*Omkāra* (Om–symbol ॐ)– The great sacred mystic symbol of all the religions of Indian origin.
315	84	***Karmas***– The aggregate material substances related to 'soul' are termed as 'karmas'. The subtlest particles of matter bind the Soul of all the living beings, according to their life-long feelings, thoughts and actions or deeds.
316	85	*The ceremonial substances*– (The Hindi word –*Vidhi-dravya*) – It denotes here a confidential symbol of pre-decision of food-taking by the sacred guest (*Munirāja*). The secret vows of the acceptable ceremonial substances in the hands of the benefactors are not known to them.

		Munirāja sees them and decides their acceptability, at once, for taking food at a particular place with a particular person or group only.
321	**86**	*The month of Sāvana/Śrāvaṇa*– It is the month of rainy season in India. It takes into its fold about 30 days– the major portion of August; while including some days of the last week of July and excluding some days of its own last week.
324	87	***Palāśa tree*** – It is a famous Indian tree, which brings forth its beautiful red-blossom in the month of March. In English language, it is called 'Butea fondosa'.
326	88	***Seven fears*** – (1) Death (2) Pains (3) Accidental or sudden fears (4) insecurity or non-safety (5) Non-control of mind, speech and body and worldly passions and emotions (6) The fears of the various troubles of the present world (7) The fears of the 'other world'.
327	89a	***Eighteen blemishes*** – (1) Birth (2) Old age (3) Discomfort (4) Hunger (5) Thirst (6) Doubt (7) Sadness (8) Disease (9) Distress (10) Prides (11) Worldly enchantments (12) Fear (13) Sleep (14) Worry (15) Sweat (16) Attachment (17) Jealousy (18) Death.
327	89b	*The spiritual or meditative*

relaxation (Hindi word *'Kāyotsarga'*)– It is a meditative relaxation, that is, the deep sense of detachment with the body, along with reciting of the *Ṇamokāra Mantra*, 09 times in 27 breathing cycles.

330 90 ***Sā, re, ga, ma, pa, dha, ni***... the musical gamut– see page number 304, and the explanatory comment number 80.

333 91 ***Śramaṇa***– It is an old Sanskrit word, which has been traditionally used for a Jaina ascetic or saint.

340 92 ***The law of Divine Destiny*** (Hindi word–*Vidhi ka vidhāna*) – This word here means 'karma', According to Jaina philosophy, 'the Functional kārmic nature' or 'karma'. as a rule, is itself the 'creator'. It is also described by some other philosophers, as the 'Law of providence' or the 'Law of Divine Destiny'.

342 93 ***Wrong habits*** (Hindi word for it is *Sapta Vyasana*)– According to Jain Ācharyas, the bad habits or (Addictions) are generally of seven types : (1) Gambling, (2) Non-vegetarian-food-taking- that is, meat-eating, (3) Intoxecation (by wine etc.), (4) Prostitution, (5) Hunting animals etc., (6) Theft and (7) Adultery / Adulteration.

343 94 ***The posture of bodily resignation*** – that is (Hindi word*Kāyotsarga*)– This word means, the practice of self-contemplation, while giving up the sense of attachment to body. After the completion of food-taking or daily ceremonials by the saint (Munirāja), it is really an observance of austerity, while standing or sitting in a motionless posture, and remembering the virtuous qualities of 'Jinadevas'.

345 95 ***The wooden water-spout***– (that is *'Kamaṇḍalu'*) –The wooden water-spout or the special wooden water-container with nozzle is used by Digamber Jain ascetics, as a means of routine calls of nature, and not for quenching the thirst. It is filled with the boiled warm water.

346 96 ***Nemīnātha***– The 22nd Tīrthaṅkara of Jainism, among the succession of 24 Tīrthaṅkaras, the founders of Jain order from time to time and the propagators of eternal religion.

347 97a **Mental excitement** (that is *Saṁvega*)– This Hindi word here means the instinct to have fear for the sufferings of worldly life.

347 97b ***Āṣāḍhī flood***– The flood which occurs in the month of *Āṣāḍha*. It covers up the major portion of the month of August, when the rainy

		season begins.
351	98	***Bindī*** – This Hindi word denotes a round-red-mark kept up by the Indian ladies on their mid-forehead as a symbol of the happy state of a wife whose husband is alive.
352	99	*'That the end...visualized'*– The saint-poet here means that the pious association of the great saints shows us the ways and means to save ourselves from the worldly sins; and to seek the true path of 'Salvation' from the bondages of worldliness.
354	100a	***The saffron dye*** – These words here mean the saffron-coloured religious flag or banner.
354	100b	***'The sharpness of the thorn'***– These words carry here the sense that there remains no purpose of revengefulness or that of being taste-greedy when the saintliness has been adopted.
359	101a	***Charaṇa***– The Hindi word '*Charaṇa*' has been used here by splitting it into two syllables— Chara + na, that is, wander not away from the venerable feet, which are venerable due to 'right conduct'.
359	101b	*Cha...ra...ṇa...> ṇa...ra...cha* – The

Hindi word (*Cha + ra + ṇa*) has been taken here in its reverse syllabic order– as– (*na + ra + cha*)– that is, never be rapt or carried away elsewhere.

362	102a	***Sat-yuga*** (*Dukhamā-Sukhamā Kāla*)–According to Jain traditional thinking, Salvation (*Mokṣa*) from the worldly bondages is possible. So, it is an auspicious Age, which is considered to be 'The Fourth *Yuga*'–that is, *Sat-yuga.*
362	102b	***The Fifth Yuga*** (*Dukhamā Kāla*) – That is, '*Kaliyuga*'– In this Age, the life of the living beings wanders and wastes itself in the sensual pleasures. So, it is a sinful Age, an inauspicious Age.
371	103a	*Flambeau*– A long rod with a burning flame of rags at the top, and caught with hand at its lower end. In Hindi, it is called *'Maśāla'*.
371	103b	*Swan* – It is an English word for the Hindi word '*Haṁsa*'. '*Haṁsa*' also denotes the 'Soul' Hence, it can be interpreted in this sense also.
373	104	***Sāvana*** (*Month*)– See comment number 86, on the back page number 321.
375	105	*Worldly objects of enjoyment* (Hindi word –***Bhogopabhogas***)–

		Bhogas+Upabhogas. 'Bhogas' are the objects which can be used only once– such as, food (eatables) and drinks etc., '*Upabhogas*' are the objects which can be used repeatedly–such as, clothes, house, vehicles etc.
377	106	*The heron* (Hindi word '***Baka***' or '***Bagulā*** ')– Heron is the Eng. name for a fishing crane. But, here, it has been taken as a symbol of a false devotee or a religious hypocrite.
381	107a	*Knowledge* – The word knowledge here means the intuitive power of cognition.
381	107b	*Knowable* – This word indicates the involvement into the knowledge of 'Soul', as well as the characteristic knowledge of 'Matter', which is the object of knowledge-sensient and the insensient elements.
382	108a	*Vessels* (*pātra or characters*)– The saint-poet has presented the different utensils, which are inanimate objects, as animated characters into a lively symbolic debate, started basically between the Earthen pitcher and the Golden pitcher.
382	108b	***Yojana*** – According to the scriptural definition of Jain Āchāryas, '*Yojana*' is an old measure of distance. It is described as follows – (I) Two

thousand measuring-rods = 01 *kroṣa* (*kosa*), (II) 04 *Kroṣas* = 01 small *yojana* (or 02 miles), (III) 2000 *Kroṣas* = 01 *Mahā yojana* (Biggest *yojana*).

383 109a ***The bright half of the lunar month***– The bright fortnight – A period of almost two weeks.

383 109b ***The dark half of the lunar month***– The dark fortnight– A period of almost two weeks.

385 110 ***The maxim of the crow and the palm*** – This maxim is symbolical of hinting at any happening taking place unexpectedly and accid entally. It originates in the unexpected fall of a palm-tree at the moment when a crow sits upon it.

386 111 ***The wedding-rite of marital hand-taking*** – In India, marriage is taken as a sacred ceremony, in which the would be husband and the would be wife express before the family-elders their firm resolve of sustaining their life-long relationship and responsibility towards each-other through the marital hand-taking ceremony, that is *Pāṇigrahaṇa.*

388 111b ***'Mana'***– A measure of weight, a Maund of 40 *seras.*

389 112 *Like a limitless ocean* (***Sāgaropama***)– These wordings have been used as

		translation of the Hindi word, *Sāgaropama.* But really, it indicates a transcendental time-limit. Ten *Koṭa-koṭi* '*Palyopamas*' go to make a '*Sāgara*'. One '*Sāgara*' is equal to ten *Koṭa-koṭi* '*Palyas*'.
391	113	*Salary (**Vetana**)* – The usage of this word here indicates the sense that the proper 'nourishment' to the bodily requirements also is very necessary.
392	114	*'Nature'*, that is, the ***'Prakṛti'***– In the last line of this page, the word 'nature' has been taken to mean as 'Mother-nature' or 'Female-nature'. But from a relative point of view, 'nature' may also indicate here 'kārmic nature' or 'Karma-Prakṛti'. On the path of asceticism 'Female-nature' (*Nārī*)–shall prove to be a hindrance, a curse. The 'Kārmic Nature' also keeps up its adverse effect upon the 'Soul' upto the last stage, that is, the 14th '*Gunasthāna*' of an accomplisher. Hence, to win over the 'kārmic nature' as a helpful companion on the path of 'Salvation' is the real accomplishment of an ascetic or *Yogi*.
393	115	*Tamarind* – In Hindi, it is called ***'Imalī'***. But, in Latin Language, its Botanical name is 'Tamarindus Indica.'

394 116 ***Puruṣa**, the Supreme Personage*– According to Jain philosophy, the 'Soul' is the '*Puruṣa*', and the 'kārmic nature' or '*Karma Prakṛti*' is the '*Prakṛti*' (nature). The Passions (Anger, pride, deceit, greed etc.) create 'bondage' of the 'kārmic nature', for the Soul–(the *puruṣa*). The *Puruṣa* ('Soul') becomes liberated after defeating the 'kārmic nature'. Hence, '*Puruṣa*', the 'Soul' is the real player and the *prakṛti* like a mere toy, to play with. Thus, the perfect observance of true religiousness overcomes the '*Karma Prakṛti*', which creates the bondage of worldliness.

395 117 ***The 'Puruṣārtha' of human existence*** – The four principal aims and objects of human life in the world as told by the ancient saints, are as follows – (1) *Dharma* (the true religiousness), (2) *Artha* (Prosperousness or money), (3) *Kāma* (Desires and Family-life), (4) *Mokṣa* (Final liberation–that is, deliverance from all the worldly bondages or shackles).

396 118 ***Kalā***– [The Hindi word]–that is, Art– The Hindi word '*Kalā*' has been analysed as– ('*ka*' + '*lā*') '*ka*'– that is, the Soul is happiness, '*Lā*', that is, 'to bring'.... 'to give'. = the life is flowered with happiness, peace and prosperity by each and every art.

397 119 Ś (श) ; Sa (स) S; Ṣ (ष)– these are three letters of Hindi alphabet used as three mystical seed- syllables. They are considered very effective through their correct and holy-pronunciations. The poet-author has explained them as *Tālavya– Śa* (श), *Danti– Sa* (स) and *Mūrdhanya– Ṣa* (ष) respectively.

398 120 'P' (प), that is, a letter of Hindi alphabet. When its stomach is cut across, it becomes '*Ṣ*' (ष) a holy symbol of 'soul', which is beyond the grip of 'Karma'. 'Karma' is the 'Kārmic molecules' which inflow into and bind a 'Soul', if it is subjected to different passions. In other words, 'karmas' are the actions for which the mundane (worldly) soul is responsible, and not the truly purified Soul.

399 121 ***'Bhū Sattāyām'***, that is 'भू सत्तायाम्'– a Sanskrit Maxim. It means that the 'Earth' is behind all existence.

401 122 ***Omkāra*** – See page number 28, Comment number 04b.

401-402 123 ***Parā-vāk*** – The Supreme power of speech.

123 (1) ***Mūlodgamā*** – Originated at the very root, that is, the *Mūlādhāra Chakra*, which is a mystical circle

situated just above the internal root of the generative organ.

123 (2) ***Paśyantī*** – A very subtle sound, like a vibrating musical wave within the internal part of the navel pit. It is a wordless measured sound.

123 (3) This very ***'Paśyantī'***, the wordless measured sound is beyond comprehension of those, who do not possess a perfect self-control, and are always busy with the thoughts and feelings of the mundane world. It is called *Vipaśyanā.*

123 (4) Then, this ***'Paśyantī'*** *(Vāṇī)* rises up, enters the lotus-heart and transforms itself into meaningful words. It is called *'Madhyamā' (Vāṇī).*

123 (5) Then, this ***'Madhyamā'*** travels from the inner world to the outer world, according to the purpose of the speaker. With the help of the throat and tongue etc., when it becomes the part of hearing, it is called *'Vaikharī'* (*Vāṇī*).

403 124 (a) ***Vai + Kharī*** (*Vāṇī*)– This Hindi word has been used here for the 'utterances' emerging from the lips of a virtuous person. They are certainly genuine.

124 (b) ***Vai + khalī*** (*vāṇī)*– This Hindi word hints at the 'speech' coming out from the mouth of a wicked person.

		It is sinful and troublesome.
404	125	***Vairī*** – The Hindi word '*Vairī*' means 'enemy', The Hindi word '*Vaikharī*'–[explained on page 403]– is broken into three syllables– *Vai+kha+rī*. On leaving aside the Hindi syllable '*Kha*', the word '*Vairī*', that is, 'enemy' comes into being.
406	126	***Tolā***– An Indian measure of weights weighing, about twelve grams.
407	127a	*The twilight-hour* (that is, ***Sandhi-Kāla***)–Whenever and wherever, 'the union-point of the solar time-element' comes into being, it is called 'conjunction-time'– as, between fore-noon and after-noon, between approaching evening and the setting of the sun–(The twilight hour); between Just after the early morning and before the early sun-rise etc., are the conjuction-times.
407	127b	***Suṣumnā*** – A particular 'Artery' of the body—(lying between the vessels called '*Eḍā*' and '*Piṅgalā*')– which plays an important role in the attainment of supreme bliss. In *Āyurveda*, it is a principal artery, lying amid the navel-point of the human body.
408	128	***Ashoka Tree***– The tree of reli-

		giousness, that is, '*Dharma Vṛkṣa*'– with ultimate fruition into Final Deliverance or *Mokṣa*.
413	129a	***Malayāchala***–*The Mount Malaya*, a forest full of sandalwood, found around the mountain range of South Indian Malābāra Zone. The part of mountain-ghats lies in the South of Mysore and East of Travancore also.
413	129b	*Suture* (***Brahma Randhra***)– An aperture in the crown of the head, through which the soul is supposed to escape. It is a seam of the bones of the skull.
421	130	***Mandodarī*** – The Queen consort– The Queen, who was installed on the throne of Laṅka with the King Rāvaṇa.
427	131	***Dhotī*** – This Hindi word means four to five meters long loin-cloth, which is generally worn around the waist by males in India.
428	132a	***Rāhu***– One of the nine astrological planets, which causes Solar Eclipse.
428	132b	***Kathiyawada***– The Hindi word '*Kathiyawada*' is used for the Western part of Gujarat province (old Saurashtra).

430	133	***Pāriśeṣya Nyāya***– It is an important word of '*Nyāya-śāstra*'. According to it, the judgment of a matter or case should be based upon all the proper facts found in the due course of time of the final decision.
433	134	***Uraga*** – It is a Hindi word, a synonym, having the meaning of a serpent-crawling creature.
438	135	***Rava-rava hell*** – According to the old Jain scriptures, the name of the third '*Paṭala*'– that is, level of the first hell is called '*Raurava hell*', where dense noisy darkness prevails.
439	136a	*The hours after hours rolled away*– That is '***Praharas***'– The Hindi word '*Prahara*' is a measure of time, equivalent to the period of three hours.
439	136b	***Bhoga–Upabhoga*** – The objects or things which are enjoyable for once only are called '*Bhogas*', as for example-flowers, fragrance, fruits, various eatable and drinkable things etc., in daily life. But, the useful things like bed, sofa, clock, Vehicles, horse, house etc., which are usable again and again are called '*Upabhogas*'.
442	137	***Omkāra*** (*Om*)– This Sanskrit word-symbol, *Omkāra* (Om), is the most sacred and mystic 'watch-word'

remembered as a supreme spiritual symbol by the ascetics or saints and meditators in India. In the ancient Jain Scriptures, 'Om' is found written as such–ॐ.

443 138 ***Lavaṇabhāskara*** (*chūrṇa*)– It is a kind of Aurocetic (or *Āyurvedic*) medicinal powder – a mixture of many kinds of salts and other things used for curing stomach disorders.

448 139 The Hindi word ***'Nālī '*** is used here as '*Nā+lī*', meaning = 'Neither taken', and the other word ***'Nadī'*** is used here as '*na+dī*',– that is, 'nor given'. It is a type of punning on letters. These words carry symbolic sense – Selfishness is like a *Nālī* (drain) and desire for fame is like a *Nadī* (river)–to fall into a 'drain' or 'river', both are undesirable and improper. Thus, this punning on '*Nālī*' and '*Nadī*' carries with it a high thought or sense also.

452 140 The Hindi word ***'Dharatī'*** – 'Earth' has been used here in its reverse order– '*Tīradha*' meaning– 'that which carries the shelter-seeker to the proper end. In its changed form of a single syllable '*tha*', in place of the single syllable '*dha*', the new word comes into being as '*Tīratha*', that is, a place of pilgrimage.

453	141	The Hindi word ***'Dharaṇī'***– 'Earth', has been put into its reverse order as '*Nīradha*', i.e., that which retains the water.
454	142a	***The Mount Meru*** – The name of a sacred fabulous mountain of gold, mentioned in old scriptures. All the planets are supposed to revolve round it.
454	142b	*The milky sea (The **Kṣīra Sāgara**)*– The seventh sea, described in the old Jain scriptures. It is called the 'sea of milk'.
454	142c	*A Heroic death* (***Vīra Maraṇa***)– that is, to die bravely and to welcome death peacefully for some great cause of true religiousness or for a great cause of Motherland.
455	143a	*Coquettish gestures* (Hindi word– ***Hāva-bhāva***)– Attractive motions of limbs or body by a woman, who trifles with a man's affection.
455	143b	*Deformed sentiments*, that is, (Hindi word–***Vibhāva***)–Passional feelings, that is, feelings contrary to real nature, due to the fruition of 'karmas'.
458	144	***Lāvā*** – (An English word)– The melted matter flowing from a volcano.
459	145	***Madada*** (*Help*)– This word of Arabic language has been used here

punningly. By breaking it into two parts (*Mada+da*)–it carries the sense of 'pride-promoting' according to its Sanskrit meaning.

460 146 ***Pātāla Loka*** – This Hindi word is translated as 'hades', that is, the lower parts of earth, pertaining to hell.

461 147 ***Samūha*** (Hindi)– That is, 'a social group'–This Hindi word carries the sense of a social group of persons, who are a part and parcel of society. It is used here punningly, by breaking it into two parts– *Sam* (rational) + *ūha* (thinking). It means a group of the persons having rational thinking, along with their good moral conduct.

463 148 ***Vikriyā*** (***Riddhi***) – That is, a strange power of transformation. In the old holy scriptures of Jainism, it is a kind of supernatural power of saints or others who may transform their bodies into different shapes. They achieve this power through the observance of penance and true religious austerities.

467 149 ***Viśalyā*** – The wife of Lord Rām's younger brother Lakṣmaṇa was the daughter of a Chakravartī King. Lakṣmaṇa was caught under swoon due to a power-hit by Rāvaṇa during Rām-Rāvaṇa war. Lakṣmaṇa's swoon

got removed by sprinkling the remnant of her bathed water over his body.

474	150	*'...the culprits'*, that is–(***Aparādhī***-Hindi word)– Culprit (*Aparādhī*) is a Hindi word which means an offender, a criminal. But it has been taken here punningly in two parts as– *Aparā* + *dhī*, which denotes 'Supreme Wisdom'.
479	151	***Sāḍī*** – This Hindi word is used for a long piece of about five to seven meters worn by Indian ladies, round their waists, passing over to the heads; a woman's garment.
480	152a	*Material cause,* that is (***Upādāna Kāraṇa***–Hindi word)–The material out of which any thing is formed. It is also called eminent cause.
480	152b	*Efficient cause*– That is (***Nimitta Kāraṇa***–Hindi word)–It is also called apparent or external cause, which assists the material cause in fulfilling its aim or objective.
482	153a	***'Sarga'***– that is, flow or canto– It is a Sanskrit word. It carries different meanings. Here, it has been taken in two senses only– (I) Flow, that is the movement of the stream of life. (II) Division and part of an Epic poem.

482	153b	*Calamity* (***Upasarga***-Hindi word) – It is a Hindi word taken from Sanskrit. According to Acharyas, it denotes disturbances caused by human or sub-human, celestial beings, animals, nature or in the form of anonymous accidents upon the great saints.
483	154a	***Anuswāra*** – This Sanskrit word denotes a nasal sign of dot (ं) dependent on others. Some of the Indian Scripts say it to be 'an after sound' the 'nasal sound' which is marked by a dot above the line, and always follows the preceding vowel. some other Hindi-Sanskrit dictionary says–'The nasal sign (written above a letter) is used in writing 'Devanagari script.'
483	154b	The Sanskrit root ('***Sṛj***') – means 'to create'– may be used in different forms and senses with different pre-fixes and suffixes-as, *Sṛj+kta* = *Sraṣṭa*, that is–the created etc.
484	155	***Chātaka*** – A famous sweet-voiced Indian bird, which drinks only the rain-drops, under *Swāti-star*, an auspicious constellation. Its pleasant voice is often heard in rainy or spring season.

□□□

णाणं पयासयं

वीर नि.सं. 2470

ई.सन् 1944

भारतीय ज्ञानपीठ